From Herodotus
to H-Net

The Story of Historiography

JEREMY D. POPKIN

New York   Oxford
OXFORD UNIVERSITY PRESS

Oxford University Press is a department of the University of Oxford.
It furthers the University's objective of excellence in research,
scholarship, and education by publishing worldwide.

Oxford   New York
Auckland   Cape Town   Dar es Salaam   Hong Kong   Karachi
Kuala Lumpur   Madrid   Melbourne   Mexico City   Nairobi
New Delhi   Shanghai   Taipei   Toronto

With offices in
Argentina   Austria   Brazil   Chile   Czech Republic   France   Greece
Guatemala   Hungary   Italy   Japan   Poland   Portugal   Singapore
South Korea   Switzerland   Thailand   Turkey   Ukraine   Vietnam

Copyright © 2016 by Oxford University Press

Published by Oxford University Press
198 Madison Avenue, New York, New York 10016
http://www.oup.com

Oxford is a registered trademark of Oxford University Press

Library of Congress Cataloging-in-Publication Data
Popkin, Jeremy D., 1948-
    From Herodotus to H-Net : the story of historiography / Jeremy D. Popkin.
      pages cm
    ISBN 978-0-19-992300-7 (pbk. : alk. paper) 1. Historiography--History. I. Title.
    D13.P569 2015
    907.2--dc23

                                                                2015010489

Printing number: 9 8 7 6 5 4 3

Printed in Canada

About the cover
Modern technology helps uncover traces of the past, and also traces of the historical
consciousness of two thousand years ago. Centuries after it was originally carved, this ancient
Egyptian statue of a sphinx was brought to Alexandria, the great center of Hellenistic learning,
along with other monuments, as a way of emphasizing the Ptolemaic monarchy's connection to
the country. Submerged during an earthquake, it remained hidden until recently.

From Herodotus to H-Net

This book is dedicated to my students, who have challenged me to find ways to communicate the excitement of history for more than forty years

CONTENTS

PREFACE

In this book, I aim to provide an introduction to historiography, accessible both to undergraduate and to graduate students in history. I understand historiography in two senses. In the first place, it defines the questions that historians must address to study and analyze the past: what constitutes a historical problem? What constitutes historical evidence, and what are the proper methods for interpreting it? How should a historical account be structured? And what purposes does history serve? In a second sense, historiography is the history of the ways historians have answered these questions in the past two and a half millennia, starting with Herodotus and Thucydides in ancient Greece and Sima Qian in ancient China and continuing to our own day. Together with learning to do historical research, acquiring an understanding of historiography is a form of initiation into the world of historians. This initiation allows students to move from simply "being interested in history" to being able to understand how history is produced and to being able to make reasoned judgments on what constitutes a successful or convincing historical account and what does not. Learning about historiography is also a way of learning what professional historians do and perhaps even a chance to consider whether this is a career one wants to pursue.

Books that try to provide an overview of historiography tend to fall into two major categories. Some approach the subject in a thematic or analytical fashion, defining the major issues that historians face and treating them separately. Some of the books in this category are more theoretical, like E. H. Carr's durable classic *What Is History?*, which has chapters on "The Historian and His Facts," "Society and the Individual," "History, Science, and Morality," and other broad topics.[1] Others, such as John Tosh's *The Pursuit of History*, divide their material according to the different stages of historical research. Tosh has sections titled "The Raw Materials," "Using the Sources," and "Writing and Interpretation," as well as more theoretical chapters on "The Limits of Historical Knowledge" and "History and Social Theory."[2] The second major approach to historiography takes a chronological approach, looking at how historians have developed different ways of researching and representing the past over time. This is the pattern of the major scholarly works on the subject, such as Ernst Breisach's *Historiography: Ancient, Medieval, and Modern* and Donald R. Kelley's three-volume study of historical writing from Herodotus to the twentieth century.[3]

Ideally, an apprentice historian should be exposed to both these approaches to historiography, but it is not easy to combine them in a reasonably short book. Two basic reasons have led me to adopt the chronological approach in this volume. In the first place, historiographical manuals organized along thematic lines run the risk of making it appear as though, in the end, all true historians should agree on the proper way of doing history. This approach has a certain practical advantage in courses where students are being taught how to do a history research project and need to learn how to define a topic, locate sources, take notes, organize their material, and write up their findings. The major drawback of the thematic approach, however, is that it treats historiography itself in an unhistorical fashion, as if history has not evolved and changed over time as the circumstances under which it has been done have altered. My second major reason for structuring this book along chronological lines has been that a chronological narrative better conveys the drama and excitement of historiographical debate. If we want to understand not only the "how" of historical methods, but also the "why" behind them, placing the historians of the past in their own historical context is the most effective approach. It is for this reason that the book concludes with a chapter on the training and careers of historians today. It is meant to help readers understand the context that their teachers and the creators of the various forms of history they encounter in their own lives live in, and, for at least a few students, it may help them decide whether they want to commit themselves to pursue similar careers.

This book is written from a perspective that accepts the diversity of ways in which history has been done over the centuries and is being done today. Diversity is often defined in terms of the groups represented in historical narratives, and the following narrative will certainly demonstrate how the working classes, women, ethnic and racial minorities, and non-Western peoples have come to stand alongside male elites as subjects of historical inquiry. But diversity also has other dimensions. There are many different ways of doing history—political history, social history, and cultural history, to name just a few major approaches—and today, more than ever, there are also many different media in which historical knowledge is communicated, from books and scholarly journals to films, museums, and even video games. This diversity is part of what gives contemporary history its vitality and intensity, but it also creates tensions and conflicts. As someone who has devoted his adult life to academic scholarship and college teaching, I have a strong commitment to the kind of professional history they represent; in the course of writing this book, I was struck for the first time by the fact that I am only three scholarly generations removed from Leopold von Ranke, often regarded as the founder of modern academic history.[4] At the same time, however, writing this book has made me more aware than I was before of the importance of nonacademic history, not only in our present-day world, but also in past eras. If there is one way in which this book differs from traditional narratives about the history of history, it is in the recognition of the plurality of ways in which stories about the past have been transmitted in every historical period. A recognition of this pluralism is more important than ever today, when university historians are increasingly worried about the future of their profession but when interest in history outside the academy is thriving.

Above all, this book has been written by an author who loves history. Many years ago, I recall meeting another American colleague on the steps of the old Bibliothèque nationale, France's national research library. The library staff had unexpectedly decided to go on strike for the day, leaving the two of us standing in front of the locked door, in the middle of Paris, with no plans for the rest of the day. We were aware that our frustration was a bit ridiculous: people all over the world dream of having free time to enjoy Paris's many attractions. The two of us, however, had really wanted to be able to continue our historical research. We had the good sense to laugh at our situation, but the story is testimony to the good fortune both of us knew we enjoyed: we had found a true vocation, a career that engaged us so much that there was nothing else we wanted to do more than to get on with our work. The majority of readers of this book will undoubtedly pursue other careers rather than becoming professional historians. I hope this book will have helped them appreciate history more, even if they only pursue it as a hobby in later life or even neglect it altogether. But I also hope it will have helped them understand what it means to find a career that really engages one, body and soul.

This book owes a great deal to the encouragement of my editor at Oxford University Press, Charles Cavaliere, who suggested the project. A stay as a scholar in residence at the Research School of Social Sciences at the Australian National University in 2012 gave me valuable time to start on the work, which could not have been completed without the assistance of the staff of the University of Kentucky library. I am grateful to innumerable friends and fellow historians for their comments and suggestions, including my colleagues at the University of Kentucky, who read one chapter in our departmental seminar in 2014, and the graduate students in my class on "Historical Criticism" in spring 2014, who served as guinea pigs for the first half of the book. David King provided valuable insights into the life of a historian writing for a general audience, and John Carland and Darrell Meadows have done likewise in helping me write about opportunities for public historians. Thanks to Valerie Barske and Fred Rosenbaum for answering my queries about their work and to the staff of the Thomas D. Clark Center for Kentucky History who took time to show me around behind the scenes at a history museum.

Most of all, however, I acknowledge the influence of the teachers who introduced me to historiographical issues, starting with my high school American history teacher, Jules Tanzer, who somehow managed to stay awake through every page of my paper on "Grover Cleveland and the Gold Standard." In my undergraduate years, I was stimulated particularly by Geoffrey Barraclough, a pioneer of contemporary world history, Carl Schorske, a virtuoso intellectual and cultural historian, and Gerald Feldman, who taught the dynamic undergraduate historiographical seminar I took at Berkeley. In graduate school, I learned from H. Stuart Hughes and Steven Schuker, the odd couple who led Harvard's introductory seminar in modern European history, Patrice Higonnet, with his highly personal take on the French past, Hans Rosenberg, a model of methodological rigor, Natalie Zemon Davis, who failed to attract me to her seminars on early modern Europe but who nevertheless managed to convey her sense of excitement about the new work in women's history she was undertaking, Judith Shklar, who introduced me to Nietzsche's *Use and Abuse of History*, Martin Malia, passionately convinced of the connection between history and present-day issues, and Richard Webster, who was always eager to convince me that the conventional wisdom was wrong. Attending seminars in Paris led by Daniel Roche and François Furet introduced me to the traditions of French scholarship. Belated thanks also to my friends in the dissertation-writing group I belonged to at Berkeley, who drew me into historiographical disputes of an intensity I have rarely enjoyed since.

Notes

1. Edward Hallett Carr, *What Is History?* (New York: Vintage Books, 1961).
2. John Tosh, *The Pursuit of History*, 5th ed. (Harlow: Pearson, 2010).
3. Ernst Breisach, *Historiography: Ancient, Medieval, and Modern* (Chicago: University of Chicago Press, 1983); Donald R. Kelley, *Faces of History: Historical Inquiry from Herodotus to Herder* (New Haven, CT: Yale University Press, 1998); Donald R. Kelley, *Fortunes of History: Historical Inquiry from Herder to Huizinga* (New Haven, CT: Yale University Press, 2003); Donald R. Kelley, *Frontiers of History: Historical Inquiry in the Twentieth Century* (New Haven, CT: Yale University Press, 2006).
4. As a graduate student at the University of California, Berkeley, in the 1970s, I was privileged to participate in the last research seminar directed by Hans Rosenberg, a major figure in modern European social history. Rosenberg had done his dissertation under the direction of the German intellectual historian Friedrich Meinecke, who in turn had been a student of Ranke's.

Jeremy D. Popkin holds the William T. Bryan Chair of history at the University of Kentucky. Popkin's passion for history began during childhood trips to Europe with his family and was deepened during his years of study at Reed College, UC San Diego, UC Berkeley, and Harvard. Popkin's books on the French Revolution, the Haitian Revolution, and the historical relevance of autobiography have won numerous awards. He has been a visiting scholar at the Collège de France, Brown University, the Martin-Luther-Universität Halle, and Australian National University, and has been awarded fellowships from the John Simon Guggenheim Foundation, the National Humanities Center, the National Endowment for the Humanities, the Institute for Advanced Study, the Fulbright Foundation, and the Newberry Library. Popkin has taught seminars on historiography for more than thirty years.

From Herodotus to H-Net

PART ONE

Historiography from Herodotus to the Twentieth Century

CHAPTER 1

What Is Historiography?

We do not know when human beings first began telling stories about striking events that had happened in the past, but
we can hardly doubt that as soon as they started to do so,
they came up against some of the same questions that historians today
encounter. How many generations ago did that especially cold winter
drive their ancestors to cross the frozen river to find game? Did the fur
pelt on the cave wall commemorate that expedition, or was it acquired
at some other time? Was that winter the worst crisis the group had ever
experienced? Did the song they knew about the great hunt exaggerate
the role of one group member's ancestor at the expense of another?
Whose memory of those events was most accurate? Questions like
these, about the nature and reliability of evidence concerning past
events, the ways of organizing stories about them, the ways those stories may be distorted, and the purposes they may serve, are the stuff of
historiography. We can define historiography as the critical assessment
of the ways in which historians try to reconstruct past events as distinguished from the statements they make about the past.

The Concerns of Historiography

Historiography deals with the various methods historians use in gathering data, analyzing it, and communicating it. The term "historiography" also refers to the history of history itself: understanding how
historians of the past conceived of their projects and the methods they

used is one of the most important ways we can gain perspective on the challenges facing historians today. Historians also speak of the historiography of particular historical topics, such as the Atlantic slave trade or the American Civil War. In this case, they are using the term to describe the way in which historical knowledge about and interpretations of those subjects have changed over time. In this book, we will be concerned with historiography in the more general sense—that is, with the common issues that confront historians, regardless of what era or aspect of the past they may be interested in.

The challenge and complexity of the subject of historiography reflects the complexity of the term "history" itself. In most languages, the word history refers both to events that took place in the past and to the accounts we give of them. In this respect, history differs, for example, from literature. The history shelves of a library do not contain the past itself; instead, they hold books that purport to contain information about the past. The fact that they often contain many different books about the same historical subjects, books that may tell quite different stories about their topics, suggests that there is not necessarily a simple relationship between "the past" and the way it is written down and remembered. By contrast, the shelves in a library's literature section contain the actual works studied by scholars of that discipline, such as the plays of Shakespeare and the novels of Virginia Woolf. Historiography is a critical enterprise that deals, in good part, with the questions raised by the difference between these two meanings of the word history. It asks what methods we can use to obtain reliable knowledge about the past, given that we cannot actually observe or recreate events that have already happened. Historiography also tries to account for the different ways in which historians have understood the past and to reconcile these conflicting interpretations with the notion that there is some core of truth about the past that can be known.

When they decide to study history, few students are particularly attracted by the prospect of taking a course in historiography. Historiography has the reputation of being a difficult topic. This reputation is not entirely deserved; some classic works on historiography, such as Marc Bloch's *The Historian's Craft* (1949) and E. H. Carr's *What Is History?* (1961), succeed in raising big issues in direct language, and even among contemporary "postmodernist" historians, who have the reputation of being hard to understand, there are some, such as Keith Jenkins, who write with admirable clarity. Nevertheless, most people are attracted to history because they are curious about some specific aspect of the past, such as the lives of women or World War I, not because they want to engage in abstract arguments about the obstacles to finding out the truth about what happened long ago. Historiography is a "metadiscourse," a "narrative about narratives" whose subject matter is other works of history, rather than historical events themselves. Historiographical analyses often move back and forth among several levels of reference—the facts of the past themselves, the ways in which those facts can be discerned and written about, and the mental processes of historians—which can make them challenging to follow.

For most students, historiography is a subject imposed on them if they want to earn a college degree in history; few people decide to study the topic for its own sake. The most common encounters that lead young people to an interest in history provide them with little preparation for understanding the issues that drive historiographical debates. History books written for young readers try to provide a sense of what life was like in days gone by, often by telling dramatic stories with colorful characters; their authors do not try to explain why it is difficult to try to reconstruct the past or why there may be different explanations of historical events. School textbooks are written to make it appear as though the information they convey is authoritative and beyond question, a set of facts that students must memorize if they want to be recognized for being "good" at history. Historical films, television documentaries, and museum exhibitions provide vivid visual images of the past that give viewers the impression of having seen things as they "really were." History books written for a popular audience emphasize spectacular events and big personalities; if they mention their sources, they often make it seem as though historical research is a matter of detective-like searches for previously undiscovered documents.

When students whose imaginations have been stimulated by these various forms of history find themselves in a historiography course, they often feel as though they are being asked to say goodbye to all the things that attracted them to the subject in the first place, above all to the assumptions that there is a clear truth about the past that we can learn and that history is primarily a matter of absorbing factual information. Professional historians who have written autobiographies about their own education often recall that they chose to study that particular subject, instead of other fields such as literature or philosophy, because they wanted to be involved with the lives of real people, rather than with imagined characters or abstract ideas. Courses in historiography confront students with the possibility that history, like literature, is about stories and that it necessarily involves philosophical questions, such as how we can actually come to know things. Once they have completed their own university studies, most history teachers also have at best a limited interest in historiographical questions. The number of historians who regularly read or aspire to publish in professional journals that specialize in such matters, such as the American-based *History and Theory*, the British journal *Rethinking History*, or the European review *Storia della Storiografia*, is much smaller than the number of those who follow periodicals that publish articles in fields defined by geography or time period.

Nevertheless, there is broad agreement among teachers of history at the college level that students should have at least some exposure to the subject of historiography. An anthropologist studying the behavior of historians might classify the historiography course required for history majors at most American colleges and universities as a rite of passage, a kind of ordeal designed to test the toughness of aspiring members of the tribe and initiate them into its secrets. Historians themselves see exposure to historiography as essential to help students transform themselves from accumulators of historical data to informed critics and potentially active participants in the historical enterprise. Historiography courses, we hope, provide the opportunity for students to realize what it means to say that the historical past is not simply "out there," waiting to be discovered, but that it must be reconstructed out of evidence that is never self-explanatory. This is why historiography courses often combine readings about the theory and history of history-writing with a hands-on exercise in which students develop a research project of their own and learn to use the methods of professional scholarship. The combination of theoretical reading, research, and presentation is meant to give students the chance to experience for themselves what it means to *be* a historian and to confront the issues that historiography raises.

An awareness of historiography is important to historians not only because it defines the difference between consumers of historical knowledge and those who have the skills to produce that knowledge, however. Historiographical debates are also where the fundamental issues involved in the reconstruction of the past are brought out in the open. For this reason, historiographical debates are often among the most intense disputes in which professional historians engage. Controversies about questions of historical fact may be heated, but they can usually be resolved by a determined search for evidence; controversies about the meaning and interpretation of the past cannot be settled in the same way. In the late 1970s, for example, as historical research on the Holocaust was becoming a major field, there was a lengthy debate about whether the German dictator Adolf Hitler had ever issued a written order for the extermination of Europe's Jewish population. After much investigation in the archives of the Nazi government, most historians accepted the conclusion that there almost certainly never had been a written "Hitler order" to this effect, that Hitler and his henchmen had developed the plans for their genocide in a series of steps rather than all at one time, and that Hitler had conveyed his intentions without putting them on paper. The debate about exactly how to define the extent of Hitler's responsibility for the Holocaust, however, is an ongoing one that will not be settled by finding more documents. Ultimately, it involves conflicting views about the relationship between political leaders and their followers, the relative importance of ideological convictions and historical circumstances in determining human actions, and differing notions of what constitutes historical evidence. In other words, it is a historiographical debate about how history should be understood.

At bottom, major historiographical debates such as the one about the responsibility for the Holocaust involve fundamental questions about human nature and human existence: Do human beings have free will, or are their actions essentially determined by external forces? Are there universal laws governing human behavior, or have societies at different times in the past exhibited different patterns of conduct and held different values? Does knowledge of the past provide us with guidance about the future, and, if not, what is the value of history? What kind of knowledge about the past can we hope to achieve, and what are the best methods for obtaining it? Because historiographical arguments are about big questions that have no simple answers, they are often among the most divisive disputes that historians engage in. (I can still remember the professor who taught my graduate-school historiography seminar challenging one of the students to a fist fight!) Although major historiographical disagreements are rarely resolved for good, in the way that questions of fact may be, these debates are not meaningless. They help to clarify the assumptions underlying different approaches to history and to make the reasons for disagreements among historians comprehensible. By challenging historians to look at the past from new angles, historiographical disagreements help keep the discipline alive. A course in historiography is a chance to discover the hidden fires that provide the energy for the discipline of history as a whole.

The big questions that historiography deals with overlap with the concerns of other academic disciplines, and participants in historiographical debates often find themselves in dialogue with, among others, philosophers, anthropologists, economists, scholars of literature, political scientists, art historians, sociologists, archeologists, and specialists in gender studies. The readings assigned in courses on historiography often include selections from the works of authors who were not themselves historians, but who raised issues that stimulated historical research, such as the sociologist Max Weber, the philosopher Michel Foucault, and the literary critic Edward Said. Although these cross-disciplinary dialogues are often fruitful, it is in historiographical debates that historians are also driven to define the unique contributions that historical research and historical thinking make to our broader understanding of human affairs. The study of historiography is thus partly a way of answering the questions of what makes history a distinctive branch of knowledge and why it is worth pursuing. By underlining the distinctive characteristics of history, historiography also emphasizes the concerns that all historians, regardless of their own special field of interest, have in common. Historiographical debates may divide historians, but the fact that these debates matter to everyone concerned with history helps to keep historians with different points of view in conversation with one another.

Learning about historiography is a way of coming to understand what history consists of; it also involves learning what defines a historian. The study of how history was recorded in the past is also a study of the emergence of a community of individuals who claim to have special skills in reconstructing the past and, consequently, special privileges to decide what should be considered reliable historical knowledge. This is why historiography courses introduce students to Herodotus and Sima Qian, the Venerable Bede and Machiavelli, Edward Gibbon and Leopold von Ranke, Marc Bloch and Mary Beard, although we may no longer read their works as reliable sources about the subjects they wrote on. Nowadays, as history is increasingly communicated in ways other than through printed books, historiography courses also must mention filmmakers, historical websites, and even historical video games. To study historiography also involves learning about the institutions that hold the historical community together: the research seminars in which academic historians are trained, the colleges and universities that employ the majority of professional historians, as well as the other venues in which an increasing number of scholars work, the process of peer review by which professional historians assess each other's work, the scholarly associations and learned journals that keep historians in touch with their fields, and the museums and other outlets through which historical findings reach a wider public.

As we can see, learning about historiography is indeed a rite of passage. Like all such rituals, it changes those who go through it. Some of the changes produced by an exposure to historiography may be painful. Once students have learned to read historical works more critically, they may look back at the books and other sources that inspired their love of history in the first place and see them as superficial or biased. Learning about the different ways in which history can be researched and presented may be dizzying and disorienting. It is not uncommon for students to react to the discovery of "the varieties of history" by concluding that all history simply reflects the preferences and prejudices of particular historians and that any perspective on the past is as good as any other. Among those students who decide to pursue historical studies beyond the undergraduate level and aim for a career in history, exposure to historiographical arguments can sometimes become almost paralyzing: faced with so many possible ways of interpreting the data from their research, they spend so much time dealing with these questions that they barely get around to discussing their own findings. History Ph.D. dissertations, at least at American universities, often begin with a dense chapter on the historiography of their topic and their author's approach to it. Students who successfully complete this difficult exercise are often dismayed when their advisors tell them that the first thing they will have to do, if they want to make their work publishable, is to drastically shorten or even eliminate those pages.

With time and experience, however, students who have passed through the ritual of exposure to historiography learn to integrate what they have learned into a broader perspective on history. We can learn to see why popular history differs from scholarly academic research and how we can be critical of propagandistic and inaccurate presentations without rejecting the importance of forms of history meant for general audiences. We can also come to see how clearly articulated professional standards can help to mitigate the biases that may arise from historians' personal investments in their subjects. The frustrated Ph.D. student who is told to discard a laboriously compiled dissertation chapter on historiography will, if all goes well, often come to realize that the perspectives generated by this work are in fact incorporated in the other parts of his or her work and have helped to make it meaningful.

Most students who major in history and take a course on historiography, as well as readers who are not students but who may decide that they want to understand something about how professional historians think, should also come away from exposure to the subject with some positive gains, although they will not go on to become professional scholars themselves. To study historiography is to begin to understand how historians think and how they do their work and to realize that one could, potentially, do that work oneself. Exposure to historiography helps us understand the complexity of the historical enterprise and gives us a deeper appreciation for the accomplishments of those who have written compelling books or produced illuminating films, museum exhibitions, or websites. Through an acquaintance with historiography, we learn to become better critics of historical work. Instead of simply saying that we like or dislike particular historical works, we are able to give reasons for our judgments. The critical skills taught in historiography courses are applicable in many other contexts as well: they can help in making political decisions, evaluating legal testimony, appraising messages in the media, and spotting the pitfalls in advertisements.

The perspective that the study of historiography provides warns us against the fallacy of assuming that our own time period is a unique era in the study of history. No one could deny, however, that historians today find themselves engaged in a wide-ranging variety of historiographical debates. For several decades now, historians have been disputing the implications for our discipline of the so-called linguistic turn in philosophy and social theory. By arguing that all our knowledge is mediated through language and that there is no necessary connection between language and the phenomena it claims to describe, historians who have adopted this perspective, such as Hayden White, have raised disturbing questions about whether we can have any access to the reality of the past. Another set of ongoing historiographical controversies has roots in opening the discipline to the perspectives of groups that were long excluded from mainstream historical narratives.

In the United States, this movement has directed attention to the history of women, African Americans, Latinos, Native Americans, homosexuals, and a variety of other "Others" whose stories, it is claimed, have been systematically silenced and repressed. On a global scale, historians have been challenged to find new ways to "provincialize Europe," as Dipesh Chakrabarty has put it, by giving more attention to the history of the non-Western world. As they turn to the history of Asia, Africa, and Latin America, historians seek to give a voice to "subaltern" groups whose lives have often left few written records and to do justice to the complexities of "postcolonial" societies deeply affected by the aftermath of the centuries in which European empires dominated the world. For some historians, the new perspectives opened up by the linguistic turn and the effort to write a more inclusive history have been stimulating challenges that have helped renew the discipline. For others, however, these historiographical developments have undermined the criteria according to which historical truth is defined and opened the door to a dangerous relativism. Whereas some historians see the multiplicity of viewpoints as a sign of the discipline's vitality, others lament that this diversity has made it impossible to construct generally acceptable narratives of the past.

Alongside the debates triggered by the linguistic turn and attempts to write a more inclusive history, the discipline is also being reshaped by changes in the ways historians access their sources and communicate their findings. Instead of relying primarily on written documents, especially those kept in official archives, and published materials found in libraries, historians are increasingly turning to visual and oral materials, often accessed via the Internet. This shift has broadened access to many historical sources, but it has also raised difficult questions about how we guarantee the authenticity of these materials and how we interpret these new forms of evidence. Whereas historical research was traditionally published in books and scholarly articles and evaluated through an elaborate process of review by other historians, nowadays historians pay increasing attention to museum exhibitions, films, websites, historical theme parks, and even historically based video games. The Internet has made ordinary readers' responses to new books easier to find than those written by professional peers. Today's media environment has made some kinds of historical knowledge more widely available than ever before, but it also posed many new questions that fall under the aegis of historiography.

This Book and Its Author

The goal of this book is to introduce readers to the history of historical thinking and to the major issues that concern historians today. We begin by sketching out the history of historical thought and writing itself, from the earliest preserved historical narratives of ancient Greece and China to the beginning of the twenty-first century. This is a way of putting our own interest in history in historical perspective. By learning how history has been done in different societies across the ages, we gain a broader appreciation of the different purposes historical narratives have served and of the different approaches to the subject that historians have developed. We can appreciate the reasons why historians have adopted certain procedures for reconstructing the past, and we develop a deeper sense of the meaning of our own historical efforts by realizing that we form part of a tradition that extends back over several thousand years.

Although history is concerned with the past, it is conducted in the present. The survey of historiography in this book concludes by describing the main themes of historiographical debate today and the new media that are playing an increasing role in the dissemination of history. Historiography is not just about how history has been done in the past: it is a live and vital subject because it informs the way we research, write, and teach history now. The final chapter of this book explains the process of training necessary to become a professional historian and describes the different careers open to those who do decide to specialize in the subject. The purpose of this chapter is certainly not to persuade all readers to become full-time historians; we acknowledge the many obstacles that even the most determined history lovers face if they decide to prepare for such a career. Reading this chapter should give all history students a better appreciation of what such a career involves, however, and why some people do decide to pursue it. Some of the lessons to be learned from reading about the process of becoming a professional historian, such as the reasons why such a career requires lengthy training and the need to be open to different kinds of employment possibilities, are relevant in many fields besides history and academia.

The author of this book has come to the subject after a lifetime spent reading, writing, and teaching about history. When my father—also a historian—died, I inherited the letters he had written to my grandmother during my childhood. One of them gives the first hint of how my interest in the past developed. My family was living in Paris for a year, and I had just turned four. As many children of that age do, I had apparently started asking my parents what happened to people after they died. In response, my father took me to see Napoleon's tomb in the church of the Invalides and tried to explain to me who he had been and why such a grand monument had been built to him. I have no personal memory of this excursion, but can it truly be a coincidence that I grew up, years later, not only to become a historian but also to study Napoleon's era, the period of the French Revolution? I first encountered the subject of historiography in a lively undergraduate seminar in 1968, and many of the authors I read in that course—Thucydides, Guicciardini, Jacob Burckhardt, Leon Trotsky, Marc Bloch—figure in the story told in this book. Looking back, it is striking to realize how few hints there were in that class of the major historiographical changes that would re-shape the field over the course of my subsequent career: no mention of women or feminism, no hint of the "linguistic turn" that would trans-form much of academia, no attention to non-Western history or even, as far as I recall, to American history. This is a reminder that historians are much better at explaining the past than at anticipating the future.

Like most history students, I only really became engaged in histo-riographical debates during my years of graduate study, during the 1970s. It is a common failing to see one's early years as a unique period in history, but certainly a lot was happening in the field of history during those years. Hans Rosenberg, one of the many German-born scholars who had immigrated to the United States to escape Hitler's Nazi regime, introduced me to the rigorous methods of source criti-cism and analysis first developed in his home country in the nineteenth century; through him, I now realize, I was only three generations re-moved from Leopold von Ranke, the founder of modern academic his-tory, who will play a major role in the pages that follow. I remember being electrified by the new approach to history suggested in a talk by Robert Darnton, one of the pioneers of what we now call cultural his-tory, and the excitement of serving as a teaching assistant for Natalie Zemon Davis, who was incorporating perspectives from women's his-tory even at the level of the introductory survey course. With fellow graduate students at Harvard and Berkeley and in Paris, I debated the strange new ideas put forward in Hayden White's *Metahistory* (1973) and the writings of Michel Foucault and compared them to the meth-odological model of the Annales school of French social historians and "cliometricians" such as the historian-sociologist Charles Tilly. I cannot claim that I was always at the forefront of these historiographical discussions; I sometimes thought to myself, "I want to play the game, not argue about the rules." But I certainly learned that historiographical considerations are present, consciously or unconsciously, in everything that historians do.

If anything about my subsequent career has prepared me to write an introduction to historiography, it is the fact that I have written and taught about a wide variety of historical subjects and employed many different approaches to deal with them. The development of my interests has taken me from the history of the press and the media in the French revolutionary era, the topic of my dissertation and several other books, to the study of slavery and abolition, which has brought me into a subfield—Atlantic history—that did not exist when I was a student. I have regularly taught a seminar on historiography, and I have written on an explicitly historiographical issue—the relationship between history and another important way of writing about the past, autobiography—which brought me into contact with the developing field of the history of memory. For many years, the most popular course I have taught has been an undergraduate class on the Holocaust. Keeping up to date on the literature in the field has given me an additional perspective on historiographical trends, as I have seen the subject grow from a marginal concern to a central issue in thinking about how we understand and transmit knowledge about the past. Among other things, it is through my engagement with Holocaust studies that I have been drawn into thinking about the role of film and of museum exhibits in communicating historical information. In recent years, I have even written a few articles on the history of my own family, an activity that has given me, among other things, the experience of having to assemble and organize my own "archive," a fancy name for the file cabinet filled with old family letters, documents, and photographs in my study.

I mention these diverse experiences here not because I think of my career as a model for anyone else, but because engaging with these many forms and subject areas of history has forced me to confront many different historiographical issues. Certainly, one lesson I would like to share with all those who read this book—both students and teachers who decide to assign it—is that thinking about history can be a deeply stimulating and rewarding activity. But deciding to spend one's life as a historian also has its limitations. To embrace any profession is to acquire what has been called a "trained incapacity": one comes to see the world in a certain framework that can be hard to transcend, and one cuts oneself off from other possibilities. When I did the research project that resulted in my book *History, Historians, and Autobiography* (2005), I was much struck by the memoir of Peter Carroll, who was in graduate school around the same time as I was but who decided to follow another career. "Wrapped in the cloak of Scholarship . . . we blithely permitted the real history of the times to pass us by," he wrote of his days in graduate school.[1] I hope there is also a second, more broadly applicable, lesson to be learned from this book, however, one that may be of value to those readers—no doubt the majority—who will pursue other paths, even while, or so I hope, maintaining an interest in history. The lesson is that one is truly fortunate if one can find and pursue a career, whatever it may be, that truly engages one's mind and one's passions. For me, that has been the study of history. For others, it will be something quite different, but hopefully something that will be as meaningful for them as history has been for me.

Justifying the Study of the Past

Studying history may be personally satisfying for some people, and it may be one way to earn a living, but creating and preserving knowledge about the past is also important for more general reasons. History is often referred to as a collective equivalent to individual memory, but the value of remembering the collective past accurately is not necessarily as obvious as the practical importance for individuals of remembering where they parked their car or stored their winter clothes. Case studies of individuals who have lost their personal memory because of brain damage have shown how incapacitating such a condition can be, preventing people from recognizing family members and depriving them of a sense of identity, but not everyone agrees that the same thing holds for groups. The nineteenth-century French historian and philosopher Ernest Renan argued that "forgetting . . . is an essential factor in the creation of a nation and it is for this reason that the progress of historical studies often poses a threat to nationality," by reviving the memory of episodes of violence and injustice that, he said, were inevitable in the establishment of any country.[2] The United States in particular, it has often been said, was founded by people who thought of themselves as creating a new nation, one that had no need of any historical heritage.

The modest place that history occupies in American school curricula shows that this attitude has by no means disappeared.

For many centuries, knowledge of the past was considered vital for those involved in public affairs because it would teach them rules about human behavior that could guide their own conduct. Thucydides, one of the founders of history in the classical world, was supposed to have said that history is philosophy teaching by example—in other words, that past events demonstrated universal rules about human life. A somewhat similar thought was formulated by the early twentieth-century philosopher George Santayana: "Those who cannot remember the past are condemned to repeat it." If this were literally true, history would certainly have obvious practical value, but modern historians are considerably less certain that knowledge of the past provides clear guidelines for action in the present and enables us to foresee the future. No two historical situations are ever exactly alike, and, in the face of a new crisis, different historical precedents can often be cited to support different courses of action.

Although few historians today would argue that the study of the past can provide us with clear rules to guide the making of public policy, most would still agree that knowledge of the past can help us understand the range of possibilities we face in dealing with contemporary problems. Knowing the history of the American, French, and Russian revolutions does not necessarily enable us to predict what will happen when a popular movement overthrows an oppressive government, but it helps us see that the outcomes of such events can be different, ranging from the establishment of a stable and enduring democracy, in the American case, to the rise of an oppressive dictatorship in the Russian one. Perhaps one of the most valuable lessons from the study of history is the importance of unintended consequences. Experts in the social sciences, such as economics and political science, often make confident predictions about the consequences of adopting certain policies; historians provide sobering, if often unwelcome, reminders that such predictions have frequently been wrong in the past. The history of U.S. foreign policy since World War II, for example, has seen repeated instances in which policy experts predicted that American military interventions would bring about the establishment of democracy in foreign countries. Historians who warned that the populations of Vietnam, Iraq, and Afghanistan might not accept American political ideas were ignored, but they turned out to be prescient.

Present-day historians are more likely to emphasize the value of history in producing a collective sense of identity than its use in terms of providing practical guidance. Communities at every level, they argue, need a shared understanding of their past. Acutely aware of how historians in the past often contributed to national myths that sometimes led to disastrous consequences, professional historians today are more likely to insist that historical consciousness should help us recognize the diverse nature of the groups we belong to. In American history, this has meant replacing a notion of American identity stressing the role of the Pilgrims, the Founding Fathers, and our most famous presidents with one that integrates the historical contributions of minority groups and women and balances emphasis on national achievements with a recognition of the darker aspects of our past. Ideally, a critical understanding of our national past will make Americans more willing to tackle the difficulties confronting us in the present in intelligent ways. At the local level, awareness of our communities' histories ought to foster efforts to preserve structures that convey a sense of the past while also showing that community identity can incorporate elements of change, as it has in previous eras. At a global level, many historians see it as our discipline's mission to show how peoples on different continents have always been connected with each other. A sense of a shared past, we hope, may diffuse conflicts and promote efforts to deal with problems of worldwide scope.

Historians are also likely to stress the importance of truthful history as a way of demolishing emotionally charged myths about the past that may have dangerous consequences in the present. As I wrote these lines, in the summer of 2014, for example, the world had been following an explosive crisis in the Eastern European nation of Ukraine. Claims that much Ukrainian territory "historically" belongs to Russia and that Ukrainians supported the German invasion of Russia during World War II have been widely circulated in the Russian media and have contributed to the acute tension between the two countries. In the United States, a half-century of serious study of the African American past has made it impossible to pretend that slaves were well treated or that there was anything inevitable about the Jim Crow laws that reduced blacks to second-class status after the Civil War.

Another important role played by history and historians is that of reminding those who hold power today that they will some day have to face the judgment of posterity. Laws in the United States and many other countries require that documentation about governmental actions be preserved and, after some interval of time, made available to historians. One of the main purposes of such laws is to ensure that politicians today know that their actions will be carefully scrutinized in the future. Although this process may not take place until after the people concerned have died, public figures are acutely concerned about how they will be remembered. Even dictators share this preoccupation. As the Nazi regime crumbled in the last days of 1945, Hitler's top officials tried desperately to destroy the records of their crimes, but the careful work of historians has made sure that there can be no legitimate doubt about the terrible things they did. In some countries, political considerations have led to the issuing of amnesties for perpetrators of injustices as part of processes designed to produce reconciliation after bitter conflicts. These amnesties may prevent legal prosecution of perpetrators, but they cannot prevent historians from investigating the past. Historians can thus contribute to respect for human rights.

These are serious contributions historians can make to public life, but history also has significance for the individuals who research it, teach it, and absorb it. Like literature, philosophy, and psychology, history is one of the disciplines that can help us understand human behavior, including, potentially, our own. It is one way of satisfying the widespread human urge to comprehend how the world we live in came to be the way it is. Learning about history can give us a sense of perspective, not only on the society we live in, but also on ourselves. It can be an inspiration to strive to achieve our goals, individual and collective, and a consolation for the fact that complete success in life is always out of reach. Finally, of course, good history is *interesting*. It immerses us in stories about other human beings that have the special attraction of being rooted in reality. History takes us to distant times and places and introduces us to personalities as vivid and varied as the ascetic female saints studied by medievalist Caroline Bynum and the murderous German policemen depicted by the Holocaust specialist Christopher Browning.

A Short Field Guide to the Varieties of History

All historians study the past, but different historians are interested in different aspects of human behavior. Like different species of animals, historians employing different approaches tend to herd together and separate themselves from other scholars. Different species of historians graze on different kinds of historical data; the government documents that are the basic diet of a political historian may be indigestible for a cultural historian. Being able to recognize to which species particular works of history belong is a basic aspect of what we might call historiographical literacy. The following chapters will explain how the different species of history have evolved over time; in this section, we will categorize the most common types of history that we will be discussing. Making these distinctions is complicated by the fact that the different kinds of historical animals often intermix, producing hybrids that cannot be neatly assigned to one species or another. Mary Renda's *Taking Haiti: Military Occupation and the Culture of U.S. Imperialism* (2001), for example, an innovative study of the American occupation of that Caribbean country between 1915 and 1934, combines political and military history with gender analysis and the interpretation of literary works, which are usually associated with cultural history. Another complication is that specimens of the same historical species do not necessarily get along well with one another. Two political historians may use similar methodology to study a topic such as Franklin Roosevelt's New Deal of the 1930s and yet come to mutually incompatible conclusions about its origins and the extent of its success.

Political history and its close cousins, diplomatic history or, as it is often called nowadays, the history of foreign relations, and military history, remain among the most vital varieties of history. Indeed, events such as the disputed American presidential election of 2000, the terrorist attacks of September 11, 2001, the U.S. invasion of Iraq in 2003, and the centennial of World War I in 2014 have reminded historians that the tools of "traditional" political, military, and economic history can still be essential for explaining the past. These forms of history go back a long way. Narrating and explaining the actions of political elites and military leaders were the principal preoccupations of the earliest historians, including Thucydides in Greece and Sima Qian in China. Similar questions preoccupied the leading historians of the Renaissance period, such as Machiavelli and Guicciardini, and they were the main focus of the nineteenth-century scholar Leopold von Ranke and the historical school he founded.

Political history and diplomatic history are sometimes criticized on the grounds that they concentrate too narrowly on "great men," leaving out the mass of the population and women. As these forms of history are practiced today, this judgment is often misguided. Political history can be and often is written about mass movements, such as the Chartists in early nineteenth-century England, and feminism has an important political history, as work on the suffrage movements of the nineteenth and early twentieth centuries, such as Karen Offen's *European Feminisms, 1700–1950,* (1999) show. Quantitative statistical methods have allowed historians to analyze voting data and explain the reasons why the United States has experienced periodic "realigning elections" that have transformed its political party system or what motivated Germans who voted for Hitler in the early 1930s. Diplomatic historians increasingly recognize that formal interactions between governments are only one aspect of foreign relations. The history of warfare has been profoundly transformed in recent decades by "new military historians," such as John Keegan, whose *The Face of Battle* (1983) applied the techniques of social history and microhistory to the subject and shifted the focus from generals and military technology to the experience of common soldiers.

Political, diplomatic, and military history remain major historical fields because scholars recognize that they deal with important aspects of human experience. Even if one tries resolutely to concentrate on the everyday lives of ordinary people in the past, one finds that they were affected by the laws of the governments they lived under, that they paid taxes, and that their lives were often drastically altered by wars and diplomatic settlements. These varieties of history lend themselves to dramatic narration, which is why they continue to dominate popular history, but the best work in these fields also has a strong analytic dimension. Understanding why Philip II of Spain launched his armada against England in 1588 or why Abraham Lincoln decided to issue the Emancipation Proclamation in 1862 requires careful evaluation of often ambiguous evidence.

Political, diplomatic, and military historians can usually draw on well-organized bodies of sources that often allow them to imagine that they can achieve a degree of certainty that is harder for other varieties of history to achieve. Documents concerning these subjects have traditionally been carefully preserved in governmental archives, and many centuries of historical practice have given scholars well-established procedures for using them. One of the attractions of these subjects is the opportunity to follow in close detail the steps that led to major political, diplomatic, or military events and to have the feeling that one can really enter into the minds of the historical actors involved in them in ways that are often not possible when doing social or cultural history. Even so, historians working in these fields still need to use their imaginations to fully understand the unfolding of events. Despite plentiful documentation, many aspects of political history remain enigmatic. Historians continue to disagree vehemently about the reasons why the French revolutionaries adopted a policy of terror in 1793, the character of the Progressive movement in American politics, and the responsibility for the outbreak of war in Europe in 1914.

Political, diplomatic, and military history have often been seen as limited because they have usually given rulers and especially nation-states a central role in their narratives. As we will see, this is no accident: over the centuries, kings and ruling elites often deliberately encouraged historians to record their deeds. "Scientific" history developed as part of the growth of nationalism in the nineteenth century, and national archives usually dwarf all other document collections in terms of the size and breadth of their holdings. Contemporary historians are acutely conscious of the limitations of nation-centered history, however. The current movement to "globalize" contemporary history stresses historical forces that transcend national boundaries. The history of international organizations, such as the League of Nations of the interwar period and nongovernmental activist groups in recent times, is currently a major growth area in the discipline, as scholars recognize that political history is not the monopoly of national governments.

Social history is another of the major species roaming the discipline's savannah, often closely associated with economic history. Once defined by the British historian G. M. Trevelyan as "the history of the people with the politics left out," social history emphasizes the different ways human beings have been connected with one another in different periods, as members of families, communities, and social classes. Economic history highlights especially the significance of the ways in which people have made a living, the technology they have used, and the effects of flows of wealth. Social and economic historians sometimes claim that their subjects deal with aspects of human life more fundamental than those emphasized by political historians. Those inspired by the ideas of the mid-nineteenth-century social theorist Karl Marx argue that conflict between social classes is the motor of historical change and that social classes themselves are the product of economic structures. During the 1960s and early 1970s, a "new social history" armed with quantitative research methods borrowed from the "hard" social sciences of economics, sociology, and political science rose to prominence in the discipline. Whereas political historians tend to concentrate on governing elites, social and economic historians often emphasized the importance of the lower classes who have made up the overwhelming majority of the population in most times and places.

In the wake of the world economic crisis of the late 2000s, concerns with the dysfunctions of the world economy and the growth of income inequality have revived interest in some of the classic themes of social and economic history. Some of the DNA of the "new social history" can also be detected in varieties of history that go by other names nowadays. Groups that historians want to rescue from what E. P. Thompson, in his *The Making of the English Working Class* (1963), called "the enormous condescension of posterity" are more likely to be defined now as racial and ethnic minorities and colonized populations or in terms of gender. Scholarship defined as "microhistory" and "the history of everyday life" often explore domains that clearly belong to the field of social history. Social history retains a strong presence in non-Western fields, such as Latin American history. In American and European history, questions about the development of social security systems and other forms of social policy have attracted historians' attention, a sign that social historians have heeded the call, sounded as early as the 1980s, to "bring the state back in" to the study of ordinary people's experiences.

Economic historians have contributed powerfully to work on global history and the connections between different parts of the world. Perhaps the most influential work of economic history published in the United States in recent years, Kenneth Pomeranz's *The Great Divergence: China, Europe, and the Making of the Modern World Economy* (2000), demonstrates what the field can contribute, both to historical understanding and to comprehension of the contemporary world. Pomeranz's argument about the reasons why industrialization began in Europe in the years around 1800 and not in China, although the two regions had had comparable levels of economic development up to that time, puts the rapid present-day development of the Chinese economy in historical perspective and challenges claims that Western cultural values and political institutions were uniquely favorable to technological innovation.

The sources that nourish social and economic history are quite different from those that political, diplomatic, and military historians normally feed on. Social and economic historians often depend on data that can be transformed into numbers and analyzed statistically: census reports, tax rolls, figures for imports and exports of goods, and records of wages and prices. Other important sources for social history can include property registers, police records, which often reveal common patterns of behavior, travelers' accounts, and private documents such as diaries. Whereas part of the attraction of political and diplomatic history can come from the sense that the sources allow the historian to see what historical actors were thinking when they made their decisions, social historians are often motivated by the challenge of showing what can be learned from documents that at first glance seem to reveal little and are often frustratingly incomplete. The genius of the French Annales school founder Marc Bloch's social history classic, *French Rural History* (1931), lies in its ability to construct a convincing picture of the life of French peasant communities from fragmentary evidence that never lets us directly hear the thoughts of the people involved.

Cultural history, the species of historical scholarship that multiplied the fastest in the last decades of the twentieth century, is another important variety of history. Whereas social history is connected to the "hard" social sciences, cultural history has closer ties with anthropology and with other humanities disciplines, such as literary studies and art history. Cultural historians study the various ways in which human groups have created meanings for themselves over the course of history. The topics of cultural history may include systems of gender identity, religious practices, and beliefs and rituals associated with death, among other issues. Whereas social history has traditionally been identified with the history of the "masses," cultural history may deal with elite culture, popular culture, and everything in between.

If political and diplomatic history draw some scholars because of the opportunity to work with sources that seem to make it possible to put together a complete picture of past events, cultural history attracts others because it offers the challenge of tracking down sources that are often widely scattered and found in places where more traditional historians would not think to look. Many cultural historians do work with printed sources and written archival materials, but others find their materials in museums and among the possessions of private individuals. Historians of memory may travel extensively to view public monuments, as the French historian Daniel Sherman did for his study of *The Construction of Memory in Interwar France* (1999), a history of memorials to the fallen soldiers of World War I. One scholar reconstructing the meaning of traditional dances performed on the Japanese island of Okinawa took lessons to learn to perform the movements she was writing about.

In the United States in the past few decades, cultural history has tended to occupy the ecological niche in the discipline that was once filled by intellectual history. The study of ideas and of intellectuals remains a significant aspect of the discipline, and indeed the perspectives associated with the "linguistic turn" in the humanities, which we will discuss in chapter 6, have given it a new vigor after a period in which it was somewhat eclipsed because of a reaction against the rather elitist character it often exhibited. Whereas cultural historians see expressions of meaning in a wide variety of human activities, intellectual historians tend to focus on formally structured texts: works of philosophy, political theory, literature, and, indeed, history; historiography forms a subspecies of intellectual history. Intellectual historians also tend to emphasize the works of individuals who devoted themselves to thought and writing; of all the major varieties of history, it is the one that has been least susceptible to the allure of "history from below." The sources of intellectual history are usually books and perhaps the unpublished papers and correspondence of thinkers and authors.

With this field guide to the major varieties of history in mind, we are now ready to begin our exploration of how and why these different species of historical literature have evolved. We presume that human beings must have developed ways of remembering past events as they created systems of language, but we can only speculate about what forms such historical memory may have taken prior to the invention of writing. We know that early civilizations recorded certain kinds of historical information, such as the king lists that have come down to us from ancient Egypt and the sculpted scenes of battles, accompanied by inscriptions, that survive from Mesopotamia, but we usually date the birth of history from the appearance of the first books devoted to the subject and the first identifiable authors who wrote histories. It is only from that point that we can begin to talk about the existence of historical thought and not merely of the preservation of the memory of certain events and the sequence in which they had occurred.

Notes

1. Peter N. Carroll, *Keeping Time* (Athens, Ga.: University of Georgia Press, 1990), 63.
2. Ernest Renan, "What Is a Nation?" 1882 (trans. Ethan Rundell, ucparis.fr/files/9313/6549/9943/What_is_a_Nation.pdf).

CHAPTER 2

History in Ancient
and Medieval Times

In view of historians' commitment to thinking about all aspects of human culture as having a history, it would seem natural that they would want to reconstruct the history of historical thinking itself, and indeed we have seen that one of the major ways in which the word "historiography" is used is to refer to the history of history, whether as a discipline or way of thinking, as a form or genre of literature, or as a profession. Curiously, history was written for several millennia before anyone first tried to write its own history, instead of treating history as just one of the many branches of literature. The history of historiography only emerged at the end of the nineteenth century, the period when, as we will see, the study of the past first came to be treated as a subject for academic research and teaching and when professional training for historians became organized in the pattern it still follows today.

Like every other aspect of the past, the development of history has looked different to historians, depending on the concerns of their own day. For much of the twentieth century, for example, the history of history was written as a story of progress, in the course of which historical thinking gradually freed itself from mythical and religious elements and adopted a scientific perspective. Historiographers working in this tradition saw the development of modern historical thinking as one of the great achievements of Western—that is, European and North American—civilization and paid little attention to the ways in which the past had been recorded in other parts of the world. In recent decades, however, there has been increased interest in alternative forms of history that existed alongside the "scientific" history taught in universities, as well as in the history of non-European historical traditions. From this perspective, the different ways in which history has been written over the centuries have taken on a new interest. Rather than simply being outmoded approaches that have now been replaced by the "proper" way of doing history, they show us that there have always been multiple perspectives from which the past can be viewed and that, like so many aspects of human culture, the predominant ways of recording history have changed over time.

Herodotus and Thucydides

However hard they strive to escape from what now often seem to be unduly narrow definitions of history, works devoted to historiography still give a privileged position to two authors who lived in the Greek city-state of Athens during the fifth century before the Common Era, Herodotus and Thucydides. They inherited a tradition of concern about the preservation of the memory of the past. Greek mythology included the goddess Clio among the nine muses of the arts. She has remained a symbol of history ever since. Herodotus and Thucydides are the earliest authors whose written works of history have come down to us largely intact. Herodotus's *The Histories*, tells of the Greek defeat of a Persian invasion that took place when the historian was a young child, and Thucydides's *The Peloponnesian War*, recounts the disastrous failure of Athens's attempt to impose its power on the other Greek city-states, an attempt in which Thucydides himself had participated. These two historians' efforts to create a realistic way of describing past events were part of a broader striving to understand the world and represent it accurately that made the Athens of their day a center of cultural innovation. The lifespans of Herodotus and Thucydides overlapped with those of the philosophers Socrates and Plato, who raised questions about the nature of knowledge in general, and with those of the playwrights Aeschylus, Sophocles, and Euripides, whose dramas were distinguished by their psychological realism.

Herodotus and Thucydides were certainly not the first people to record information about historical events or to construct stories about the past. Herodotus, who traveled throughout the Mediterranean world of his day, noted that the Egyptians had kept records of their rulers going back for many centuries and that the Persians had their own traditions of recording the past. Both he and Thucydides were intimately familiar with the poetic epics of Homer, the *Iliad* and the *Odyssey*, which told the story of the Trojan War, a conflict that had supposedly taken place many centuries earlier. Although the two Greek authors did not know it, members of other civilizations had also constructed historical narratives. In another part of the eastern Mediterranean, the Jews had preserved the story of their own origins and the deeds of their rulers, which would eventually be written down and incorporated into the Bible. At the other end of the Asian continent, in China, the philosopher and religious sage Confucius had insisted on the importance of remembering past events to draw lessons from them that would guide appropriate conduct in the present.

What made the works of Herodotus and Thucydides different from previous records and stories about the past was their attempt to define history as a distinct method of telling the story of the past, unique above all because of its devotion to discovering and transmitting the truth about bygone events. Herodotus and Thucydides had to define for themselves what history should take as its subject, what materials it should draw on, and what purposes it should be designed to achieve. Although Herodotus recorded the myths and legends of the Egyptians and Persians and noted that Greek beliefs in oracles often influenced their actions, both he and Thucydides defined history as the story of the thoughts and deeds of human beings; unlike Homer, they eliminated the gods from their explanation of events. Herodotus and Thucydides agreed that history should concern itself with exceptional events that affected the lives of whole societies, not with the lives of individuals, and indeed each of them claimed that the war he wrote about was the most important conflict the world had ever known.

The Greek word "istoria" that Herodotus used for his work can be translated as "inquiry," and Herodotus devoted a good part of his writing to recounting the travels he had undertaken to collect information about the various peoples involved in the Persian wars. Herodotus often indicated the sources of his information and critically evaluated them for his audience, telling them what he thought was true and what he considered doubtful. Thucydides said less about his sources, but he did promise readers that he had included only incidents that he had personally observed—in one passage, he soberly described a defeat for which he had been personally responsible and which had forced him to go into exile from Athens for many years—or that had been reported to him by reliable witnesses.

The purpose of his work, Herodotus wrote, was to ensure "that what human beings have done will not fade through the passage of time and . . . that the great and amazing actions of the Greeks and the barbarians will not lose their fame, and in particular the reason why they went to war against one another."[1] Of the importance of the Greek victory over the Persians he had no doubt: it had preserved the independence of the small Greek city-states and permitted the extraordinary development of Athenian democracy that had followed, until the outbreak of the Peloponnesian war that Thucydides would record (and during whose early years Herodotus himself died) put an end to the city's "golden age." Nevertheless, Herodotus treated the Greeks' Persian enemies with respect and attempted to explain the motives for their actions fairly; in his view, history's commitment to telling the truth required that it be something different from partisan propaganda. Herodotus's wide-ranging interest in human behavior led him to include, among other things, stories in which women played an active role; his method suggested that all aspects of human life could potentially be of historical interest.

Thucydides, a generation younger than Herodotus, was even more single-minded in his devotion to reconstructing a true story about the past. His criticism of storytellers who mixed fables with verifiable facts was probably aimed at his predecessor. Thucydides limited himself to writing about things that had taken place during his own day, asserting that these were the only events about which certain knowledge could be obtained, and he had no interest in the entertaining anecdotes that livened up Herodotus's work. Thucydides had no doubt, however, that the story of the great war between Athens and its rival Greek city-states, particularly Sparta, was a drama worth recording. Whereas Herodotus had told the heroic story of how the Greeks had successfully defended their freedom from a foreign enemy, Thucydides recounted the tragic tale of how internal conflicts and Athens's unbridled ambitions had brought disaster upon his native city. Readers ever since have taken *The Peloponnesian War* as a warning against the dangers that can befall a society that overestimates its own strength and allows its policies to be determined by irresponsible demagogues.

Thucydides limited the scope of his narrative more narrowly than Herodotus; with few exceptions, he wrote only about war and politics, thus excluding women from his story. His prose style was clear and precise, without rhetorical flourishes, and it continues to serve as a model for serious history writing even today. On the other hand, however, he included in his narrative a number of speeches given by leading actors in his story, although he conceded that he had rarely been able to capture the actual words they had spoken. "My method has been," he wrote, "while keeping as closely as possible to the general sense of the words that were actually used, to make the speakers say what, in my opinion, was called for by each situation."² In these speeches, such as the funeral oration in honor of soldiers killed in the war delivered by the Athenian leader Pericles, Thucydides allowed his characters to explain the motives for their actions. The speeches are among the most powerful passages in *The Peloponnesian War*, and Thucydides's example inspired many subsequent historians to resort to the same device, but such invented material later became seen as blurring the line between history and fiction. The elimination of imaginatively reconstructed speeches from historical narratives after the eighteenth century was one of the signs of an increasing separation between history and other forms of literature. When makers of historical films create dialogue for their characters, however, they can be seen as reviving one of Thucydides's practices.

The works of Herodotus and Thucydides provided important models for subsequent historians in the ancient Greek and Roman world and for their successors ever since. Largely forgotten during the Middle Ages, the books of Herodotus and Thucydides were rediscovered during the European Renaissance and have been recognized since as the foundations of the Western historiographical tradition. Along with their definition of the nature of history, the most important contribution the two men made to history was the fact that they put their narratives in writing. The preservation of their words on permanent materials—parchment or papyrus—meant that those words survived to influence readers long after their authors' deaths. Written historical accounts could also be reproduced in multiple copies, giving them the potential to reach a widely dispersed audience, and they could potentially be compared with other documents, opening a path to a more critical understanding of the challenges of recording events.

Herodotus has been praised as the first historian to single out the struggle for freedom as a central theme and also because of his wide-ranging interest in the cultures of the different peoples he wrote about; on the other hand, he was sometimes denounced as "the father of lies" because of the many tall tales he incorporated into his work. Thucydides's essentially tragic vision of human existence and his clear understanding of how politics works also continue to speak to present-day readers, and his ruthless elimination of fables and anecdotes makes him a model for those who think history should stick strictly to facts about serious matters. Because Herodotus and Thucydides represent two different, but equally compelling, visions of how history should be written, present-day historians' reactions to their works are often a clear sign of what they consider most important in the writing of history. The authors of two important recent surveys of European historiography provide a good example of this. Ernst Breisach's references to Thucydides's "splendid narrative" and to the "magnificent unity of style and content" in his work leave little doubt about his preference. Donald R. Kelley, on the other hand, devotes nine pages to Herodotus's work, concluding that "its value is more appreciated than ever today," whereas he gives Thucydides only two pages, writing that he "had a much narrower conception of human thought and action" than his predecessor.[3] It is tempting to conclude that Thucydides appeals to more traditionalist scholars and Herodotus to those more open to innovation, but this is not always the case. The German historiographical theorist Reinhart Koselleck, for example, a major contributor to the "linguistic turn" that shook up history-writing in the 1970s, saw Thucydides as a forerunner of postmodernism because "he demonstrated that the gathering of facts is not identical with what is said or written about them."[4]

History-Writing in the Hellenistic and Roman Worlds

The Athenian city-state whose fortunes had been the subject of their works lost its primacy after the Peloponnesian War, but for several centuries after Herodotus and Thucydides, history-writing in the Mediterranean world remained a specialty of Greek intellectuals. A half-century after Thucydides's death, the famous Greek philosopher Aristotle offered one of the first and most influential characterizations of the nature of history and its relationship to other forms of thought. "The distinction between historian and poet is . . . that the one describes the thing that has been, and the other a kind of thing that might be. Hence poetry is something more philosophic and of graver import than history, since its statements are of the nature rather of universals, whereas those of history are singulars," Aristotle wrote.[5] Although Aristotle clearly considered poetry and, by implication, philosophy superior to history because the latter was limited to the more or less accidental sequence of actual events, whereas the former dealt with general issues, his formulation did concede that history had a special connection to empirical truth that was missing in other genres of literature.

The later Greek historians had much to write about, including the conquests of Alexander the Great in the fourth century BCE and the breakup of his empire after his death. In the meantime, the city-state of Rome was rising in importance; by the beginning of the second century BCE, after its victory over its North Africa rival Carthage, it was clearly the strongest power in the Mediterranean, and it soon began to exert direct influence in the Greek world. Although the Romans took pride in their military superiority over the Greeks, they admired Greek cultural achievements, including their sophisticated tradition of historical writing. The first important work on the history of Rome, that of Polybius, was written in the middle of the second century BCE by a Greek who had been deported to Rome because of his family's opposition to Roman authority and who wrote about the Roman past in his own language.

Polybius and his successors, of whom the most important, Livy and Tacitus, wrote in Latin, inherited the models of history forged by Herodotus and Thucydides, but they faced some new challenges of their own. To explain Rome's rise to greatness over a period of several centuries, they had to collect and evaluate sources from the distant past. They were able to draw on some documents, such as the texts of laws from earlier periods, but they all recognized the difficulty of separating truth from legend. Herodotus and Thucydides had dealt with the history of one small city-state; the historians of Rome had to widen their scope to the whole of the known world. Among other things, this required them to attempt to reconcile the different chronologies of Rome, where dates were counted from the supposed founding of the city and, for more recent times, according to the names of the annually elected officials called consuls, and the various Greek city-states, where the most widely used system was based on the records of the Olympiads, the athletic contests held every four years. In our world, accustomed to calculating dates according to the now almost universally accepted calendar based on the birth of Jesus (BC and AD or, more recently, BCE and CE), it is hard to imagine how difficult it was for earlier historians to match up dates originally handed down in different systems.

Polybius's history, although it emphasized the rise of Rome, strove to cover the whole of the known world of his day. "By far the greater number of historians concern themselves with isolated wars and the incidents that accompany them: while as to a general and comprehensive scheme of events, their date, origin, and catastrophe, no one as far as I know has undertaken to examine it," he wrote.[6] His successors, who concentrated more exclusively on Roman history, invented the genre of the national history, the story of a single political community over an extended period of time. From Polybius onward, historians of Rome were drawn to the question of the causes of that state's extraordinary success, and then, especially after the Roman Republic was replaced by the one-man rule of emperors, beginning with Augustus in 27 BCE, to the reasons for its decline. "What is really educational and beneficial to students of history is the clear view of the causes of events, and the consequent power of choosing the better policy in a particular case," Polybius wrote, making an argument for the usefulness of history that continues to be advanced today.[7] Polybius's argument that all forms of government inevitably tend to degenerate, but that the combination of elements of monarchy, aristocracy, and democracy in the Roman Republic's constitution had made it more resistant to decline than any of its rivals, provided a framework for the understanding of political history that had immense influence on politics and history-writing in the European world, especially in the centuries from the Renaissance to the era of the French Revolution.

Polybius wrote while the power of the Eternal City was still rising. As the Roman state continued to expand and as its domestic conflicts became more serious, conservative critics blamed its troubles on the abandonment of its historic institutions. Unable to revive the past, these so-called antiquarians nevertheless contributed to the refinement of historical methods by developing better methods for interpreting evidence from the distant past, such as old laws and inscriptions. A century after Polybius, Livy's massive history of Rome, which was completed during the troubled years leading to the collapse of the Republic in the first century BCE and of which only a fraction now survives, drew a contrast between the simplicity, patriotism, and honesty of the early Romans and what he saw as the corruption of his own day. Livy was acutely aware of the problem of writing the history of events such as the founding of Rome that had taken place centuries before his own lifetime, a challenge quite different from what Herodotus and Thucydides had done. The early parts of his history, he wrote, dealt with "matters obscure, as well by reason of their very great antiquity, like objects which from their great distance are scarcely perceptible, as also because in those times the use of letters, the only faithful guardian of the memory of events, was inconsiderable and rare."[8] Livy's lifetime overlapped with that of Julius Caesar, whose *Gallic Wars* recounted his conquest of a vast new territory for Rome. Caesar's work, with its famous opening line, "All Gaul is divided into three parts," established a precedent for memoirs written by military and political leaders to describe their own accomplishments. Caesar portrayed himself as a thoughtful and humane leader, devoted to the interests of Rome rather than his own ambitions. Like many later imperial conquerors, he claimed that his occupation of foreign lands brought benefits for their inhabitants. Although political memoirs are always suspect of bias in favor of their authors, they remain, to the present day, a major form of writing about the past. Unlike historians, memoirists can claim to have participated directly in the events they describe and to offer readers insights into their thinking. Even as they question memoirs' one-sidedness, historians cannot neglect their value as sources.

Once the Republic had been replaced by the empire, after the reign of Augustus, Tacitus's eloquent denunciations of the corrupt and tyrannical rule of the emperors reinforced the idea that the duty of a historian was to use the past to demonstrate the shortcomings of his own day. Tacitus's terse style, expressing complex thoughts in just a few words, as in his description of the effects of Roman conquests—"they make a desert and call it peace"—was to inspire many imitators over the centuries. The contrast he drew between the decadent Romans of the empire and the simple lives of the freedom-loving Germans who defeated Augustus's legions in 9 CE would later serve to shape historical depictions of the "barbarians" who eventually overran Rome. An important contemporary of Tacitus was Plutarch, often considered the inventor of the genre of biography, one of the close relatives of history. His *Parallel Lives*, in which the life stories of notable figures from Greek and Roman history were paired together to reinforce moral lessons, demonstrated the literary power of this genre. Whether biography constitutes a form of history or whether biographers' tendency to concentrate on their subjects' lives at the expense of context inevitably leads them to exaggerate individual agency have been debated ever since. The fact that educated Europeans, from the time of the Romans onward, were more likely to read Latin than Greek meant that for many centuries, Livy, Tacitus, and Plutarch were better known and more influential as historical models than Herodotus or Thucydides.

By the end of the second century CE, Greek and Roman authors had created an extensive tradition of historical writing and even a tradition of critical writing about historical methodology. Roman authors such as the famous orator Cicero and the theorist of rhetoric Quintilian wrote about the functions of history and the proper way to compose it, and Plutarch wrote a scathing denunciation of Herodotus's biases and inaccuracies. A Greek writer, Lucian of Samosata (c. 125 CE–200 CE), produced a longer work, *How to Write History*, that shows that ancient historians had already considered many of the issues that continue to preoccupy historians today. According to Lucian, the historian should be "fearless, incorruptible, free . . . an impartial judge . . . independent, subject to no sovereign, not reckoning what this or that man will think, but stating the facts." History should be well written, but it should "keep its feet on the ground" rather than "being swept down into poetry's wild enthusiasm." The historian should only start to write after "much laborious and painstaking investigation" and careful note-taking. "Above all, let him bring a mind like a mirror, clear, gleaming-bright, accurately centered, displaying the shape of things just as he receives them, free from distortion, false coloring, and misrepresentation," Lucian advised.[9]

By Lucian of Samosata's day, the sophisticated tradition of historical writing created in Athens and expanded by historians of Rome had already endured for nearly six hundred years. It constituted a significant aspect of the culture of classical world. Starting in the era of the Renaissance, the historians of antiquity would inspire a "modern" history that attributed the causes of events to human agency or impersonal forces, rather than to the will of an omnipotent divinity; their works would also serve as examples of literary elegance. As much as they admired the historians of the ancient world, however, the historians of later centuries who took them as models failed to understand some major aspects of the ancient world's approach to the recording of the past. The Greek and Roman historians were not modern rationalists: they lived in a world that believed in various supernatural powers and took omens seriously. They also wrote for a limited audience. Although the written word allowed their works to be reproduced and to survive their authors, manuscripts were expensive and their circulation was far more limited than that of historical works written after the invention of printing would be. Although the writings of Herodotus, Thucydides, and their successors loom large in our understanding of historical thought, whatever most of the population of the ancient world knew about history was largely transmitted through other means, such as public monuments and oral tradition. Written history was the preserve of a small, cultivated elite.

The Origins of Chinese Historiography

While important forms of history-writing were developing in the Greek and Roman world, another distinctive historical tradition took shape in China. The name of the great sage Confucius, who lived from 551 to 479 BCE, somewhat earlier than Herodotus, is associated with the *Chunqiu* or *Spring and Autumn Annals*, a chronicle of several centuries of events in one Chinese kingdom. Later authors added commentaries to the rather dry account in the original work, emphasizing the moral lessons to be learned from the events it related. In the second century BCE, when history-writing was flourishing in the Roman world, Sima Qian (c. 145–86 BCE) compiled the most influential work of early Chinese history, one that shaped historical writing there for many centuries. Just as the Roman historians had been inspired by that state's success in imposing its rule on the whole of the world they knew, Sima Qian's *Shiji* was a response to the unification of China under the Han dynasty after 206 BCE. Sima Qian's father had begun a history of China, from its origins onward, and Sima Qian was determined to complete this project after his father's death. Few other historians have made such a personal sacrifice to be able to devote themselves to their craft: arrested for political reasons and forced to choose between an honorable death or the humiliating punishment of castration, Sima Qian accepted the latter. "I could not accept dying, if that meant that the high points of my writing were going to be lost to posterity," he wrote to a friend, although he knew that the disgrace he had suffered meant that his work would only be appreciated long after his death.[10]

Much longer than the works of Herodotus or Thucydides, Sima Qian's *Shiji* was more like an encyclopedia than a coherent historical narrative. "I have cast a universal net to gather together all the old traditions of the world that were scattered and lost," he wrote.[11] Along with an account of the various dynasties that had ruled parts of China for the previous two thousand years, Sima Qian included a remarkable set of chronological tables, a vast collection of miscellaneous information, and biographies of important historical figures. Like Herodotus, Sima Qian included all aspects of human life in his collection and recognized the role that women had often played in history. He was not concerned to rigidly separate legends about the past from documentable facts, and it was sometimes possible to draw contradictory conclusions from the different sections of his work. More explicitly than the early Greek and Roman historians, Sima Qian commented on the lessons to be drawn from historical episodes, in passages beginning with the words "the Grand Historian says." He did not lay down simple rules and was always sensitive to the fact that differing circumstances might dictate different courses of action, but he left no doubt of his conviction that the past was the best guide for action in the present. Sima Qian's hope that his writing would survive him was fulfilled: the *Shiji* became a model for the long tradition of Chinese historical writing.

History, Judaism, and Christianity

In the Western world, the tradition of historical writing created by the Greeks and Romans faced a new challenge with the rise of the new faith of Christianity. Once Christianity became the dominant religion of the Roman Empire, following the conversion of the Emperor Constantine in 312 CE, historians developed a new vision of the past, closely linked to Christian teachings about the world's future. Greek and Roman historians had rarely asked themselves whether the overall course of human history was leading in a particular direction. Herodotus and Thucydides, whose works dealt with relatively short spans of time, did not consider the question. Polybius's theory of the inevitable degeneration of political systems suggested a history consisting of repeated cycles in which one dominant state would rise and then decline, to be replaced by another. By contrast, the Jewish Bible, whose historical books had been written down roughly in the era in which Herodotus and Thucydides had been active and which Christians incorporated as part of their own scriptures, offered a different vision of history. According to the Bible, God had created the world at a specific moment in time, and the events in human history were all part of a divine plan that would lead, according to the Jews, to the coming of the Messiah or, as Christians reinterpreted the divine message, to the second coming of Jesus. In either case, history in this framework had a clear plot line, beginning with Adam, the first man, and leading, after various catastrophes caused by human resistance to God's will, to redemption and the end of the world. In their thinking about history, Christian authors were heavily influenced by the prophetic passages in the Bible and especially by the prophecy in the Book of Daniel that the world would be dominated by a succession of four empires before the end of days. Although there was some disagreement about the identity of the first three empires, there was general agreement that the Roman Empire should be counted as the fourth and that there would be no successor to it before the divinely foretold end of history.

Having incorporated this linear vision of history and the account of their first centuries of existence into their holy books, Jewish thinkers largely lost interest in further developments in history. The one important Jewish historian to take up history-writing on the Greek and Roman model, Josephus, was considered a traitor by most of his fellow Jews because he had abandoned the Jewish cause after the unsuccessful Jewish revolt against Roman rule in Palestine in 67–70 CE. Josephus's books introduced Roman readers to the Jewish past. In a demonstration of how later events can give a centuries-old work of history a new meaning, after the creation of the modern state of Israel in 1948, his history of the unsuccessful Jewish revolt, and particularly his description of the one Jewish extremist group's suicidal defense of the mountaintop fortress of Masada against the Romans, became part of a new national myth. Soldiers being sworn into the Israeli armed forces take their oath to defend the country at the ruins of Masada.

Although Josephus proved to be the last important writer of Jewish history for many centuries, Christian authors developed an important historical tradition that grew to dominate the European world for more than a millennium. Once Christians abandoned their original hope for the imminent return of Jesus and resigned themselves to the fact that history would continue for a period of unknown duration, however, they began to confront the problem of integrating their own history into the larger historical framework they had inherited from the Bible and from the Greeks and Romans. Eusebius, who lived at the time of Constantine, shaped the pattern of Christian history for centuries afterward. For Eusebius, and for all the Christian historians who followed him, the purpose of history was to show the working out of God's plan for humanity. Whereas the historians of ancient Greece and Rome had explained events in terms of human actions or the structures of governments, Eusebius attributed them to divine providence. The military victories achieved by Constantine and his forces, for example, came about because "God proved their ally in the most wonderful manner."[12] Eusebius took over the account of the creation of the world from the

Jewish Bible and joined it to the story of the spread of the Christian faith
from the time of Jesus onward. Eusebius devoted considerable attention
to chronology, attempting to show that the Jewish tradition was older
and therefore more reliable than that of the Greeks. His *History of the
Church* was a highly polemical defense of orthodox Christian doctrine,
as it had been defined at the Council of Nicaea in 325 CE, a meeting
of theologians in which Eusebius participated. In contrast to the pre-
Christian historians of the Greek and Roman world, Eusebius did not
pretend to impartiality, but, on the other hand, to buttress his arguments,
he made more use of direct citations from his sources—the theological
arguments of his predecessors—than they had and provided a model
for what would nowadays be called intellectual history.

By Eusebius's day, the Roman Empire had become divided into a
western half, governed from Rome, and an eastern Byzantine Empire
whose capital, Constantinople, is now the city of Istanbul in Turkey. The
Greek-speaking Byzantine Empire survived until it was captured by
the Turks in 1453 and produced a significant historical tradition, including such notable works as Procopius's scathing portrait of corruption
at the imperial court in the sixth century CE and the empress Anna
Comnena's *Alexiad* (c. 1148 CE), one of the few historical works written
by a woman author, in the twelfth century. In the western half of Europe,
however, knowledge of the Greek language disappeared, cutting historians off from the traditions that continued to influence Byzantine writers,
and changing political conditions created new challenges to historical
writing. The sack of the city of Rome by the Goths in 410 CE raised serious
questions about the notion that God would protect the empire until the
end of the world. The great theologian Augustine, in his masterwork
The City of God, provided a theoretical response to this problem: he argued
that the world exists on two levels, a "city of man" in which evil, caused
by sinful human beings, may appear to triumph and a "city of God," in
which divine justice prevails. History, in the Augustinian schema, takes
place on the human level, although God determines its course, and its
catastrophes do not invalidate the promise of eventual salvation for the
faithful. Indeed, the sufferings of human history serve a higher purpose
by preparing humanity for its eventual redemption.

Augustine's teaching implied that earthly history is ultimately not
as important as events in the city of God. Nevertheless, by acknowledging that human actions can be secondary causes of historical events,
Augustine provided some justification for the study of the subject in its

own right. Augustine did not write any historical works himself, but he did help invent another important form of writing about the past. His *Confessions*, in which he related the story of his own life, is usually considered the first example of autobiography. As Augustine's work showed, an autobiographer, unlike a biographer, could give a history of his inner thoughts and feelings as well as the things he had done. In modern times, historians have sometimes tried to show that they, too, can probe the subjective dimensions of human experience; a number of them have also followed Augustine's example and written personal histories of their own lives.

History in the Middle Ages

From the time of the Renaissance in the 1400s until recently, the kinds of history written in Europe during the Middle Ages were usually regarded as an unfortunate detour on the path leading from the works of the Greek and Roman historians to the more critical history of modern times. In 1895, Lord Acton, one of the great promoters of "scientific" historical scholarship in Britain, allowed that the Middle Ages "possessed good writers of contemporary narrative," but complained that they "were careless and impatient of older fact. They became content to be deceived, to live in a twilight of fiction."[13] More recent scholars of historiography have shown more understanding of the motives of medieval history writers. They adapted history to a new framework, dominated by religious belief, but they still saw themselves as serving the cause of truth. Their purpose, however, was to present truths that would convince their readers of appropriate moral and religious lessons. What the medievalist Walter Goffart wrote of the early medieval historian Gregory of Tours applies to most of those historians who lived in the Middle Ages: "Gregory's goal was pastoral, and contemporary history was his means of persuasion."[14]

Among the consequences of the disintegration of the western Roman Empire was a decline in the number of those who received the kind of education that would allow them to become historians. Without knowledge of the Greek language, it was impossible to read the works of authors such as Herodotus and Thucydides, and almost the only people still capable of reading and writing in Latin were the members of the clergy. Their ranks would provide almost all of the authors of history for the next several centuries. The breakup of the empire deprived these writers of the familiar framework that had guided their predecessors since the time of Polybius. Instead of a universal empire whose fate affected the whole known world, they now had to deal with the histories of separate kingdoms ruled by "barbarians" whose ancestors had lived outside the boundaries of Rome. Medieval historians often began their works with a summary of world history, drawn from the Bible and Roman sources, and they often tried to connect their countrymen to this universal past by claiming that they were descended either from offspring of the Biblical Noah or from figures from antiquity: both British and French authors claimed that their nations had been founded by survivors of the Trojan War. In this way, medieval historians linked their local histories of their own region and of the "barbarian" peoples who had supplanted the Romans to the broader picture of the past they had inherited from the culture of antiquity. Gregory of Tours's *History of the Franks*, written in the sixth century CE, was the first chronicle of the region that would eventually become the nation of France, for example, and told the story of how the Frankish chieftain Clovis had created a unified kingdom. Gregory of Tours was more interested, however, in religious questions and the history of the church; in his eyes, the most significant of Clovis's acts was his conversion to Christianity.

The most important of these early medieval national histories, written around 735 CE, was Bede's *Ecclesiastical History of the English People*, which founded the tradition of British history. More than Gregory of Tours, Bede understood that he was writing the history of a distinct national group, the English, that was not descended from the Romans and that the history of the spread of the Christian faith in England, his principal topic, was inseparable from the political history of the various rulers in the island who had promoted that process. Bede was unusual among medieval historians in his scrupulous concern for accuracy and his acknowledgment of his sources. He was the first historian to adopt the practice of dating events from the time of the birth of Jesus, creating the division of time into "BC" (before Christ) and "AD" (*anno Domini* or "year of our Lord"), a practice that would not be widely imitated for several centuries after his death. Bede's clearly written work ended with the successful unification of the church in the British Isles and reflected a confidence in the future of his country, a confidence that his successors would struggle to maintain in the face of the Viking invasions and other disasters in subsequent centuries.

After Pope Leo III crowned the Frankish ruler Charlemagne as emperor in Rome in 800 CE, historians in the West, ignoring the claims of the Byzantine Empire, argued that the legacy of the Roman Empire had been passed or "translated" to him and his successors and that the world was still in the age of the fourth empire predicted in the Biblical prophecy of Daniel. Charlemagne's vast empire, which had included most of present-day France, Germany, and northern Italy, split apart after his death, but a succession of German rulers claimed the title of Holy Roman Emperor, and historians, such as Otto of Freising, who lived in the twelfth century, could still confidently write that it would last "until the end of the ages." Despite the development of traditions of national history, exemplified by Bede's work, this imperial framework continued to dominate historical thinking. Among other things, it kept medieval historians from recognizing clearly the differences between the society in which they lived and that of the classical world that had preceded it.

Bede's *Ecclesiastical History* was a well-thought-out narrative leading to a clear ending point. The form of history-writing most associated with the Middle Ages, however, were annals and chronicles, in which events were recorded in the sequence in which they happened, without any attempt to connect them to each other. A typical entry from a medieval chronicle, for the year 1239, tells us that "William Raleigh was elected Bishop of Norwich on 10th April. That horrible race of men known as the Tartars, which had once come swarming from remote fastnesses and overrun the face of the earth, laid waste Hungary and the neighboring territories. On 18th June Eleanor, queen of England, gave birth to her eldest son Edward."[15] Such accounts were often compiled, sometimes over the course of several centuries, by the monks of particular monasteries, meaning that they had multiple authors rather than reflecting the thoughts of a single writer, as Bede's history did. Their laconic entries were not necessarily unbiased: chronicles kept in a particular monastery often reflected the influence of local rulers who protected the institution. Annals and chronicles often recorded valuable historical information, and modern historians regularly use them as sources, but unlike the historical works of antiquity, they had few literary qualities and made no attempt to explain the causes of the events they described, leaving it to readers to make sense of them.

History in the Chinese and Islamic Worlds

Whereas history-writing in Western Europe in the early Middle Ages was mostly confined to monasteries and usually seemed to have lost the sophistication it had achieved in the ancient world, the narrating of the past flourished in other parts of the world. In China, the rulers of the Tang dynasty (618–906 CE) created an official History Bureau, charged with recording the events of their reign. For the Tang and the dynasties that succeeded them, history-writing served important political functions, especially that of demonstrating that the preceding rulers they replaced had lost "the mandate of heaven" and deserved to be overthrown. The Tang's successors, the Song dynasty (960–1279 CE), continued to support history-writing, and this period also saw the development of a sophisticated critique of historical methods that would not be equaled in Europe for another four centuries. The eleventh-century authors Ouyang Xiu and Sima Guang argued for the importance of evidence from archeology and inscriptions as a way of verifying claims made in written sources and for the superiority of older sources, written closer to the time of past events, over more recent compilations.

Another tradition of history-writing took shape in the Islamic world, beginning with accounts of the life of Muhammad and the early Muslim conquests during the seventh century. Muslims dated events according to their own calendar, beginning in 622 CE, the date of the *hijra*, Muhammad's departure from Mecca to Medina. Concerned with preserving the precise words of Muhammad, Muslim scholars paid unusual attention to the details of how sayings attributed to him had been transmitted. They were familiar with the tradition of Greco-Roman history and with the Jewish and Christian scriptures and drew on these sources for their chronicles of the pre-Islamic past; whether evidence from non-Islamic sources could be cited for later periods was a subject of controversy. In the late Middle Ages, the Tunisian-born scholar Ibn Khaldun (1332–1406) produced a systematic critique of historical thought that was far more probing than anything written in the European west until the era of the Renaissance. Ibn Khaldun analyzed the reasons why historians might give erroneous accounts of the past, including "partisanship toward a creed or opinion," "over-confidence in one's sources," a failure to understand a source's true meaning, "the inability rightly to place an event in its real context," and the desire to please those for whom one was writing. The most important source of error, he asserted, was "the ignorance of the laws governing the transformations of human society." Human behavior, Ibn Khaldun argued, was sufficiently consistent so that historians, drawing on their own experience, could "distinguish what is naturally possible from what is impossible" when dealing with the past.[16]

The Late Middle Ages in Europe

The Crusades, a series of attempts by warriors from Western Europe, beginning in 1095, to capture and defend the Christian holy sites in Palestine from the Muslims who had conquered the area in the seventh century, provided the inspiration for a number of historical works in Europe and in the Islamic world as well. "Never, I believe, has a more glorious subject been given to historians of warfare," one author wrote.[17] Most of the European historical accounts of the Crusades portrayed them as heroic endeavors to defend the true faith, but more sober chroniclers found themselves compelled to admit that the expeditions were poorly organized, that instead of coming together in a spirit of religious unity, the participants were often divided along national lines, and that they sometimes massacred innocent victims. The greatest of the historians of the Crusades, Geoffrey de Villehardouin, found himself recording one of the most controversial of the Crusaders' actions, their attack on the capital of the Christian Byzantine Empire in 1204, carried out at the behest of the government of Venice, which hoped to profit from the looting of the city. As they departed for the First Crusade in 1096, German warriors began their campaign against infidels by exterminating the Jewish communities in several cities along the Rhine River. The Jewish chronicler who recorded the effort of the Jews in Mainz to defend themselves and their decision to commit collective suicide when they saw that they were about to be overwhelmed and forced to abjure their faith provided a rare example for this period of history written from the perspective of victims rather than conquerors.[18] His work founded a specifically Jewish tradition, sometimes called "lachrymose history," emphasizing the sufferings of an oppressed minority group, that has found its most important modern expression in the history of the Holocaust.

The dryness of medieval annals and chronicles may help explain the popularity of Geoffrey of Monmouth's *History of the Kings of Britain*, written around 1130, which provided the earliest written version of the legend of King Arthur, his wife Guinevere, and his loyal knights. These stories were probably Geoffrey of Monmouth's own inventions, but the mythical past that he created was far livelier than that found in the period's chronicles. Even at the time, critics denounced Geoffrey of Monmouth's stories as "mendacious fictions, invented to gratify the curiosity of the undiscerning," but this did nothing to diminish their success.[19] Subsequent authors elaborated on the Arthurian legends, fashioning the warlord of Geoffrey of Monmouth's narrative into a model for the values of chivalry that developed in the later Middle Ages and making this fictional ruler better known than any of the actual figures of medieval British history. Another largely legendary account of past events that enjoyed a wide readership in the Middle Ages was Jacobus de Voragine's collection of stories about the lives of Christian saints, the *Golden Legend*, compiled around 1260 CE. These stories, filled with miraculous elements, emphasized the close involvement of God in human affairs. They inspired many works of art and clearly had a strong appeal to medieval audiences, who were less concerned with their literal truth than with their edifying religious message.

By the time the Arthurian tales and the *Golden Legend* were written down, a new and more complex society was developing in Western Europe, and the ability to read and write was no longer confined to monasteries. The eleventh and twelfth centuries saw the establishment of the first universities, which provided education not only for future clergy but also for laymen who wanted to become lawyers or doctors. History, however, was not part of university studies and would not become so for many centuries. More important for the practice of history was the growth of cities, a product of medieval society's increasing prosperity. The merchants and guildsmen of these urban communities fought against church authorities and feudal lords to establish their right to govern themselves, and in the process, they also became historical subjects in their own right, who assumed that the events in which they had participated deserved to be recorded.

Urban chronicles, often written by laymen, were especially common in Germany and Italy, with their powerful and competitive city-states; the tradition of local history in the Tuscan city of Florence would strongly influence the two most famous history writers of the Renaissance period, Machiavelli and Guicciardini. Whereas chronicles of monasteries and kings had emphasized religious issues and wars, urban histories were more inclusive, recording the concerns and actions of local officials and guildsmen and noting events such as crimes and fires. These medieval city chronicles can be considered the first examples of social history. At the other extreme from these local compilations were "universal" chronicles that attempted to include the history of the entire known world. In view of the difficulty of obtaining accurate information on so broad a subject, these universal chronicles were often highly inaccurate, but they reflected a desire to achieve a vision of history that took in at least the whole of Christiandom and provided a framework for understanding narrower national and local events. In France, Christine de Pizan's *Book of the City of Ladies* (1405 CE) argued that a truly comprehensive history ought to include the deeds of women as well as men, but her appeal had little impact until many centuries later.

By the 1400s, the approaches to history that developed over the course of what later generations would call "the Middle Ages," especially the recounting of events in a religious perspective and the emphasis on chronicle in preference to analytical narrative, had been part of European culture for almost a thousand years. Talented writers continued to throw themselves into the production of such narratives, and they still found receptive audiences. Jean Froissart, who recorded many of the episodes of the Hundred Years' War between England and France, was proud to state that he "had labored at this history thirty-seven years," and he insisted that "the greatest pleasure I have ever had, was to make every possible inquiry, in regard to what was passing in the world, and then write down all that I had learnt."[20] Aware of the importance of truthfulness in the composing of history, he explained how his close connections with leading political figures of the time had enabled him to observe events firsthand and claimed that his dedication to accuracy was shown by his inclusion of incidents that cast his own patrons in an unfavorable light. Neither Froissart nor his readers anticipated that his style of historical writing would soon come to seem more dated and less relevant to the understanding of the past than the works of the Greek and Roman historians who had lived more than a thousand years before him.

Notes

1. Cited in Thomas R. Martin, *Herodotus and Sima Qian: The First Great Historians of Greece and China* (Boston: Bedford/Saint Martin's, 2010), 31–32.
2. Cited in John Burrow, *A History of Histories: Epics, Chronicles, Romances and Inquiries from Herodotus and Thucydides to the Twentieth Century* (New York: Random House, 2008), 38.
3. Ernst Breisach, *Historiography: Ancient, Medieval, and Modern* (Chicago: University of Chicago Press, 1983), 16, 17; Donald R. Kelley, *Faces of History: Historical Inquiry from Herodotus to Herder* (New Haven, CT: Yale University Press, 1998), 30.

4. Reinhart Koselleck, *The Practice of Conceptual History*, trans. Todd Presner (Stanford, CA: Stanford University Press, 2002), 68.

5. Aristotle, *Poetics*, cited in Donald R. Kelley, ed., *Versions of History from Antiquity to the Enlightenment* (New Haven, CT: Yale University Press, 1991), 62.

6. Polybius, cited in Peter Gay and Victor G. Wexler, eds., *Historians at Work*, 4 vols. (New York: Harper & Row, 1972), 1:112–3.

7. Polybius, in Gay and Wexler, eds., *Historians at Work*, 1:114.

8. Livy, in Gay and Wexler, eds., *Historians at Work*, 1:171.

9. Lucian of Samasota, *How to Write History*, cited in Kelley, ed., *Versions of History*, 66–67.

10. Cited in Martin, *Herodotus and Sima Qian*, 92.

11. Cited in Martin, *Herodotus and Sima Qian*, 92.

12. Cited in Gay and Wexler, eds., *Historians at Work*, 1:263.

13. Lord Acton, "Inaugural Lecture on the Study of History," in John Emerich Edward, Lord Acton, *Lectures on Modern History* (London: MacMillan, 1906), 4.

14. Walter Goffart, *The Narrators of Barbarian History (AD 550–800): Jordanes, Gregory of Tours, Bede, and Paul the Deacon* (Princeton, NJ: Princeton University Press, 1988), 228.

15. Cited in Burrow, *History of Histories*, 218.

16. Ibn Khaldun, *An Arab Philosophy of History: Selections from the Prolegomena of Ibn Khaldun of Tunis*, Charles Issawi, trans. (London: John Murray, 1950), 27–29, 34.

17. Cited in Breisach, *Historiography*, 133.

18. See "The Crusaders in Mainz," in Jacob R. Marcus, *The Jew in the Medieval World: A Sourcebook* (New York: Atheneum, 1969), 115–20.

19. William of Newburgh, cited in Kelley, ed., *Versions of History*, 186.

20. Cited in Joseph Dahmus, *Seven Medieval Historians* (Chicago: Nelson–Hall, 1982), 218.

CHAPTER 3

The Historiographical Revolution of the Early Modern Era

The transformation, beginning in the fifteenth century, that made Jean Froissart's chronicle of the Hundred Years' War seem dated only a few decades after it was written was part of the great intellectual shift that thinkers of the time called the "Renaissance" or the "rebirth of learning." Present-day historians are more likely to call the historical period beginning around the year 1450 "the early modern era," a more neutral label that avoids implying that the preceding centuries had been a "dark age" or adopting the view, espoused by many of the authors of the period, that it was truly a revival of the culture of ancient Greece and Rome. Indeed, the early modern period was characterized not only by an obsession with antiquity, but also by the impact of profound historical novelties, such as the discovery of America and the invention of printing. At the same time, there were important continuities between the Middle Ages and the new era that was taking shape after 1450. Religious belief remained fundamental to European civilization, and indeed the outbreak in the early sixteenth century of a massive conflict within Christendom, the Protestant Reformation, made questions of faith even more explosive than they had been during much of the Middle Ages. The practice of history could hardly fail to be affected by these great transformations; at the same time, new ways of understanding history contributed to broader changes in culture and society.

The Renaissance Revolution in Historiography

By the beginning of the nineteenth century, when a new elite of professionally trained scholars began to define history as a "science" based on the systematic study of archival documents, the historical practices of the early modern era came to look as outdated in some respects as the writings of their medieval predecessors. Whereas Lord Acton could dismiss the history written during the Middle Ages as almost worthless, however, the "modern" historians of the period since 1800 have always recognized their debt to the scholars of the early modern period. Contemporary scholars of historiography, such as Donald Kelley and Anthony Grafton, often argue that the historians of the Renaissance period already anticipated most of the critical methods that would become the defining features of modern academic history. In studying the historians of the period between 1450 and 1800, we are examining the origins of many of the features of history as it is researched and presented today.

The profound shift in historical methodology that occurred in Europe in the fifteenth and sixteenth centuries is often illustrated by reference to the Italian scholar Lorenzo Valla's *Discourse on the Forgery of Constantine*, written in 1439–1440. At issue was Valla's demonstration that the so-called "donation of Constantine," a document cited in numerous medieval histories as proof that the Emperor Constantine had given sovereignty over the city of Rome to the Pope in the fourth century, was a forgery, written several centuries later to buttress papal claims to authority. Valla's innovation was to apply the new critical methods of humanism, the intellectual movement for close study of the culture of classical antiquity, that had begun to develop in Italy in the 1300s, to a historical question. Because of his thorough knowledge of classical Latin, Valla was able to show that the donation of Constantine used words and turns of phrase that had not existed at the time when it was supposedly written and that this momentous document was not mentioned by any other sources from its supposed time of origin.

Valla's demonstration that the Latin language had changed substantially since the fourth century carried a broader historical message: it questioned the notion that the world of his own day was still a direct continuation of the ancient past and the claim that the medieval Holy Roman Empire was substantially the same as its predecessor. Renaissance historians stopped dividing history according to the framework of the "four empires" inherited from the Bible and began instead to speak of three periods, antiquity, a "middle age" from the fall of the western Roman Empire to their own day, and the new era in which they themselves lived, a way of dividing history into periods that is still prevalent and is sometimes applied even to non-European civilizations, although its relevance to other parts of the world is doubtful. Finally, the success of Valla's critical method of careful scrutiny and comparison of sources showed how scholars of the past could use the power of reason to question even long-established traditions and thereby come closer to an age-old goal of history, the discovery of the truth about the past. Valla himself was mostly concerned with philology, the study of language, but other Renaissance humanists applied the same critical spirit to the study of other remains from the past. Specialized fields of antiquarian research such as numismatics, the study of coins and medals, and epigraphy, the study of inscriptions from ancient buildings and monuments, gave scholars increasing confidence in their ability to reconstruct the past on the basis of the traces it had left behind, rather than relying on written accounts compiled much later.

Valla was just one of many writers and artists associated with the Renaissance, or "rebirth," that began in northern Italy and spread, by 1500, to affect intellectual life throughout Europe. Although most of the writers of the Renaissance remained sincere Christians, they redefined the place of religion in human life in a way that left more place for purely human concerns, in particular for political engagement. Whereas the Christian scholars of the Middle Ages had regarded the culture of classical antiquity as essentially flawed because it lacked knowledge of the true faith, Renaissance intellectuals admired the intellectual achievements of the ancients, particularly the elegance of their language. After many centuries during which knowledge of the Greek language had died out in Western Europe, the humanists revived it and rediscovered many long-forgotten texts, including the historical works of Herodotus and Thucydides, as well as Latin works like those of Tacitus. Renaissance historians strove to emulate these models, adopting practices such as the composition of fictitious speeches like those Thucydides had inserted into his narrative.

Renaissance humanism first arose in the independent city-state republics of northern Italy, especially the prosperous city of Florence. Like the citizens of the ancient Roman republic, those of Renaissance Florence argued and fought over political issues and reacted with alarm to the growing power of one of the city's leading families, the Medici, who would eventually establish themselves as rulers of the city. In these circumstances, the historians of republican Rome, especially Livy, had a special appeal to Italian humanists. When France invaded the Italian peninsula in 1494, setting off a series of conflicts that undermined the independence and prosperity of the Italian city-states, Livy's meditations on the fall of the Roman republic looked even more pertinent.

The two historians who responded most eloquently to this crisis were Niccolo Machiavelli and Francesco Guicciardini, both from Florence. The two men's histories broke radically with the framework of medieval history-writing. Both were purely secular narratives that made no pretense of trying to fit events into a divinely ordained plan or a grand scheme of universal history. Both treated the Italian city-states as autonomous entities and explained their histories as the result of human power conflicts. Machiavelli's *History of Florence* (1526) was part of his broader interest in the workings of political power, a subject he had analyzed in his famous treatise *The Prince* (1513) and in his *Commentaries* (1517) on Livy's Roman history. By the time he turned to the history of his city, the Medici family, briefly driven out of Florence by a republican revolution in the 1490s, had returned and established firm control over the city. Machiavelli, who had had to go into exile for some years for supporting the movement against them, was careful not to criticize their regime openly, but his history blamed a loss of patriotic commitment or *virtù* for the weakness of Florence's republican institutions. Guicciardini's *History of Italy* (1537–1540), which drew heavily on his own experiences as a diplomat, offered a detailed narrative of the political events that had led to the domination of the formerly independent Italian city-states by outside powers, particularly Spain and France. Based on the assumption that rulers invariably seek to increase their power and weaken that of their rivals, it has remained a model for the writing of diplomatic history, the study of the relationships between states.

Whereas Machiavelli and Guicciardini concentrated on political history, another Florentine of the period, Giorgio Vasari, gave the study of the past a new dimension in his *Lives of the Artists*, first published in 1550 and intended to document "the renaissance of the arts, and the perfection to which they have attained in our own time."[1] Vasari's collection of stories about leading Italian artists and their major works founded the study of art history and provided a model for historical works dedicated to specific forms of cultural activity. In modern times, art history, the history of science, and a number of other specialized genres of history have grown into disciplines of their own, requiring training in historical methods but also expertise concerning their specific subject matter.

The new, secularly oriented humanist history first developed in the context of the Italian city-states, but it soon spread to other parts of Europe, particularly to the increasingly powerful monarchies of France and England. In France, Claude Seyssel and Robert Gaguin followed the new critical spirit in rejecting the old legends that linked the founding of the kingdom to refugees from ancient Troy and attributed miraculous accomplishments to earlier rulers, particularly Charlemagne. Their works, much more readable than the medieval chronicles from which they drew much of their information, glorified the victories of more recent French monarchs over the English (in the Hundred Years' War) and their dangerous rivals, the Burgundians. Humanist historians in France paid special attention to the evolution of French law, demonstrating that it had become quite distinct from Roman legal codes; this was one of the many ways in which the new history of the Renaissance era created an increasing consciousness of difference between the past and the present. Across the Channel, Polydore Vergil threw out the story of Brutus, the mythical Trojan ancestor of the Britains, and the legends of King Arthur. In both countries, the way was cleared for a national history, often deliberately encouraged and sponsored by their rulers, that would acknowledge their autonomy from the ancient past and the tradition of the Roman Empire.

Historians in a New World

The emergence of new national monarchies in Western Europe made it increasingly difficult to conceive of history in the framework inherited from the Middle Ages; so did the discovery of the Americas, beginning with Columbus's voyage in 1492. It was not easy to see how these new peoples and new territories could be fitted into the familiar narrative constructed on the basis of the Bible and the history of the ancient world. In his *History of the Indies*, written in 1542, Bartolomé de Las Casas argued that the Indians had souls, and their past therefore had to be considered part of any true universal history. As they tried to integrate the peoples of the Americas into the history of humanity, Europeans discovered that the peoples of this new world had their own traditions for recording the past. The native peoples of the Americas had their own historical records, some of them preserved in pictographic books, and indeed in 1425, one Mexican ruler had demonstrated his appreciation of the political importance of history by ordering the destruction of all earlier chronicles, so that only accounts he approved would survive. Among the texts produced by indigenous authors are several accounts of the conquest of Mexico as seen from the Aztec point of view, lamenting that "Broken spears lie in the roads; we have torn our hair in our grief."[2]

After the conquest of Mexico and Peru, several historians of Indian descent who had learned Spanish wrote important chronicles drawing on pre-Conquest traditions, although they were also influenced to some extent by European models. The works of Fernando de Alva Ixtlilxochitl, who came from a royal family that had fought on the side of the Spanish against the Aztecs in Mexico, and Guaman (or Huaman) Poma and El Inca Garcilaso de la Vega (1539–1616), two descendants of Peruvian Incan noble families, had considerable influence on later accounts of the history of Spanish America. A Spanish priest, Bernardino de Sahagun, relied heavily on information gathered from Nahuatl-speaking informants in compiling works about the history and customs of the people of Mexico. As they sought to create a distinct "Creole" history of their region, "the heroes of Spanish American authors were ancient or sixteenth-century Amerindian historians," the modern explorer of this literature Jorge Cañizares-Esguerra has written.[3]

In the same years in which Machiavelli and Guicciardini were writing their analyses of the secular power conflicts in Italy, a new religious conflict that would dominate European life for the next two centuries was breaking out in Germany. The German monk Martin Luther's challenge to basic church teachings and practices, announced in his *Ninety-Five Theses* in 1517, quickly grew into a sweeping religious upheaval that affected the writing of history along with every other aspect of life and thought. Luther and his Protestant followers called for a "reformation" that would return the church to the purity of Jesus's original teachings, which they claimed had been corrupted over the centuries. Both sides in the Catholic–Protestant quarrels that followed turned to the past to justify their arguments, producing voluminous publications to support their respective points of view. The warring religious parties also used historical writings to glorify the actions of their adherents. John Foxe's *Book of Martyrs*, an account of the persecution of English Protestants under the reign of Queen Mary in the mid-sixteenth century, was for many decades the second most widely read book in that country, after the Bible. The bitter conflicts growing out of the Reformation further divided Europeans and made the writing of anything resembling an agreed-upon general history more difficult than ever. The "confessionalization" of history—the division of scholars into pro-Protestant and pro-Catholic camps—lasted well into the twentieth century, affecting the writing of history not only in Europe but also in the United States.

One group of pro-Protestant historians, the compilers of a general history known as *The Magdeburg Centuries*, published in the mid-sixteenth century, made an important historical innovation that was eventually accepted by scholars of all camps. In the course of compiling a mass of historical data to prove the corruption of the Catholic Church, these authors divided their account into volumes that each covered a "century" of a hundred years. Whereas periodizations based on biblical prophecies or the sequencing of history into ancient, medieval, and modern eras or the reigns of Chinese dynasties implied judgments on the divisions they established, the "centuriators'" procedure created intervals of "empty" time, defined strictly by the calendar. On the other hand, they created a tenacious habit of thinking of centuries as periods with distinctive characteristics, a frame of mind that persists even when historians recognize that years ending in "oo" rarely coincide with major historical transformations. The tendency of historians to divide the past into hundred-year-long units is an example of the importance of periodization: the intervals historians choose to frame their narratives often affect the way they see the phenomena they study.

The Age of Print

The new methods of critical inquiry developed by the humanists, the greater familiarity with the literature of the ancient Greeks and Romans, the discovery of the New World, and the conflicts resulting from the Reformation transformed the ways in which historians wrote their books and the frameworks in which they set their narratives. The invention of the printing press by Johannes Gutenberg, around 1460, changed the way in which texts circulated, greatly expanding access to historical knowledge. The new medium of print also had important implications for the ways in which historians did their work. Until then, written historical works had circulated only in manuscript. Few libraries had major collections of them, and history writers could not easily compare the different accounts produced by earlier authors. The printing press greatly multiplied the number of copies of historical books in circulation, and the audience for stories about the past grew rapidly. The fundamental texts of the ancient Greek and Roman historians, many of them preserved in only a handful of manuscript copies during the Middle Ages, now became broadly available, contributing to the transformation of historical writing associated with the Renaissance. Medieval works, too, including both serious productions and pseudo-history like the Arthurian legends, poured from the presses. Printing made it possible to publish not only works written by historians, but also historical documents, such as old laws and charters. Instead of relying on secondhand accounts by earlier chroniclers, history writers could now read the original sources for themselves. At the same time, however, the new technology raised new questions: how could one be sure of the authenticity of a document reproduced in printed form if one did not have access to the original it purported to represent? The existence of the printing press also provoked rulers and religious authorities to make new efforts to control the circulation of reading material, including historical writings. Formal systems of censorship, which had not existed in the Middle Ages, now required authors and publishers to submit books to examination before they were printed and placed limits on what could be said about the past.

The impact of printing on historical thought continued to expand in the seventeenth century. Even before 1600, enterprising printers had published illustrated broadsheets about important current events, such as wars, natural catastrophes, and the deaths of monarchs; printed almanacs, another inexpensive form of publication that was marketed even to peasants, also included summaries of the past year's most notable occurrences. These kinds of inexpensive news accounts allowed even members of the lower classes to think of themselves as living in the midst of historical events. At least one of them, the leather tanner Miquel Parets of Barcelona, even became a historian himself, keeping a manuscript chronicle of events in his own life and that of his city for more than thirty years.[4] The first decade of the seventeenth century saw the invention of the periodical newspaper, which provided readers with an ongoing narrative of events; readers who kept their copies and had them bound now had a kind of "instant history" of the most recent occurrences in the world around them in the chronicle form that historians had largely abandoned, but that journalists kept alive. Another form of chronicle that appeared in the seventeenth century was the private diary, of which the first important example was kept by the English writer Samuel Pepys in the years from 1660 to 1669. To modern readers, diaries like Pepys's have a freshness that news accounts and histories written at the time cannot match, and historians often find them to be irresistible sources, although they recognize that diary writers frequently provide a partial and subjective viewpoint on the events they describe.

The years around 1600 also saw the rise of a new medium, the modern theater, that provided a new form for the representation of historical events. The origins of the theater in Europe lie in religious ritual: during the Middle Ages, "passion plays" depicting the events leading up to the crucifixion of Jesus were often performed around Easter. Increasingly, however, actors found eager audiences for stories about secular subjects, including history. Written in the years just before and after 1600, William Shakespeare's historical plays, both those dealing with English history, such as *Richard III* and *Henry V,* and those set in ancient Greece and Rome, such as *Julius Caesar,* have had an indelible impact on how we remember their protagonists. Even professional scholars cannot write about the historical Richard III without conjuring the ghost of Shakespeare's scheming tyrant or think about the assassination of Caesar without remembering the funeral oration Shakespeare composed for Marc Antony, beginning, "Friends, Romans, and countrymen, lend me your ears." Until the invention of film in the twentieth century, theater remained the most powerful way of bringing history to life. Because plays with historical settings often had clear political implications, rulers kept a close eye on the theater, censoring what could be performed and sometimes prohibiting controversial productions altogether.

By the late seventeenth century, a new form of periodical, the learned journal, was beginning to affect the writing of history. Many of the early journals, such as the French-born philosopher Pierre Bayle's *Nouvelles de la République de Lettres,* consisted largely of reviews of newly published books, including works of history. The system of "peer review," destined to become such a significant aspect of professional historians' lives in subsequent centuries, thus began to take shape. Another medium for the transmission of historical knowledge, the museum, also started to appear in this period. Historical artifacts and documents were part of the "cabinets of curiosities" assembled by wealthy rulers and learned intellectuals. The Franckesche Stiftung museum in Halle, Germany, preserves the display opened there in 1698, in which medieval charters and other objects from the past were exhibited alongside stuffed animals and unusual mineral specimens as part of an effort to impress viewers with the full range of God's creations.

The historical events of the seventeenth century, including the Thirty Years' War between Catholics and Protestants that devastated Germany, the Puritan Revolution in England and the trial and execution of King Charles I, and the series of wars in northern Europe that marked the emergence for the first time of Russia as a major player in European affairs, all inspired their historians, most of whom now wrote in the deliberately literary style popularized by the humanists rather than in the chronicle form preferred in the Middle Ages. The early English colonists in North America recorded the history of their settlements from the beginning. John Smith's *A True Relation of Such Occurrences and Accidents of Note as Happened in Virginia*, which included the story of how his life was saved by the Indian woman Pocahontas, was published in 1608, just one year after the founding of the colony, and William Bradford's *Of Plymouth Plantation* (1630–1651) memorialized the early years of the Puritan settlement in Massachusetts.

Three seventeenth-century histories of major events in Europe that continued to be read for decades afterward were the Venetian Paolo Sarpi's account of the Counter-Reformation, notable for its critical view of the Papacy despite its author's Catholicism, the moderate English royalist Edward Hyde, earl of Clarendon's *History of the Rebellion* (first published in 1720), an account of the English civil war of 1640–1660 by a man who had participated in many of its events, and the French Cardinal Bossuet's *Discourse on Universal History* (1681), one of the last great efforts to place all of human history in a framework derived from the Bible. The political dramas that played out in mid-seventeenth-century England and France, where a series of revolts known as the Fronde threatened the stability of the monarchy, inspired some elite women to write "family histories," with the justification that they were recording the deeds of their husbands. Lucy Hutchinson's *Life of Colonel Hutchinson* (not published until 1806), the story of one of the English "regicides" who supported the execution of king Charles I, also recorded his wife's engagement in events.[5] The Protestant Jacques Basnage's *Histoire des Juifs* (1706) was notable for its attention to the history of the Jews in the centuries since the rise of Christianity: for the first time, a Christian author considered that Jewish history after the time of Jesus might have some meaning despite the Jews' rejection of him as the messiah.

Cardinal Bossuet's *Universal History* furnished, among other things, a defense of the absolute power of the French king, Louis XIV. This strong-minded monarch took advantage of all the ways in which European kings of the Renaissance period had learned to use history to bolster their legitimacy. Royal officials combed the royal archives to find documents that could justify Louis's claims to additional powers within his kingdom and to territories disputed with other states. Royal historiographers were appointed to produce laudatory accounts of the king's accomplishments, and a special institution, the Académie des Inscriptions, was founded to promote historical erudition; among its assigned functions was the designing of historical medals that would preserve the memory of the major events of Louis's reign. The decor of the royal palace Louis XIV constructed at Versailles included elaborate paintings of his military victories and other achievements. Other European rulers took similar initiatives, but none of them could match the resources Louis XIV poured into exploiting history for propaganda purposes.

Probably none of the serious works historical works written by members of Europe's educated elites or sponsored by its rulers in the seventeenth century had as many readers, however, as the many editions of Alexandre Oexmelin's *History of the Buccaneers of America*, the first book about the pirates who roamed the Caribbean in the seventeenth century. Oexmelin was a French indentured laborer in the colonies who had joined a pirate crew himself. His swashbuckling popular history, whose first edition appeared in Dutch in 1678, was quickly translated into English, French, and Spanish by publishers who had no compunction about adding their own material to it. The great success of Oexmelin's tales showed that there was now a large enough reading audience to support historical publications that were not underwritten by rulers or the church. Oexmelin's stories, reworked many times over the intervening centuries by other authors and in other formats, including the popular *Pirates of the Caribbean* film series, continue to amuse and enthrall modern audiences. At the same time, academic researchers interested in the lives of members of the lower classes in the seventeenth century have also resurrected Oexmelin's work, mining it for information about how poorly paid sailors became pirates and how racial attitudes developed in the colonial world.[6] The ongoing impact of Oexmelin's book demonstrates that it is not only the "serious" historical writing of the past that continues to have a role in shaping our own vision of history.

Most readers of Oexmelin's thrilling stories were hardly concerned with the questions of historical accuracy and the meaning of history that preoccupied the increasingly scrupulous antiquarian researchers and the philosophers of his day. Even as the humanists developed increasingly elaborate methods of evaluating historical evidence, their work raised new concerns about the possibility that the documents on which historians depended might be forgeries, like the donation of Constantine, or that they might have been altered for various reasons as they were copied and recopied over the centuries. Pierre Bayle, in addition to founding one of the first learned periodicals, compiled a massive *Historical and Critical Dictionary* (1686–1687), in which he systematically exposed the errors in previous publications, including many works of history, raising doubts as to whether any dependable knowledge of the past was possible. Bayle's work was part of what has been called "the skeptical crisis of the seventeenth century," a movement that called into question the possibility of acquiring reliable knowledge of any kind.

A French Benedictine monk, Jean Mabillon (1632–1707), concerned that all historical research could be discredited by such fears, tried to establish rules for the practice of diplomatics, or the study of documents from the past. Mabillon admitted that even seemingly conclusive evidence, such as the age of the paper or parchment on which a document was written, might not be sufficient, since forgers could acquire old materials and learn to imitate older forms of writing. Nevertheless, he argued, a trained scholar with experience in working with old documents, who had learned to evaluate all their characteristics together, rather than relying on any single criterion, and to compare different documents with each other rather than studying them in isolation, would be able to make reliable judgments. Mabillon's guidelines for the evaluation of evidence are still echoed in the training professional historians receive.

The development of modern science and philosophy in the seventeenth century posed other problems for history-writing besides that of the evaluation of sources. The pioneering scientist Galileo, determined to put knowledge of the natural world on a basis of experimental evidence and mathematical formulas, raised the question of whether assertions based essentially on memory and not subject to demonstration according to scientific rules could really constitute knowledge. The philosopher Descartes's famous phrase, "I think, therefore I am," anchored certain knowledge in an analysis of the workings of the human mind, rather than on information entering the mind from the outside world. Like Galileo,

Descartes was doubtful of the reliability of memory and thought that the past had little to teach those who were prepared to use their powers of reason. Not all seventeenth-century philosophers were so contemptuous of history, however. Francis Bacon, another important contributor to the development of modern scientific thought, valued empirical evidence more highly than Descartes and saw no essential difference between the careful observation of nature and the critical use of documents to reconstruct the past. The Dutch philosopher Baruch Spinoza's rejection of the divine inspiration of the Bible had important implications for history. By arguing that the Bible was a historical document like any other, written by men and designed to further certain human interests, Spinoza challenged the Jewish and Christian traditions of providentialist history, opening the way for an entirely secular view of human existence. Among other things, if the Bible was not the word of God, there was no need to construct elaborate explanations of how all the peoples of the earth were descended from Adam or to try to explain how the chronologies of other civilizations, such as the Egyptians and the Chinese, could be made to fit with the story in the book of Genesis. Projects like that of the English bishop James Ussher, who painstakingly calculated that the creation of the universe could be dated to October 23, 4004 BCE, began to appear as subjects of ridicule rather than heroic exercises of erudition.

History in the Age of the Enlightenment

Pierre Bayle's critical method and Spinoza's rejection of the authority of the Bible foreshadowed the major intellectual movement of the eighteenth century, the Enlightenment. Enlightenment thinkers were usually more cautious than Spinoza in dismissing the bases of religious belief, but they had little hesitation about challenging the authority of established churches and in insisting that the motor forces of history were human rather than divine. Perhaps the most important feature of Enlightenment historical thought, however, was its orientation toward the future rather than the past. Roman historians lamenting the corruption of republican values, Christian writers for whom human history began in the Garden of Eden, and Renaissance humanists for whom classical antiquity represented the pinnacle of human achievement had all agreed that the passage of time had left human beings worse off than they had once been.

Enlightenment thinkers instead began to conceptualize human experience as a story of progress, pointing toward a better future. The last decades of the seventeenth century were marked by a wide-ranging controversy, the "quarrel of the ancients and the moderns," which pitted those who admired the cultural achievements of the Greeks and Romans and believed that they could never be surpassed against those who argued that modern authors and artists had shown the ability to produce equally great masterpieces. As the "moderns" began to prevail in this debate, they opened the way to a new vision of the meaning of time in which the future, with its possibilities for further achievement, loomed larger than the past. For some authors, this put the value of studying history in question: if previous ages had been thoroughly benighted, what could their experience teach the present? Others, however, still saw the study of the past as crucial for identifying the factors that had made progress possible and the obstacles that had to be overcome to facilitate it.

In the long run, the eighteenth-century thinker who has had the greatest influence on subsequent history-writing was a man who stood outside the mainstream of Enlightenment thinking, the Italian philosopher Giambattista Vico (1668–1744). Vico challenged the claim, put forward by rationalist philosophers such as Descartes, that the surest form of knowledge was that derived from scientific study of the natural world and argued instead that since men make history, they can know it from the inside in a way that they can never know facts about nature. His argument that knowledge in the human sciences rests on a different basis from the understanding of the natural world has inspired many subsequent schools of historical thought, from the historicist scholars of the nineteenth century to the cultural historians of recent decades. The issue Vico raised is at the heart of debates today about whether computers will ever be able to achieve anything resembling human consciousness. Perhaps one test of this will be whether computers begin to take an interest in history.

Vico also elaborated a cyclical theory of history, arguing that all societies progressed through three stages: an age of gods, in which people believed in supernatural powers, an age of heroes, in which authority was held by elites who claimed a divine origin, and finally an age of men and "human government."[7] Each of these stages was equally valid in its own terms, according to Vico, but any one civilization inevitably progressed from one to the next. In time, however, nations that had reached the third stage of development would inevitably decline, and new nations would take their place and go through their own cycle of growth and decay, *corso* and *ricorso*, as he put it in Italian. Unlike most Enlightenment historians, then, Vico did not espouse the idea that humanity as a whole progressed over time. Rather than concentrating on forms of government, Vico conceived of societies as holistic cultures, making customs, language, and beliefs as important for history as political institutions and events. Vico's model of a history structured around the story of a society's evolution, understandable to historians because of the humanity they share with their subjects, had little immediate impact, but it has served as an inspiration for many scholars in subsequent centuries, down to the cultural historians of our own time.

Rather than following Vico, the most widely read historians of the Enlightenment era claimed to make use of the critical methods developed by their predecessors from the Renaissance onward, but they complained that the careful analysis of sources recommended by Mabillon too often resulted in dry antiquarian publications that discouraged readers and failed to teach useful lessons. The most celebrated historians of the Enlightenment era, like the French author Voltaire, practiced history as a form of literature, striving to infuse it with drama and a clear message. His history of the *Age of Louis XIV* (1751), Voltaire wrote, would not spend time on the obscure details that obsessed antiquarian scholars: "We shall confine ourselves to that which deserves the attention of all time, which paints the spirit and customs of men, which may serve for instruction and to counsel the love of virtue, of the arts and of the fatherland." In addition to chronicling the wars and political events of Louis XIV's reign, Voltaire emphasized the cultural achievements of the period, although his interest was largely confined to elite culture. His attitude toward religion was clear from his remark that religious wars were "a madness peculiar to Christians and unknown to pagans."[8] In his other major historical work, the *Essay on the Customs and the Spirit of the Nations* (1756), Voltaire broke out of the European framework that had confined most previous writers in the West. Indeed, it served his purposes to portray Chinese and other non-Christians in a positive light, so as to underline his criticism of Christianity.

Voltaire's glorification of the cultural achievements of the age of Louis XIV had a lasting impact in France, but the literary nature of his historical works and their strong polemical flavor limited their impact on the development of historiography. More original contributions to the tradition of historical writing and research were made in Britain and Germany during this period. British historians produced outstanding examples of history-writing that were more persuasive than Voltaire's works, and philosophical writers in Scotland gave the Enlightenment doctrine of historical progress its most convincing formulations. The biography of the English author Samuel Johnson written by a Scottish-born author, James Boswell, gave new vigor to a genre closely related to history. In Germany, the study of history became a university specialty for the first time, foreshadowing the conversion of the subject into an academic discipline in the nineteenth century. The new university of Göttingen, founded in 1734, was a pioneer in promoting research based on critical methods. Göttingen professors such as August Ludwig von Schlözer edited several scholarly journals devoted to history, although their content consisted primarily of source documents rather than the research articles that would be the main feature of the academic journals created in the nineteenth century.

Three British authors, David Hume, William Robertson, and Edward Gibbon, are generally acknowledged to have been the most distinguished exemplars of Enlightenment history-writing. Hume's *History of England* (1759–1761), which dealt with the events of the seventeenth century, was remarkable for its author's evenhandedness toward the contending parties whose conflicts had made that period so tumultuous. Members of the Whig Party that dominated British politics during the years when Hume was writing and that considered itself the heir to the parliamentary side in the English civil war objected to his relatively positive portrayal of the Stuart kings they had fought against. Hume replied by insisting that, as a historian, he could not take a partisan point of view. "Even that party amongst us, which boasts of the highest regard to liberty, has not possessed sufficient liberty of thought in this particular, nor has been able to decide impartially of their own merit, compared with that of their antagonists," he told his critics.[9]

Hume's history sold much better than the philosophical writings for which he is better known today. Thanks to its success, he wrote, "I was become not only independent, but opulent."[10] Hume's example showed that a sufficiently talented historical author could hope to make a respectable living from his writing without having to depend on private patrons or a government job. Hume's skeptical view of the political values that dominated British life in his day did bring him criticism. Whig sympathizers preferred the more openly partisan *History of England* (1763–1783) of Catharine Macaulay, one of the first woman authors to make a name for herself as a historian. Macaulay's writings inspired many of the American revolutionaries, and she visited the United States shortly after the end of the war of independence. Among those profoundly influenced by Macaulay was Mercy Otis Warren, who met her during her trip. Warren went on to write a *History of the Rise, Progress, and Termination of the American Revolution* (1805), modeled after Macaulay's work.

William Robertson's major work was his *History of the Reign of the Emperor Charles V* (1769), the first attempt at a comprehensive history of sixteenth-century Europe that went beyond the framework of national history. He also wrote a *History of America* (1777), which told the story of the European conquests there. Robertson was not the only author to attempt an "Atlantic" or "global" history encompassing the expansion of European influence overseas. Another historical bestseller of the Enlightenment era was the *Philosophical History of the Two Indies*, a collaboratively written multivolume overview of European colonialism published in 1770 under the name of the abbé Guillaume Raynal. Both Robertson and Raynal condemned the cruelty of the Spanish *conquistadores* who had destroyed the indigenous populations of the Americas and some sections of Raynal's work criticized slavery, but the two authors also emphasized the economic importance of overseas colonies to Europe. The negative view of Spanish colonial society purveyed in these works inspired a number of authors from the region to write responses: for the first time, historians located outside the European world turned European historical methods against the Europeans themselves. The Mexican-born Francisco Clavijero's *Historia antigua de México* (1781), for example, argued that Raynal and other European authors had systematically misrepresented the achievements of precolonial American civilizations. In Spain itself, the desire to respond effectively to outside critics led scholars to turn to primary sources from the era of the Conquest, which were brought together in one of the first modern archival institutions, the Archivo de Indias, in the 1780s.

The third of the major British history writers of the Enlightenment era, Edward Gibbon, devoted most of his life to the writing of his *Decline and Fall of the Roman Empire* (1776–1789). Gibbon occupies an important position in the history of historiography not only because of the scope of his scholarly work, but also because of his lively *Memoirs* (1796), considered the first modern British autobiography, which allow us to follow the stages by which a history writer acquired his skills and carried out his project. In one magnificent paragraph, Gibbon condensed years of hard work, recalling what he had done "to methodize the form, and to collect the substance of my Roman decay." The writings of the Romans themselves "were my old and familiar companions," he wrote, as he "investigated, with my pen almost always in my hand, the original records, both in Greek and Latin. . . . The subsidiary rays of medals and inscriptions, of geography and chronology were thrown on their proper objects" as he strove to "fix and arrange within my reach the loose and scattered atoms of historical information." The writing was as hard as the research: "At the outset all was dark and doubtful: even the title of the work . . . and I was often tempted to cast away the labour of seven years. . . . Many experiments were made before I could hit the middle tone between a dull chronicle and a rhetorical declamation." His great historical endeavor, Gibbon told readers of his memoirs, had given meaning to his life. When he finally finished the manuscript, "a sober melancholy was spread over my mind by the idea that I had taken my everlasting leave of an old and agreeable companion."[11]

The underlying theme of Gibbon's narrative was fully in line with the Enlightenment's critique of religion: he showed how the spread of Christianity had undermined the values on which the Roman Empire depended. In contrast to Voltaire's overt sarcasm toward religion, however, Gibbon adopted a solemn and ironic style that made a more lasting impression. "The clergy successfully preached the doctrines of patience and pusillanimity; the active virtues of society were discouraged; and the last remains of military spirit were buried in the cloister," he wrote in his conclusion. By contrast, the Europe of his day no longer faced the same dangers. Without saying so openly, he implied that religious beliefs no longer had the same hold on people's minds, and "the general manners of the times" seemed to him to provide security against a relapse into barbarism.[12] Like the works of Voltaire, Hume, and Raynal, Gibbon's *Decline and Fall* was a commercial success. Modern scholarship has rendered Gibbon's history out of date, but it is still considered a literary masterpiece and an outstanding expression of Enlightenment thought.

Gibbon's confidence that the Europe of his day would not suffer the fate of ancient Rome reflected the Enlightenment faith in progress and especially the increasingly widespread conviction that history revealed a steady rhythm of human advancement. In Scotland, whose capital, Edinburgh, was one of the main centers of Enlightenment thought, Adam Ferguson, in his *Essay on the History of Civil Society* (1782), elaborated a "conjectural history" according to which all societies inevitably moved through a series of economic and cultural stages, starting with a simple life based on the tending of flocks. This pastoral stage developed into one organized around agriculture and then to a society based on trade and manufacturing. Economic progress was accompanied, Ferguson and other Scottish theorists maintained, by the refinement of social customs; among other things, they emphasized improvements in the condition of women as one of the most important indices of cultural development. The most emphatic statement of this optimistic philosophical history was provided by the French philosopher Condorcet, in his *Sketch for a Historical Picture of the Progress of the Human Mind* (1794), which he wrote in the midst of the upheavals of the French Revolution. Although the experience of the Revolution was to make many thinkers question the inevitability of progress, Condorcet was sure that "nature has set no term to the perfection of human faculties." History, or "observations upon what man has been and what he is today," Condorcet insisted, "will instruct us about the means we should employ to make certain and rapid the further progress that his nature allows him still to hope for."[13]

The developmental scheme of history proposed by the Scottish philosophers and Condorcet had its critics even at the time. The most important of these was the German thinker Johann Gottfried von Herder (1744–1803), who objected to the idea of measuring the distinctive cultures of different nations according to a universal standard of civilization derived from the experience of Western Europe. Herder's insistence that every nation had its own unique characteristics, and that these were best reflected in the folk culture of its ordinary people rather than by its educated elites, suggested a relativist or historicist approach to history, in which each nation's past was considered only on its own terms. Herder's interest in popular culture owed a good deal to his reading of Vico, whose notion that historians could achieve an intuitive understanding of past societies that was deeper than the knowledge that reason alone could construct appealed to him. By making the nation, defined primarily in terms of a shared language, the fundamental unit of human society, Herder also anticipated the strongly nationalist character of most European history-writing in the nineteenth century. One of Herder's German contemporaries, Justus Möser, provided an influential example of this approach to history in his account of the development of his home town of Osnabrück. Rather than critiquing the provincialism of the city's population, Möser contended that their actions grew organically out of the specific circumstances of their lives.

The critical approach to the study of the past that developed in Europe during the seventeenth and eighteenth centuries was not unique. It had its analogue in China, where the overthrow of the Ming dynasty by Manchu invaders in 1644 caused a crisis among the country's intellectuals. Under the succeeding Qing dynasty, a school of "evidential scholars" developed more exacting standards for the evaluation of historical sources in the hope of recovering the true nature of the Confucian tradition, which they argued had been overlaid with later additions in intervening centuries. Members of this school used skills similar to those of the European humanists to identify errors in the long-accepted classics of Chinese historical writing, including the work of Sima Qian, and denied that the main function of history was to teach moral lessons. "Rather, one should examine the veracity of regulations and institutions and ensure the factuality of events and records in order to see the truth," Wang Mingsheng (1722–1798) wrote.[14]

The early modern period was thus a highly creative one for the understanding of history and the practices used to represent it. The separation of history from the religious framework characteristic of the Middle Ages gave the story of the human past a new autonomy, although the need to satisfy rulers, embattled parties in the religious struggles of the Reformation, and even the standards of "reason" as defined by the Enlightenment often influenced the way historians told their tales. The rediscovery of the historians of the ancient world inspired authors, and the critical methods developed during and after the Renaissance helped define more clearly what constituted historical truth. The printing press allowed historical works to reach audiences much greater than ever before, and a few historians became wealthy from the sale of their works. The discovery of the Americas forced historians to confront the problem of integrating its past into their picture of the development of mankind, and the spread of the idea of progress challenged historians to defend the value of their discipline by arguing that it could contribute to the construction of a better future for humankind.

The historians of the early modern era were, as that label suggests, "modern" in some ways, but the historical enterprise today is, in other respects, quite different from what it was anywhere in the world up to the time of Gibbon and his contemporaries. In their day, history was not a regular part of school curricula. There were only a handful of university teaching positions specifically dedicated to the subject, and there was no regular program of training for people interested in becoming historians.

The distinction between scholarly and popular history did not exist, and the institutions that make scholarly history possible—public archives of historical documents, specialized journals, professional associations—were just beginning to come into existence. Nor could the historians of the past have imagined the many media through which historical knowledge is disseminated in the modern world, ranging from historical museums to websites. To fully understand the environment in which we study history today, we must turn to the important developments in the study of the past since the end of the eighteenth century.

Notes

1. Vasari, "Preface," *The Lives of the Painters, Sculptors and Architects,* 8 vols. (London: J. M. Dent, 1900), 1:xxxvi
2. Cited in Miguel Leon-Portilla, ed., *The Broken Spears: The Aztec Account of the Conquest of Mexico* (Boston: Beacon Press, 1962), 137.
3. Jorge Cañizares-Esguerra, *How to Write the History of the New World: Historiographies, Epistemologies, and Identities in the Eighteenth-Century Atlantic World* (Stanford, CA: Stanford University Press, 2001), 4.
4. James Amelang, *The Flight of Icarus: Artisan Autobiography in Early Modern Europe* (Stanford, CA: Stanford University Press, 1998), 1.
5. Mary Spongberg, *Writing Women's History since the Renaissance* (New York: Palgrave Macmillan, 2002), 73.
6. See Doris Garraway, *The Libertine Colony: Creolization in the Early French Caribbean* (Durham, NC: Duke University Press, 2005), 103–19.
7. Cited in Kelley, *Versions,* 476.
8. Cited in Gay and Wexler, eds., *Historians at Work,* 2:287, 289.
9. Cited in Gay and Wexler, eds., *Historians at Work,* 2:252.
10. David Hume, "My Own Life."
11. Edward Gibbon, *Memoirs of My Life* (Middlesex: Penguin, 1984), 151, 158, 169.
12. Edward Gibbon, *The Decline and Fall of the Roman Empire,* ed. Dero A. Saunders (New York: Penguin, 1952), 622, 626.
13. Condorcet, cited in Kelley, ed., *Versions of History,* 491.
14. Cited in Daniel Woolf, *A Global History of History* (Cambridge, UK: Cambridge University Press, 2011), 322.

CHAPTER 4

The Nineteenth Century and the Rise of Academic Scholarship

The nineteenth century inherited traditions of writing about the past that were already more than two millennia old. In Europe, China, and other parts of the world, historians had developed sophisticated methods for evaluating evidence and creating coherent narratives about the past. Neither historians nor their audiences could have anticipated, however, how the study of the past was going to be transformed in the course of new century. The nineteenth century would see history transformed into an academic discipline and elevated to a central position in European thought. In the decades after 1800, historical scholars would achieve greater prestige and more influence in politics and culture than they had ever had before or would ever have again. To gaze at the multiple volumes of nineteenth-century works such as Thomas Babington Macaulay's history of England, Adolphe Thiers's history of the French Revolution, or Heinrich von Treitschke's history of Germany on a library's shelves today is to be reminded of an era when historians wrote on a grand scale and readers were prepared to follow them on epic journeys through the past. The historians of the period were not just scholars. Macaulay was a longtime member of the British Parliament, Thiers led the French Revolution of 1830, which toppled one French government and created another, and Treitschke was close to many of his nation's political leaders.

The distinction between older forms of historical writing and the historical writing of the nineteenth century indicates a profound shift in the ways in which history is conceived. Nineteenth-century historians were confident that their discipline's insights into the ways in which change and development occurred were fundamental to the understanding of every aspect of existence. Whereas previous eras had looked to religion or philosophy to find timeless general truths, the historians of the nineteenth century argued that change was the essence of reality and that each society and every era needed to be understood in terms of its own unique individuality, rather than being seen as an example of some broader category. This way of understanding the world is often called "historicism." The twentieth-century German historian Friedrich Meinecke, whose *Historism* (1936) is the most detailed study of the origins of nineteenth-century historicism, defined its essence as "the substitution of a process of *individualizing* observation for a *generalizing* view of human forces in history."[1]

For Meinecke, this "was one of the greatest intellectual revolutions that has taken place in Western thought . . . The world and all its life take on a new aspect once one has become used to looking at them along these new lines."[2] In Meinecke's view, the key insight of historicism was that the outcome of events is not determined by general laws that human beings cannot alter. "Individual historical development," he wrote, "is no mere evolution of tendencies already present in the germ-cell. Rather does it possess a large measure of plasticity, of capacity to change and be regenerated as it is worked upon by the ever-changing forces of time." In present-day terms, Meinecke was arguing that historicism recognized the power of human agency in ways that previous systems of thought had not. Only the historicism of the nineteenth century, according to Meinecke, was able to do justice to the "endless variety" of human experience and appreciate every era of the past in its own terms, rather than subordinating them to some overall scheme of progress or decline.[3] Meinecke's insistence that historicism represented a sharp break from earlier forms of historical thinking has been challenged by more recent scholars, and the horrors of the Nazi era led even Meinecke himself to criticize the relativism inherent in its insistence that historians should not apply universal moral rules to the judgment of past eras. Nevertheless, many insights derived from nineteenth-century historicism remain alive in present-day historical thinking; the late twentieth century even saw the growth of a "new historicism" bent on recovering the nineteenth-century movement's appreciation of the importance of historical context.

As important to the confidence of nineteenth-century historians as the notion that historical development was the most fundamental phenomenon of human existence was their equally strong conviction that new methods were enabling them to understand the past with an accuracy that their predecessors had never obtained. Few historians today describe their discipline as a "science," but all historians for the past two centuries have been deeply affected by the attempts, beginning in the early nineteenth century, to put historical knowledge on a more secure foundation and to professionalize its methods of research. These changes have been associated with the development of programs of specialized academic training for historians. University-trained scholars are not the only ones who practice history in the modern world, but their standards have become the benchmarks against which the validity of all other forms of history as accurate representations of the past are judged.

Together with the insights of historicist thinking and the development of modern professional methods, a third major change in historiography during the nineteenth century was the development of history conceived as the story of nation-states. To be sure, the history written in earlier periods often focused on particular states and their rulers. Prior to 1800, however, few historians defined their task as writing the history of a people, a community with a distinctive character and destiny. This began to change with the American and French revolutions, two movements dedicated to the idea that governments were the representatives of the people who made up their nations. These revolutions depended on the willingness of populations to see themselves as citizens capable of making their own history. The notion of nationalism also drew on ideas such as those of the eighteenth-century German thinker Herder, who had argued that every people had its own specific cultural traditions and ought to maintain its distinctive identity. Herder's notion of national communities as individual entities developing over time fit easily into the historicist framework. The explosive conflicts set off by the French Revolution and Herder's cultural nationalism would spread the idea of nationalism to the rest of the European continent and ultimately the rest of the world. Everywhere, historians would play a major role in these developments.

The Revolutionary Era and the Development of Historical Consciousness

All aspects of Western civilization, including the study of history, were deeply affected by the American and French revolutions of the late eighteenth century. The American revolutionaries claimed to be forging a new nation, one that by definition was not rooted in history. The French revolutionaries, imbued with the optimistic spirit of the Enlightenment, also rejected the authority of the past. "Don't try to follow the conduct of your ancestors, they had no principles to follow," one of their leading spokesmen wrote, urging his fellow citizens to "consult only good sense, which is the same in all countries and all epochs, and the law of nature."[4] In 1793, as the Revolution became increasingly radical, its leaders introduced a new calendar, making the proclamation of the French Republic on September 22, 1792, the start of Year I. Symbolically, the new calendar was a way of dismissing the whole of human history prior to that time as essentially meaningless. The revolutionary movement was not entirely hostile to history, and indeed chronicles of the Revolution, many of them compiled from the reports in the numerous newspapers founded to promote the movement, began to appear almost as soon as the movement started. In 1790, the revolutionaries established a national archive, meant to preserve official documents and make them accessible to all citizens, including historical researchers. In 1795, alarmed by the excesses inspired by the Revolution's repudiation of the past, which included the destruction of some of France's historic churches and artworks dedicated to the now-abolished monarchy, the new French government backed the establishment of a museum of historical monuments to preserve the cultural achievements of previous eras, which were reclassified as a national "patrimony" testifying to the creativity of the French people. Nevertheless, the French Revolution's relationship to a past that the revolutionaries dismissed as "the old regime" was obviously problematic.

The most fundamental contributions the French Revolution made to the conception of history, however, resulted from the movement's redefinition of the notions of "the people" and "the nation" and from the dramatic changes the Revolution brought about throughout Europe and the world. Events such as the storming of the fortress of the Bastille by a Paris crowd on July 14, 1789, showed that profound historical changes could be brought about by the collective actions of ordinary individuals; history could no longer be thought of essentially in terms of the actions of rulers and members of elite groups. In the long run, the events of the French Revolution would stimulate an interest in history written "from below," with an emphasis on the role of the masses. The French Revolution also welded the French people into a new kind of self-conscious community, whose members were supposed to identify with their "nation" and be ready to defend it against foreign enemies. Unlike subjects of a king, who might have little in common besides loyalty to their monarch, citizens of a nation were expected to regard each other as "brothers"—the role of women in national life was left undefined—and to abandon distinctions among themselves, such as historic ties to their home regions or social status groups. The nationalism inspired in France by the Revolution helped spread the idea that history was the story of the emergence of distinct national communities, organized into unified political states, and of the conflicts among them.

As the ideas of the Revolution spread across Europe and even to some overseas territories and as French armies toppled old governments and legal systems, Edward Gibbon's confidence that Western civilization could not experience any changes as profound as those that had caused the fall of the Roman Empire no longer appeared valid. Napoleon's campaigns, which took him as far as Egypt and Russia, ended in defeat, but for the first time in millennia, the Western world was dominated by a conqueror whose deeds were comparable to those of Alexander the Great and Julius Caesar. When Napoleon rode through his small German town of Jena, the philosopher G. W. F. Hegel wrote that he had seen "the World Spirit on horseback." Napoleon deliberately stoked the interest in his own historic accomplishments, through the *Bulletins of the Grand Army* he published during his campaigns and then through the memoirs he dictated during his years of exile after 1815. Historians were challenged to explain how such dramatic ruptures as the French Revolution and such spectacular events as Napoleon's conquests had been possible and what they meant.

It was the Revolution's opponents, however, more than the revolutionaries themselves, who paved the way for a new appreciation of history. As the Revolution's sweeping attempt to restructure society according to abstract principles encountered increasing difficulties, its critics, such as the British conservative Edmund Burke, argued that the revolutionaries' fundamental error had been to ignore the lessons of history. In his *Reflections on the Revolution in France* (1790), Burke insisted that even seemingly irrational institutions and patterns of conduct handed down from the past reflected an accumulation of practical experience that made them a better guide for the present than rational maxims. Burke emphasized the importance of understanding the legacy of the past, especially that of one's own nation. The French revolutionaries had also stressed the importance of national identity, but Burke defined the nation in historical terms, as a "partnership not only between those who are living, but between those who are living, those who are dead, and those who are to be born." Especially in Germany, where his emphasis on the uniqueness of each nation's past and the value of continuity fit in with ideas such as those expressed earlier by Herder and Möser, Burke's emphasis on the importance of history was welcomed. When French armies invaded Germany and imposed revolutionary reforms there, many Germans reacted defiantly by insisting on the value of their own traditions, including their devotion to the past. It was certainly no accident that Germany would become the country where new approaches to the study of history would develop most strongly in the course of the nineteenth century.

Among the most important reevaluations of the importance of history inspired by the events of the revolutionary era was the philosophical thought of Hegel, who had called Napoleon "the World Spirit on horseback." In contrast to previous philosophers, who had searched for timeless truths, Hegel argued that thought itself was historical and that the public events recorded by historians marked the unfolding of the Spirit or Idea behind reality. In contrast to Enlightenment thinkers, with their optimistic faith in progress, Hegel admitted that finding a meaning in the record of the past was not easy. "In contemplating history as the slaughter-bench at which the happiness of peoples, the wisdom of states, and the virtue of individuals have been sacrificed, a question necessarily arises: To what principle, to what final purpose, have these monstrous sacrifices been offered?" he wrote.[5] His answer was that, through what he called "the cunning of Reason," even the worst historical catastrophes had, in the long run, promoted the development of properly regulated human freedom. The outcome of the violence of the French revolutionary era, for example, had been the development of governments regulated by laws and dedicated to the welfare of their subjects, of which he claimed that the Prussian kingdom in which he lived was the best model.

Hegel was not a historian, and most scholars of the past rejected his contention that historical events could be explained as the working out in reality of some deep philosophical principle. His insistence that, in any given era, only a handful of states or individuals come to embody the essence of world history led him to dismiss the peoples of the non-European world as having nothing to contribute to the fulfillment of humanity's higher purposes. Hegel's exaltation of the importance of the state, at the expense of individual freedom, has often been blamed for the later excesses of German nationalism. Nevertheless, Hegel's insistence that all aspects of reality undergo development over time gave a new philosophical importance to history. His notion of dialectical development, in which the assertion of any principle inevitably leads to the articulation of an opposing one, asserted that change over time was built into the very structure of reality. Hegel's dialectical thinking inspired the mid-nineteenth-century socialist thinker Karl Marx's analysis of history as a series of conflicts between rival socioeconomic classes, which has had wide impact on historical scholarship. More recently, the provocative passage on "the master–slave relationship" in one of Hegel's works has had a profound impact on historical studies of movements against slavery and colonialism.

Whereas Hegel's system gave history a philosophical meaning, the literature and art associated with the cultural movement of romanticism also spurred interest in the past. Rejecting the Enlightenment's emphasis on reason, the romantics valued emotion. They saw the past, especially the Middle Ages, as a time when men and women had been freer to follow their passions. No one exploited the romantic allure of the past more than the historical novelist Walter Scott, whose best-selling books gave bygone times a new popularity and challenged historians to distinguish their narratives from his. Scott's portrayal of the Middle Ages did much to change attitudes toward a period that the writers of the Enlightenment had described as an age of superstition and intolerance. In the preface to his novel *Ivanhoe*, which, among other things, gave the story of Robin Hood its modern form and generated sympathy for Europe's Jewish minority by including a beautiful young Jewish woman as one of its heroines, Scott defended himself against critics who claimed that by "intermingling fiction with truth, I am polluting the well of history with modern inventions, and impressing upon the rising generation false ideas of the age which I describe." He had, he insisted, studied historical documents closely before beginning to write and had used them to recreate "the private life of our ancestors," a topic that scholarly historians scorned but that he sensed would interest his readers. Above all, however, he had tried to write about the past in such a way "that the modern reader will not find himself . . . much trammelled by the repulsive dryness of mere antiquity."[6]

The vogue for historical novels coincided with a fashion for elaborate paintings of dramatic scenes from medieval and early modern history and for architecture inspired by the buildings of that era. Some history painters, obsessed with accuracy, became collectors and experts on the clothing, furniture, and architecture of the past, anticipating the interests of today's historians of material culture.[7] In 1837, the French government opened a museum devoted exclusively to French history, the Historical Museum of Versailles, located in the former royal palace. French artists were offered commissions to create large-scale paintings illustrating major episodes in the country's history, from the early Middle Ages to the Revolution, with the object of dramatizing the development of national identity. The issues raised in debates about the historical validity of novels and films, the modern-day equivalents of historical paintings, continue today, with professional historians objecting that novelists and filmmakers distort the past in the interest of making their stories accessible and historical novelists and film creators replying that they bring the past to life for audiences who would otherwise take no interest in it.

One of the most lasting testimonies to the nineteenth century's absorption with the past was the vogue for architecture inspired by the Romanesque and Gothic styles of the Middle Ages. Architects such as the British Augustus Pugin carefully studied the surviving monuments of that era and strove to create environments that would revive its religiously inspired sense of community. Their designs reflected a new attitude toward history: for the first time, architects deliberately sought to imitate the styles of the past. The earnestness of these nineteenth-century "neo-Romanesque" and "neo-Gothic" structures, a number of which still stand on British and American university campuses, contrasts sharply with the suppression of historical references in much of twentieth-century architecture or the self-conscious use of them in a kind of pastiche in contemporary design. Today, whole-hearted imitations of medieval architecture are found in theme parks that attract viewers because they evoke a past from which we are completely separated; in the nineteenth century, it was still possible to imagine that all of modern life could be lived in such a setting. In such a cultural atmosphere, it is not hard to understand why the study of history would be regarded as a matter of the highest importance.

Ranke and His "Revolution"

The historian whose name is most associated with the new "scientific" history of the nineteenth century, the German Leopold von Ranke, was one of those who credited Walter Scott's books with attracting him to the study of the past, but who then came to insist on the importance of distinguishing between history and fiction. Ranke is the central figure in Friedrich Meinecke's *Historism*; for Meinecke, one of Ranke's students, it was Ranke who truly realized the potential of history as the supreme method for the understanding of human life. In the history of historical writing, Ranke is also the first important figure to be celebrated as much for of his contributions as a university professor as for his writings. For most of his long life—he lived from 1795 to 1886—Ranke taught at the University of Berlin, founded in 1810 as part of a deliberate program to promote German national identity in opposition to the influence of the French, who had conquered Prussia in 1806. The founder of the University of Berlin, William von Humboldt, considered history an extremely important part of the curriculum; his essay "On the Tasks of the Historian," published in 1821, set out a program that anticipated many of Ranke's ideas. At Berlin, Ranke trained several generations of younger scholars, both German students and foreigners attracted by the growing reputation of the new scientific history, in the methods of historical research and the values he had embraced.

Ranke is most remembered today for a single sentence: his insistence that the task of the historian was "to show what actually happened" (*"wie es eigentlich gewesen"*). For him, this meant that the historian was not to judge the past critically, according to the principles of his own time, as Enlightenment historians such as Voltaire and Gibbon had done, or to shape events into a story with a moral lesson for the present. Instead, Ranke insisted that every era of the past was "immediate to God" (*"unmittelbar zu Gott"*), meaning that each age had its own set of values and that no one of them could claim superiority to all others. To achieve the goal of truly understanding past events, the Rankean historian needed to reconstruct them as much as possible on the basis of documents from the time when they had occurred. For Ranke, this meant above all the sources preserved in archives, which were becoming accessible for the first time to scholars as other European governments followed the example of the French and granted public access to their records. One of the consequences of the insistence that historians needed to use original documents, or what we now call primary sources, in preference to other materials was that the entire history of the past suddenly cried out to be rewritten. Barthold Niebuhr, a German historian who had anticipated many of Ranke's ideas a few decades earlier, justified his decision to compose a new history of ancient Rome by writing that authors who relied on the celebrated historians of the past, such as Livy, were like "people [who] take maps and landscapes for reality itself."[8] The notion that the entire past was waiting to be properly researched by historians trained in new methods lent the historical enterprise a sense of novelty and excitement. Ranke spoke of searching for "virgin" archives and, when he gained access to one collection, wrote that he "had a sweet, magnificent fling with the object of my love."[9]

Ranke put strong emphasis not only on the search for original historical documents, but also on objective reporting of the information they provided. "The strict presentation of the facts, contingent and unattractive though they may be, is undoubtedly the supreme law," he wrote. But the historical scholar could not be satisfied with a dry chronicle of isolated facts; he also had to write them up in such a way that the "unity and progress of events" would be evident to readers. Beyond this, the historian needed to avoid becoming so absorbed in the details of any one episode of the past and in the "pleasure in the particular for itself" that he lost track of the broader meaning of his findings and "the universal aspect of things."[10] In his publications, Ranke showed readers the archival and interpretive work that had gone into his writing by accompanying his narrative with footnotes that identified his sources and discussed their reliability, thus producing what the intellectual historian Anthony Grafton has called "a distinctively modern, double story": the story of the past and the story of the historian's efforts to reconstruct it.[11] Grafton argues that the humanist antiquarian scholars of the Renaissance era and their successors in the seventeenth century had already anticipated Ranke's emphasis on the critical reading of primary sources and that Gibbon, among others, had already made masterful use of the footnote as a form of commentary on his main narrative. Nevertheless, he admits that Ranke was more successful than any of his predecessors in integrating these two levels of historical inquiry.

Ranke's importance in historiography is the result not only of his articulation of a critical method for the study and narration of the past, but also of his development of a new model of historical education: the research seminar. Until Ranke's time, when history was taught in schools and universities, it was presented in the form of lectures: students were given a narrative of the past, but they learned little about how to construct such a story. Ranke's innovation was to systematically engage students in the process of source interpretation by having them closely study primary documents and present their conclusions to other scholars, who would subject them to criticism. Instead of a lecture hall, university seminars on the Rankean model met in smaller rooms that facilitated discussion and argument; as the seminar model became established, seminar rooms were usually also equipped with a library of reference works on which participants could draw. Part of the appeal of the Rankean seminar was the sense of being initiated into an elite club, limited to those who had mastered the exacting techniques of scientific scholarship. This new method of training in historical scholarship attracted students from all over the world, lured by the excitement of gaining a new kind of mastery of the past. As an American student of Ranke's described the experience, "There the student appears, fortified by books and documents borrowed from the university library, and prepared with his brief of points and citations, like a lawyer about to plead a case in the court room . . . Authorities are discussed, parallel sources are cited; old opinions are exploded, standard histories are riddled by criticism."[12] Many of Ranke's students went on to establish historical training seminars at other universities. In the United States, for example, Johns Hopkins University established the first Ph.D. program in history in 1876.

Along with his insistence on the need for research using archival sources and his development of the history seminar, Ranke made a third vital contribution to the development of modern history by insisting on the autonomy of history as an academic discipline and the necessity of its professionalization. Until his day, the study of history had often been considered a branch of the broader study of literature or a subsidiary subject to be learned as part of philosophy. In a polemic against Hegel, who taught philosophy at the University of Berlin during Ranke's early years there, Ranke articulated the difference between the two disciplines by arguing that philosophers were only interested in specific events insofar as they demonstrated some universal principle, whereas "history recognizes in each existence something infinite, in each condition or being something eternal coming from God" and therefore worthy of study in its own right. History therefore needed its own methodology, distinct from that of philosophical reasoning: according to Ranke, philosophers proceed by deducing consequences from general propositions, whereas historians work inductively, starting with specific instances that may eventually lead to general conclusions.[13] Ranke's insistence that historical research had to be judged according to its own rules, and that these rules could only be learned through systematic training, pointed the way to the creation of a community of professional historians, something that had never previously existed. The success or failure of historians' projects would henceforth be determined by the judgment of their professional peers, rather than by the reactions of the public or honors awarded by rulers.

Like Herodotus and Thucydides, Ranke is one of those symbolic figures who evokes different reactions from scholars of history, depending on their own views of how history should be done. One of Ranke's own students, the Swiss-born Jacob Burckhardt, was the nineteenth century's most articulate critic of the heavy emphasis on political history characteristic of the Rankean school. The title of the first chapter of Burckhardt's *Civilization of the Renaissance in Italy* (1860), "The State as a Work of Art," underlined the difference between his approach and that of his teacher. For Ranke, the state was an essential aspect of reality; for Burckhardt, it was a human cultural creation, to be judged essentially on aesthetic grounds. Burckhardt's work revived the tradition of cultural history, in terms reminiscent of eighteenth-century authors such as Vico and Voltaire. Burckhardt tried to show that all aspects of the Renaissance period—its politics, but also its art, its thought, and the pattern of everyday life—reflected a common spirit. To understand the new individualism that, according to Burckhardt, was the distinctive feature that separated the Renaissance from the Middle Ages, the historian had to rely as much on an intuitive understanding of the spirit of the past as on a careful study of documents. Ranke's methodological insights are still appreciated, but his books are rarely read nowadays. Burckhardt's masterwork, on the other hand, is still considered essential reading for the study of the period it treats, and remains an inspiration for more recent cultural historians.

Although Burckhardt's work was admired even in its own day, it was generally seen as an isolated exception rather than as a model for other historians to follow. Early in the twentieth century, the British historian G. P. Gooch, whose *History and Historians in the Nineteenth Century* (1913) became the standard English-language account of historiography for many decades, announced that Ranke was "the master of us all." Friedrich Meinecke rated him as "one of the immortals," and in the 1980s, Ernst Breisach called him the "key figure" in the definition of a modern approach to history, not only because of his contributions to historical methodology but also because of "the universality of his historical vision."[14] More recent historians of historiography, such as

Peter Reill, Donald Kelley, and Anthony Grafton, have questioned Ranke's originality, arguing that he did little more than systematize the use of the critical methods pioneered by the humanists and antiquarian scholars of the Renaissance and the seventeenth century and build on the insights of eighteenth-century German scholars who had already elaborated historicist insights. The feminist scholar Bonnie Smith has stressed that the Rankean model of the university research seminar excluded women, who did not gain access to higher education until the twentieth century, and the postmodernist theorist Hayden White has asserted that Ranke's historical narratives were dictated less by the facts than by the desire to shape past events into a certain kind of story.[15] Ranke's emphasis on political and diplomatic history militated against consideration of women's role in the past, and he had no doubt that the history of what he called "racially kindred nations either of Germanic or Germanic–Latin descent" was "the core of all modern history," thus dismissing non-European civilizations as unimportant.[16] Even as historical research has broadened its scope to take into account other parts of the world and other forms of human experience, and even as admission to university programs has been opened to women and other excluded groups, however, Ranke's definition of what constitutes proper use of sources and his seminar model of teaching have remained influential.

The Rankean model of historical research, with its emphasis on the study of primary sources, was closely associated with the development of modern standards for the conservation and publication of such documents. In 1819, as part of its program for strengthening national consciousness after the Napoleonic wars, the Prussian government initiated the *Monumenta Germaniae Historica*, a series of volumes dedicated to the publication of carefully edited historical sources, particularly those concerning the Middle Ages, which was seen as a high point of German civilization. The *Monumenta Germaniae Historica*, which continues to appear today, became a model for similar projects in other countries. Historians' new concern for sources led to the development of a new profession, that of the professional archivist, specifically trained to preserve and organize documents in such a way that historians can make use of them. The French *Ecole des chartes*, established in 1821 and still in existence, was the first institution established to train such specialists.

Another important consequence of the Rankean model of historical scholarship was the establishment of professional associations for academic historians and scholarly journals for the publication of historical research. The periodic meetings of historical associations, such as the Société de l'histoire de France, established by the politician and historian François Guizot in 1834, brought scholars together and helped disseminate new scholarly standards. The narrowly focused and heavily documented studies produced by historians devoted to the new methods were often exciting to other professionals, but they did not appeal to a wider public. Journals such as the *Historische Zeitschrift*, founded in 1859 by one of Ranke's leading students, Heinrich von Sybel, provided an outlet for such scholarship. "We demand from our contributors strictly scientific methods of exposition, with each assertion accompanied by proof, by source references and quotations . . . we severely exclude vague generalities and rhetoric," the editors of the French *Revue historique*, founded in 1876, warned.[17] Book reviews were an essential part of these professional journals and served as a mechanism for defining the standards that academic historians were expected to follow and judging which new publications met them. During the second half of the nineteenth century, journals on this model appeared in Italy (*Rivista Storica Italiana*, 1884), Britain (*English Historical Review*, 1886), Japan (*Shigaku Zasshi*, 1889), and the United States (*American Historical Review*, 1895).

The standards that historical research had to meet to be considered professional were most succinctly laid out in the *Introduction to the Study of History*, published by the French scholars Charles-Victor Langlois and Charles Seignobos in 1897. Their book was quickly translated into other languages and remained an authoritative guide for decades. The preface to the 1898 English version announced that "the student will learn . . . to have no mercy on his own shortcomings, to spare no pains, to grudge no expenditure of time or energy in the investigation of a carefully chosen and important historical problem, to aim at doing the bit of work in had so thoroughly that it will not need to be done again."[18] Langlois and Seignobos's instructions on how to locate sources, their breakdown of the "analytic operations" of external and internal criticism of sources and the proper procedures for taking and organizing notes, and their discussion on the "synthetic operations" necessary for the "grouping of facts" and their "exposition" in accordance with "the modern scientific ideal" still underlie most of the "how-to" manuals assigned in classes on historical methods today.

Nationalism and Historical Scholarship

Together with the rise of university-based scholarship and training in history informed by historicist principles, the increasing prevalence of historical writing dominated by nationalist perspectives was the leading development in the discipline during the nineteenth century. A leading modern scholar of historiography, Donald Kelley, has seen the rise of nationalist history that "enhanced notions of national identity or antiquity as well as modern superiority" as a example of a new kind of "mythistory," successful because of its emotional appeal rather than its factual basis.[19] At the time, however, the two developments of professional history and of nationalism were related to each other, since the increasingly professionalized scholarly history of the nineteenth century was heavily dependent on national governments for support. In most countries, governments funded the universities where the new history was taught and the archives where the documents historians needed were made available. Historians in turn saw the writing of national history as their most important task. It is true that Ranke, the leader of the new methodological approach to history, did not limit himself entirely to national history; his ambition was to write a "universal" history of Europe as a whole, integrating the research he had done on the different European national states. Most of his German students, however, concentrated more narrowly on the history of their own country and actively supported the growing movement to unite into a single nation the separate small states into which Germany had long been divided. They saw unification as an expression of the individuality of the German nation, expressing itself as historicist teaching indicated. The most notorious of Ranke's students, Heinrich von Treitschke, identified himself wholeheartedly with the cause of German unification under the leadership of Prussia, the most powerful of the German states, and strongly supported the aggressive policies of the Prussian chancellor, Otto von Bismarck, who established the German Empire in 1871. Treitschke's *German History in the Nineteenth Century* (1879–1896) told the story of the country's recent history in a way that made Bismarck's accomplishment appear necessary and inevitable. Treitschke insisted that Germany was destined to become Europe's dominant power; he was also actively hostile to the country's small Jewish minority, which he saw as a foreign element that threatened to weaken the newly founded national state. Among the evidence he cited to support his attack were passages from the first comprehensive modern history of the Jewish people, written by Heinrich Graetz, a German-Jewish scholar also inspired by the methods of the "new" scientific history. By showing that the Jews, despite their lack of a territory of their own, were nevertheless a national community, Graetz demonstrated, according to Treitschke, that they could never be loyal citizens of any other nation. The nationalist and anti-semitic outlook propagated in Treitschke's influential works helped create the climate that led many Germans to support the policies that led to World War I and later made the rise of Hitler possible.

Nationalist perspectives also permeated the history produced in other countries, both among scholars who embraced the new scholarly paradigm identified with the "German school" and among those who continued to write for a broader public. Whereas German nationalist historians emphasized the role of the state and the military, the most celebrated French, British, and American nationalist historians of the nineteenth century were more sympathetic to constitutional government and, sometimes, to democratic movements. After the fall of Napoleon, liberal French historians such as Augustin Thierry and François Guizot sought to show that the French Revolution's ideas of liberty and equality were not abstract philosophical principles, as Edmund Burke had claimed, but instead grew out of traditions of local self-government that went back to the Middle Ages. Their works gave these modern ideas a respectable historical pedigree. The most famous French nationalist historian, Jules Michelet (1798–1879), saw the common people of France as the embodiment of the country's spirit and the early years of the French Revolution as their moment of triumph. His lyrical description of how the common people of Paris prepared the site for the celebration of the first anniversary of the fall of the Bastille in 1790, demonstrating "equality in action," is a classic evocation of the spirit of democracy.[20] Michelet was strongly influenced by the eighteenth-century Italian historicist philosopher Vico's ideas about the development of national cultures. Michelet's writings and his public lectures made him a hero to students and opponents of the elitist July Monarchy regime. He enthusiastically supported the Revolution of 1848, which brought about the institution of universal manhood suffrage in France, although, like many republican radicals, he strongly opposed the extension of political rights to women, who, he claimed, were too easily influenced by superstitions and religious beliefs to make rational decisions. Not all French historians shared Michelet's enthusiasm for revolutionary democracy, however.

Alexis de Tocqueville, famous for his analysis of *Democracy in America* (1835/1840), acknowledged that traditional social hierarchies were breaking down in Europe as well. In his classic analysis of *The Old Regime and the French Revolution* (1856), published after the hopes generated by the Revolution of 1848 had been dashed, he warned that the advance of social equality, exemplified by the principles of the Revolution of 1789, might pose a greater threat to individual liberty than monarchical rule. Tocqueville's demonstration that the outcome of historical movements is often different from what their participants intended has resonated powerfully with historians of many subsequent revolutionary movements.

Whereas French nationalist historians like Michelet were convinced that the experience of the Revolution of 1789 made their country uniquely qualified to show the rest of the world the road to historical progress, the leading British historian of the first half of the nineteenth century, Thomas Babington Macaulay, celebrated the achievements of his country's parliamentary system. In his view, the special genius of the English was their ability to make progressive reforms without the accompanying violence of the revolutions that France had experienced. Describing the relatively bloodless "Glorious Revolution" of 1688 in England at a moment when the memory of the 1848 revolutions in France and other parts of Europe was still fresh, Macaulay wrote, "the speeches presented an almost ludicrous contrast to the revolutionary oratory of every other country. Both the English parties agreed in treating with solemn respect the ancient constitutional traditions of the state . . . and yet this revolution, of all revolutions the least violent, has been of all revolutions the most beneficent."[21] In the United States, nationalist history took the form of narratives exalting the makers of the constitution and the territorial expansion of the new nation after independence. George Bancroft's *History of the United States*, which began to appear in 1834, announced that the country's past showed that it was the bearer of a universal message, "for the advancement of the principles of everlasting peace and universal brotherhood."[22] Although nineteenth-century American historians promoted a patriotic version of the national past, in contrast to those in Europe, they received little encouragement from the government. The United States would not have a centralized national archive until 1934, and the federal government did not directly support universities. It was left to private associations, of which the oldest, the Massachusetts Historical Society, had been founded in 1790, to collect and preserve historic documents.

The nationalist framework for historical writing proved to be an important influence on the writing of history in the non-Western world as well as in Europe and the United States. At the time of Napoleon's invasion of Egypt in 1798, the historian Abd al-Rahman al-Jabarti, schooled in the Islamic tradition of chronicle writing, grasped the importance of this confrontation between two different cultures. Among other things, he was impressed by the systematic way in which the French collected information about the Egyptian past. In his own writings, he celebrated the achievements of Mehmet Ali, a ruler who challenged Ottoman rule in Egypt in the early nineteenth century and is remembered as the creator of modern Egyptian nationalism. A younger Egyptian historian, Rifa'ah al-Tahtawi (1801–1873), followed the pattern of European nationalist historians by emphasizing the deep roots of Egyptian identity, going back to the time of the pharaohs. This represented a break with the tradition of Islamic history-writing, which had treated the centuries prior to the coming of the new religion as unimportant and stressed the shared values of all Muslims, regardless of their nationality.

In India, although there were older indigenous traditions of writing about the past, British administrators employed by the East India Company were the first to conceive of the region's history in "national" terms. James Mill's *History of British India* (1817), written to praise the benefits of British rule, treated the subcontinent as a geographic unit and had a strong influence on subsequent Indian writing. As nineteenth-century Indian authors began to write history according to the nationalist model imported from Europe, they often took over assumptions from Mill and other European authors about the absence of serious historical thought in precolonial India and the oppressive nature of the Muslim rule that had preceded the British. In the 1840s and 1850s, two Haitian authors living in exile in France, Thomas Madiou and Alexis Beaubrun Ardouin, produced early examples of "postcolonial" history, defending the accomplishments of the former slaves who had defeated Napoleon's troops and made their country the first independent black state in the Americas a half-century earlier. At a time when the history of Africa still seemed to defy study, because of the absence of written documents, Madiou and Ardouin used the story of the revolt led by Toussaint Louverture to demonstrate, as Ardouin put it, that blacks "were capable . . . of imagining and doing whatever men of the white race could imagine and do."[23]

The combined impact of the new historical methods developed in Western Europe in the nineteenth century and the export of European notions of nationalism was equally significant in East Asia, where long traditions of historical writing already existed. In eighteenth-century China, the so-called "school of evidential learning" had already introduced critical methods for the study of the past that had many similarities with those developed by European scholars from the Renaissance period onward.[24] In the nineteenth century, as European interactions with China increased, the reaction of many Chinese historians was to insist more strongly than ever on the value of their own traditions, including the characteristic practice of writing about the past in the form of annals rather than in more structured narratives.

In Japan, whose rulers had tried even more strongly than the Chinese to keep out foreign influences, the impact of the Western world arrived more suddenly after the country's "opening" to the world in 1854 and the "Meiji Restoration" of 1868 that gave power to an emperor bent on modernizing the country. Part of this modernization process was the adoption of Western historical methods. In his *Outline of a Theory of Civilization*, published in 1875, the Japanese historian Fukuzawa Yukichi (1835–1901) called for the abandonment of Confucian traditions and the writing of a history that would show how Japan could play its part in the overall progress of world civilization. In 1887, a German scholar, Ludwig Riess, was appointed the first history professor at the newly established Tokyo University, where he was soon joined by Japanese colleagues eager to adapt the new methods to their own country's history. As Japan began its rapid rise to the status of a major power, however, historians were increasingly pressured to stress the continuity between the country's distant past and the present and to emphasize the uniqueness of its traditions, while minimizing the influence that its larger neighbor China had played shaping its culture. Japanese history thus took on a strongly nationalist coloring.[25]

History and the Sciences of Society

Ranke and his disciples considered history a *Wissenschaft*, a form of objective knowledge, but they argued that history differed from the natural sciences in that it dealt with singular events and did not aim at discovering general laws. Many nineteenth-century thinkers, however, insisted that the same scientific principles that were leading to striking advances in the understanding of natural phenomena could also be applied to the study of society, including its historical development.

At the same time, however, these social theorists were heavily influenced by the prevailing historicist atmosphere. Instead of basing their theories on timeless notions about society, the social philosophers of the nineteenth century tried to give general explanations of why historical change occurred.

The French thinker Auguste Comte called his version of social science "positivism," meaning that it was based only on rational observation of positively established facts. According to his doctrine, this observation showed that all branches of human knowledge progressed from a stage of religious belief through a "metaphysical stage," in which phenomena were explained in terms of abstract forces, and finally reached a "positive" stage, in which the search for ultimate causes was abandoned in favor of an empirically based understanding of the laws governing occurrences in the world. Comte's doctrine seemed in many ways to fit the development of the natural sciences, and it gave a powerful impetus to the development of social sciences such as sociology. Many historians shared Comte's notions of the inevitability of progress and the need for scholarship about the past to model itself on the procedures of the natural sciences, and elements of Comte's thinking can be found in more recent overall frameworks for explaining history, such as the "modernization theory" that influenced much American historical research in the mid-twentieth century. In debates among historians since the end of the nineteenth century, however, the term "positivism" has become a pejorative one, used by proponents of theoretically oriented forms of history to denounce rivals who, they claim, believe "that if you got the 'facts' right, the conclusions would take care of themselves."[26] Used in this sense, the term positivism comes closer to describing the views of Ranke than those of Comte.

One of the "positive" facts that many nineteenth-century thinkers claimed that science had established was the assertion that there were fundamental differences in intelligence and character among the different human races and between the sexes. Popular books such as the French author Arthur de Gobineau's *Moral and Intellectual Diversity of the Races* (1855) and the collaboratively written *Types of Mankind*, published in Philadelphia in 1854, spread the notion that racial differences explained all important aspects of social life. The notion of biological races with fixed characteristics was in many respects antithetical to historical thinking since it denied the possibility that human groups could change and evolve over time. Nevertheless, racialist thinking pervaded much of Western culture during the nineteenth and much of the twentieth century, and racial explanations were frequently advanced to justify historical developments such as European imperial conquests in the rest of the world, the westward expansion of the United States, and slavery and segregation in the American South. Racialist thinking was often associated with the evolutionist ideas of Charles Darwin, although Darwin's key idea was that the characteristics of biological species changed over time in response to environmental conditions and he did not believe in the existence of fundamental differences between human groups. Darwin's idea that evolution was powered by a competition among individuals of the same species for resources that resulted in "the survival of the fittest," however, could easily be misinterpreted as suggesting that history was the result of a contest between rival human groups and that those groups that triumphed were more "evolved" than others.

Another approach to history that was also presented as "scientific" was that of the German socialist thinker Karl Marx (1818–1883). Marx combined the philosopher Hegel's doctrine of dialectical development with advances in economic thought to create a complex doctrine that explained historical change as the result of changes in the economic structure of society. Each stage of economic development, Marx argued, generated a specific form of society divided between classes with conflicting interests. The agricultural economies of the European past had been dominated by a ruling class of landlords, who exploited the labor of peasants; the modern industrial world that had begun to develop in the eighteenth century gave rise to a property-owning bourgeois class and an exploited class of laborers or proletarians. By a dialectical process similar to that postulated by Hegel to explain the development of philosophy, the inherent contradictions in the capitalist economic system would, Marx insisted, inevitably lead to its breakdown and its replacement by an egalitarian socialist society in which there would be no more class conflicts. Politics, Marx claimed, was fundamentally governed by conflicts between rival socioeconomic classes. He demonstrated how his ideas could be applied to the analysis of historical events in the books he wrote about the unsuccessful revolution in France in 1848, *The Class Struggles in France* (1850) and *The Eighteenth Brumaire of Louis Napoleon* (1852), in which he explained that event as the result of conflicts between the interests of the bourgeoisie, the "petty bourgeoisie" of small shopkeepers and artisans, and the industrial working class or proletariat.

In contrast to Comte's positivism and the racialist ideas of the period, Marx's system was thoroughly historical, and indeed his collaborator Friedrich Engels claimed that Marx had "discovered the law of development of human history."[27] Marx's famous statement, "Men make their own history, but they do not make it as they please; they do not make it under self-selected circumstances, but under circumstances existing already, given and transmitted from the past," is a powerful formulation of the need for historians to balance the importance they grant to human agency with a recognition of the conditions under which it must be exercised.[28] Marx's theories about economic and social development suggested numerous topics for historical investigation, and even historians who rejected his socialist ideas were influenced by his insistence on the close connection between economic changes and transformations in social structure and politics. Marx's own ventures into historical writing focused more on politics than on society, but his ideas inspired other historians to study topics such as the nature of feudalism in medieval Europe, the connections between the growth of trade and manufacturing in the early modern period and the decline of the landed nobility, and the rise of trade unions and working-class movements in the nineteenth century. Particularly in the nineteenth century, when much of Europe was being transformed by the spread of large factories and railroads, Marx's propositions seemed to have a good deal of plausibility. The statistics-filled pages of his major work, *Capital*, gave his claims the appearance of a scientific grounding that Hegel's philosophical arguments about the impact of ideas did not possess. At the same time, Marx's claim to speak for the oppressed working class whose growth was one of the most visible features of the period gave his doctrine a moral appeal.

From the start, however, there were criticisms of Marx's ideas. His prediction that capitalism was inevitably bound to create a society dominated by the conflict between two hostile classes, the property-owning bourgeoisie and the laboring proletariat, does not explain major aspects of the actual history of the modern world, such as the strength of nationalist sentiments, which often created unity among members of classes whom Marxist theory taught should be each other's enemies. Marx's expectation that the capitalist economy's potential for growth would soon be exhausted, leading to a general crisis of the system, has also not come to pass, or at least not yet. Marx's assumption that the pattern of economic development in Western Europe showed the path that the rest of the world would inevitably follow led him to see European imperialism as a historically progressive force, and the adoption of his ideas by the dictatorial Communist regimes that seized power in Russia after 1917 and in China after 1949 undermined the notion that Marxism was always on the side of human freedom. Nevertheless, in a world where social inequalities generated by the capitalist economic system remain glaringly evident, Marx's doctrines still have an appeal, both to social activists and to a number of historians.

Nineteenth-century academic historians and social theorists were largely in agreement that the inferiority of women to men was rooted in the biological differences between the sexes. Among other things, this was taken to mean that women were unfit for the higher forms of intellectual activity, such as historical research. Even some women endorsed this view, such as a British author, M. A. Stodart, who wrote in 1843 that women's "powers of mind are hardly fitted to enter this field for the sake of instructing others . . . her feelings usurp the seat of judgment, and she is carried away by their power. She feels keenly, and then decides promptly, instead of calmly weighing facts and deciding upon evidence." Stodart did allow that "the humbler walk of Biography is less unfitted to feminine power," presumably because it dealt with its subjects' private lives.[29] In fact, nineteenth-century women wrote not only biography but also popular history and historical novels. Charlotte Yonge (1823–1901), for example, has been called the "mother of historical fiction for children," the "first to reorient history from a child's perspective" by creating realistic stories about the past in which children figured as the heroes.[30] In France, Augustine Fouillée's elementary school textbook, *Le Tour de France par deux enfants* ("Two Children's Tour of France"), first published (under a male pseudonym) in 1877, taught history, geography, and patriotism to several generations of French pupils.

Despite their contributions to other genres of history, however, women remained almost entirely excluded from the university seminars that had now become crucial for the achievement of academic status in the historical profession. In the second half of the nineteenth century, a few anthropologists and social theorists began to challenge the notion that women's condition was a permanent and unchanging aspect of human life. Among the first was Johann Jakob Bachofen, a Swiss scholar, whose *Mutterrecht* ("The Law of the Mother"), published in 1861, argued that at one stage in the development of human society, matriarchy, rather than patriarchy, was the general rule and that female deities were widely worshipped. In 1884, Karl Marx's longtime collaborator, Friedrich Engels, integrated Bachofen's argument into a broader socialist theory, claiming that in primitive societies, women's economic contributions were important enough to guarantee them a certain respect, but that as society became wealthier and women's work became less necessary, men were able to impose their domination and reduce women almost to the status of property. Bachofen's and Engels's arguments had little impact at the time, but mid-twentieth-century feminists found them inspirational when they set out to challenge the notion that gender inequality has been a constant throughout history.

A Historical Civilization

Just as the development of science and technology in nineteenth-century Europe appeared to have demonstrated that there were no limits to human potential, the development of history written according to the new methods developed after 1800 appeared to have given human knowledge about the past new scope and new certainty. At the same time, other cultural developments were creating a picture of the universe in which change over time appeared to be a general phenomenon. Advances in geology replaced the Biblical story of the creation of the world with an account emphasizing how slow natural processes had shaped the planet over hundreds of thousands or even millions of years. Darwin's theory of evolution posited that plant and animal species were the products of lengthy processes of development. New archeological findings extended the story of the human past back many millennia, replacing the temporal framework inherited from the Bible and Enlightenment philosophers' speculations about an original "state of nature" with evidence about how "cave men" had actually lived. Like some of the proponents of the present-day movement to construct a "big history" incorporating the evolution of humanity into a story beginning with the creation of the universe, nineteenth-century scholarship thus claimed to give an account of the world from its creation to the present.

As the story of the world's past began to extend further back in time, historians separated themselves from specialists in "natural history" and from archeologists, who dealt with the period before the invention of writing, and limited their own domain to the study of societies that had left written records. The nineteenth century witnessed striking developments in the understanding of the history of the world's earliest civilizations. The French invasion of Egypt in 1798 opened the era of modern Egyptology. Among the objects discovered by the French scholars who accompanied the army was the Rosetta Stone, a large stone tablet inscribed in both Greek and Egyptian hieroglyphics that became the key to translating the mysterious symbols of that language. Once they could read hieroglyphic inscriptions and papyri, scholars could begin to reconstruct the life of the society that had produced them. Other scholars succeeded in translating the cuneiform inscriptions that recorded the past of the civilizations of the Middle East. Comparative study of languages, inspired by the English philologist William Jones's demonstration that ancient Greek and Latin shared many features with the Indian language of Sanskrit and his hypothesis that these languages and most European tongues had developed out of a common "Indo-European" linguistic ancestor, shed new light on the connections between ancient civilizations.

Nineteenth-century historical science also turned its attention to the religious and mythical texts that had long been regarded as the basis of Western civilization and that had for centuries influenced the understanding of its past. The historical approach to the Bible, first suggested by the seventeenth-century philosopher Spinoza and some of his contemporaries, undermined the notion that that document provided a privileged access to truth about the human past. Radical critics even suggested that there was no solid evidence that Jesus himself had ever existed, a proposition that an English churchman, Richard Whately, tried to subvert in his *Historic Doubts Relative to Napoleon Buonaparte* (1819), in which he used skeptical arguments to show that, by the same standards, there was no convincing proof that the French emperor had ever lived. In his *Life of Jesus* (1835), the German scholar David Strauss accepted the existence of a "historical Jesus," but argued that the miracles recounted in the four Gospels of the New Testament should be regarded as myths and that Jesus's life could be reconstructed through the application of the critical approach used in dealing with other historical subjects, an approach extended and popularized later in the century by a French author, Ernest Renan, whose own *Life of Jesus* (1863) presented its subject as a human being without divine attributes.

Later in the century, a German scholar, Julius Wellhausen, employed historical and linguistic analysis to show that the Torah, the first five books of the Hebrew Bible, was a composite of several earlier documents written at different time periods, but in any case long after the events they claimed to describe. Another German, Heinrich Schliemann, excavated what is now generally accepted as the site of the ancient city of Troy and insisted that he had found relics proving the historical validity of the *Iliad*. Although subsequent research has shown that Schliemann misdated his major finds and that his crude methods probably led him to destroy most actual remnants of the Trojan city described by Homer, his work showed that archeological exploration could provide a new picture of the Greek past that had previously been known only through its surviving literature and art.

The nineteenth century's intense interest in the past was fueled by new discoveries but also by new ways of presenting history to the public. Madame Tussaud's wax museum, presenting tableaux of the French revolutionary Terror and other dramatic scenes, was opened in London in 1835 and still exists today. Photography, introduced in the middle of the century, brought a new degree of realism to the depiction of current history, exemplified by Matthew Brady's pictures of Civil War battlefields. Photographs appeared to preserve images in an objective form, allowing viewers direct access to the scenes they depicted, although the limitations of Brady's equipment meant that his pictures were all taken after the battles they purportedly illustrated. Panoramas and cycloramas—huge paintings shown in special circular buildings that gave spectators the illusion of being in the middle of historical scenes—enjoyed great popularity. Paul Dominique Philippoteaux's depiction of Pickett's charge, the final turning point of the battle of Gettysburg, painted in 1883, is still one of the major attractions for visitors to the site. In Sweden, Artur Hazelius, concerned that the rapid urbanization of the country was destroying the memory of its rural heritage, began buying up peasant cottages and other material objects to preserve them. In 1891, he opened the Skansen open-air museum, the first historical theme park, which remains one of Stockholm's principal tourist attractions.

By the last decades of the nineteenth century, history had come to pervade Western culture to an unprecedented extent. Educated people everywhere had come to think of themselves and their countries as the product of historical development. Although few actually read the scholarly journals inspired by Ranke's methods, general readers assumed that the more accessible works of history they purchased rested on a solid basis of scientific scholarship. University-trained historians remained relatively few in number, but the institutions that would provide the basis for the expansion of the discipline were rapidly taking shape.

It was in this optimistic mood that American historians met in 1884 to found the American Historical Association, still the major organization of history professionals in the United States. Looking back on its founding fifty years later, J. Franklin Jameson, one of the association's major leaders, remarked that, in 1884, there had been only "a few historians . . . in the real sense" in the country. But the founders had been optimistic. They had the support of the country's leaders—former president Rutherford B. Hayes was among the forty-one original members of the association, and Congress enthusiastically voted to grant the association an official charter in 1889—and they counted on the new generation of younger scholars who had gone to study in Germany, "from which they returned with eager ambition to raise American scholarship to higher levels."[31]

At its second meeting in 1885, the American Historical Association made von Ranke its first honorary member; it was the last honor he received before he died in 1886. Ranke's historicist outlook, his critical methodology, and his pedagogical innovations seemed to have triumphed throughout the civilized world. The new academic history would indeed continue to develop throughout the decades that followed Ranke's death, but as the twentieth century unfolded, its practitioners found themselves confronted with an ever-increasing number of challenges. The centrality of history in the understanding of the world would be contested from many points of view. Ranke's research methods would be questioned, and the emphasis on national history he had promoted would be assailed. Even the seminar system he had developed would be criticized. Nevertheless, Ranke's historicist principles—judicious evaluation of evidence, with careful attention to its historical context, and a recognition of the distinctiveness of the different periods of the past—remain an important part of historical practice.

Notes

1. Friedrich Meinecke, *Historism: The Rise of a New Historical Outlook*, trans. J. E. Anderson (New York: Herder & Herder, 1972 (orig. 1936)), lv. Anderson's decision to translate the German word *Historismus* as "historism" rather than the more commonly used "historicism" was widely criticized.
2. Meinecke, *Historism*, lv, liv.

3. Meinecke, *Historism*, 504, 505.
4. Paul Rabaut de Saint-Etienne, *Considérations sur les intérêts du Tiers-Etat* (Paris, 1789), p. 37, trans. Jeremy D. Popkin.
5. G. W. F. Hegel, *Reason in History*, trans. Robert S. Hartman (Indianapolis, IN: Bobbs–Merrill, 1953), 27.
6. Walter Scott, "Dedicatory Epistle," *Ivanhoe* (1820).
7. The early nineteenth century's history painting was the subject of a major exposition at the Musée de Beaux-Arts in Lyon, France, in 2014. See the catalog of the exposition, Stephen Bann and Stéphane Paccoud, eds., *L'Invention du passé. Histoires de coeur et d'épée en Europe, 1802–1850* (Paris: Hazan, 2014).
8. Cited in Fritz Stern, *The Varieties of History: From Voltaire to the Present* (New York: Meridian Books, 1956), 51.
9. Cited in Bonnie G. Smith, *The Gender of History: Men, Women, and Historical Practice* (Cambridge, MA: Harvard University Press, 1998), 119.
10. Ranke, cited in Stern, *Varieties of History*, 57, 59.
11. Anthony Grafton, *The Footnote: A Curious History* (Cambridge, MA: Harvard University Press, 1997), 27.
12. Cited in Burrow, *History of Histories*, 435.
13. Frederick C. Beiser, *The German Historicist Tradition* (New York: Oxford University Press, 2011), cit. p. 260.
14. G. P. Gooch, *History and Historians in the Nineteenth Century* (Boston: Beacon Press, 1953 (orig. 1913)), 97; Meinecke, *Historism*, 496; Breisach, *Historiography*, 232, 235.
15. Smith, *Gender of History*, 103–29; Hayden White, *Metahistory: The Historical Imagination in Nineteenth-Century Europe* (Baltimore: Johns Hopkins University Press, 1973), 163–90.
16. Ranke, cited in Stern, *Varieties of History*, 56.
17. Cited in Stern, *Varieties of History*, 173.
18. F. York Powell, "Preface," in Charles Victor Langlois and Charles Seignobos, *Introduction to the Study of History*, trans G. G. Berry (New York: Holt, 1966 (orig. 1898)).
19. Donald R. Kelley, *Fortunes of History: Historical Inquiry from Herder to Huizinga* (New Haven, CT: Yale University Press, 2003), 342; for Kelley's definition of "mythistory," see his *Faces of History: Historical Inquiry from Herodotus to Herder* (New Haven, CT: Yale University Press, 1998), 1.

20. Jules Michelet, *History of the French Revolution*, trans. Charles Cocks, ed. Gordon Wright (Chicago: University of Chicago Press, 1967), 459.

21. Cited in Burrow, *History of Histories*, 354.

22. Cited in Breisach, *Historiography*, 256.

23. Aléxis Beaubrun Ardouin, *Etudes sur l'histoire d'Haiti, suivies de la vie du général J.-M. Borgella* (Port-au-Prince: Dr. François Dalencour, 1958 (orig. 1853)), 2:92.

24. Georg G. Iggers and Q. Edward Wang, *A Global History of Historiography* (Harlow, UK: Pearson Education, 2008), 52–57.

25. Ibid., 137–39, 142–47.

26. Eric Hobsbawm, *Interesting Times: A Twentieth-Century Life* (London: Allan Lane, 2002), 288.

27. Cited in Breisach, 298.

28. Karl Marx, *The Eighteenth Brumaire of Louis Bonaparte* (1852).

29. M. A. Stodart, *Female Writers: Thoughts on Their Proper Sphere and on Their Powers of Usefulness* (London: R. B. Seeley and W. Burnside, 1843), pp. 124–25, 128.

30. Suzanne Rahn, "An Evolving Past: The Story of Historical Fiction and Nonfiction for Children," *The Lion and the Unicorn* 15, no. 1 (June 1991), 4.

31. J. Franklin Jameson, "Early Days of the American Historical Association," *American Historical Review* 40 (1934), 1, 2.

CHAPTER 5

Scientific History
in an Era of Conflict

B y the time he died in 1886, Leopold von Ranke had become the
symbol of a new approach to history, in which the study of the
past was defined as a scientific enterprise to be conducted by
professional scholars systematically trained in universities. Thanks in
large part to Ranke and his students, an elaborate infrastructure to
support this kind of history was developing throughout the Western
world and even beyond its boundaries. Public archives preserved historical documents and made them available to researchers, professional
associations and scholarly journals helped them to share their findings
with one another, and graduate seminars conducted along the lines
of Ranke's courses at Berlin gave them opportunities to train younger
colleagues. The number of full-time academic historians was still
limited—in 1884, the four hundred colleges and universities in the United
States employed only twenty full-time history professors—but it was
growing rapidly as systems of higher education expanded. Governments and elites throughout the world saw the promotion of scientific
historical scholarship as crucial for the development of a sense of national identity and cohesion. They were prepared to support and encourage university-trained historians, who would in turn provide
narratives of the past that schoolteachers could transmit to their students. Embedded in a general culture in which historical thinking had
achieved a central place, the discipline of history appeared to have
established an unassailable position.

Over the next three-quarters of a century, up to the decade of the 1960s, academic history on the Rankean model did indeed achieve great successes. The number of professional historical scholars and students increased in almost every part of the world. Some representatives of the new academic history were prepared to concede that it might not produce many works of great genius, but, as the American professional leader J. Franklin Jameson argued in 1891, this was not what the discipline required. Instead, he wrote, "it is the spread of thoroughly good second-class work . . . that our science most needs at present; for it sorely needs that improvement in technical process, that superior finish of workmanship, which a large number of works of talent can do more to foster than a few works of literary genius."[1] Jameson was unduly pessimistic, however: the period from 1890 to 1960 saw the publication of many historical works that have become enduring classics, such as Johan Huizinga's *Autumn of the Middle Ages* (1919), Charles Beard's *Economic Interpretation of the Constitution of the United States* (1913), and Fernand Braudel's *The Mediterranean and the Mediterranean World in the Age of Philip the Second* (1949).

For all the achievements of professional history, however, the period from the 1880s to the 1960s was also a time of trial for the discipline as a whole and, at times, for its practitioners. Even as the new methods of research and teaching entrenched themselves in academia, they came under criticism from many directions. Starting in the last decades of the nineteenth century, an increasing number of thinkers began to question the premises of the historicist outlook that had come to dominate Western thought during Ranke's lifetime. New questions about the possibility and the value of historical knowledge challenged historians to defend the significance of their work. Within the discipline, some historians rebelled against Rankean history's emphasis on politics and the nation-state and called for new attention to the history of the working classes, women, and minority groups. Professional historians debated whether their new scientific methods were cutting them off from the general public, and they sometimes lamented the influence of the new media such as film, which brought the past to a mass audience in ways that scholars often considered distorted. The cataclysms of the twentieth century's two world wars undermined the unspoken faith in historical progress that had powered so much of the nineteenth century's enthusiasm for the study of the past. Antidemocratic political movements pressured historians to conform to their ideological demands, and many historians' lives and careers were disrupted by historical events in ways that their predecessors in the nineteenth century had rarely experienced.

Critiques of Scientific History

A decade before Ranke's death, a then-obscure German philosopher, Friedrich Nietzsche, delivered the first and one of the most telling blows against the nineteenth century's faith in the value of history. In his 1873 essay, "The Use and Abuse of History," Nietzsche warned that an excessive obsession with knowledge about the past for its own sake could become dangerous. "There is a way of practicing history and a valorization of history in which life atrophies and degenerates," he wrote. Nietzsche distinguished among three forms of history, which he called monumental history, antiquarian history, and critical history, each of which, he argued, could be useful in some contexts but harmful in others. What he called "monumental" history, the celebration of the great deeds and epochs of the past, could, he thought, inspire people in the present by showing them what humanity was capable of, but it could also have the effect of making the present appear insignificant compared to the past. Antiquarian history, the second of Nietzsche's categories, valued the past for its own sake and could provide a sense of identity, but, taken to excess, it led to the rejection of change and development. Critical history, "bringing this past before a tribunal, painstakingly interrogating it, and finally condemning it," might help rouse movements against long-standing injustices, but, Nietzsche warned, those who tried to separate themselves completely from the past, "tak[ing] a knife to its roots," denied the extent to which all human beings are shaped by their previous history and tried to give themselves "a new past from which we would prefer to be descended, as opposed to the past from which we actually descended." Nietzsche's insistence that history, in all its forms, "stands in the service, not of pure knowledge, but of life,"[2] was a critique of excessively dry and abstruse academic research, but it could easily be twisted into an argument that ideological movements could shape history to suit their own purposes. In the twentieth century, Adolf Hitler's Nazi movement in particular often used Nietzsche's name to justify its distortions of the past.

Although Nietzsche was himself a university professor, in his polemical essay he posed as an outsider to the academic enterprise. But critiques of the kind of scholarly history that had developed in the wake of Ranke's "revolution" also came from within the ranks of university scholars. Rankean history's concentration on politics and his school's insistence that history had a unique methodology of its own, distinct from that of all other forms of research, was challenged by scholars in a number of countries. In Germany itself, the historians' guild was shaken in the years around 1890 by Karl Lamprecht's call for a broader approach that paid more attention to social and economic factors and one that went beyond the explanation of individual historical phenomena to articulate general laws, as other sciences did. Lamprecht's opponents accused him of socialist sympathies and of importing "foreign" positivistic ideas into German scholarship. After a bitter public controversy, they succeeded in blocking his appointment as editor of German historical scholarship's flagship journal, the *Historische Zeitschrift*, in favor of the nationalist political historian Heinrich von Treitschke. Mainline German historical research and teaching thus came to be identified not only with the defense of the Rankean tradition but also with political conservatism.

Meanwhile, philosophers and social scientists were raising other questions about some of the assumptions built into the Rankean approach. Ranke had posited both that the historical past had an objective existence that could be brought to light through the proper use of sources and that, despite his insistence that every period had to be judged on its own terms, historical development reflected an overall trend of progress, culminating in the modern nation-states of his own day. In the 1880s, the philosopher Wilhelm Dilthey, strongly influenced by the eighteenth-century Italian thinker Vico, questioned the assumption that the past could really be understood through objective methods. For Dilthey, the only meaningful route to the understanding of the past was through personal experience, which made the subjective genre of autobiography more reliable rather than reconstructions based on documents. "We are first of all creatures of history, before we become observers of history," Dilthey wrote, "and only because we are such creatures, can we become such observers."[3] Dilthey thus argued that historical knowledge had a different basis from knowledge of the natural world.

Dilthey's writings inspired a tradition of "idealist" historical thought, so called because its adherents argued that it was the historian's imaginative idea or mental reenactment of the past, rather than the documentary evidence itself, that made historical understanding possible. The best known of these idealist thinkers was the Italian historian and philosopher Benedetto Croce (1866–1952), who dominated his own country's intellectual life for much of the first half of the twentieth century and attracted many foreign admirers. Like Dilthey, Croce emphasized the importance of his countryman Vico's ideas. His concentration on the mental activity performed by the historian led Croce to argue that the past really had no existence outside the minds of those who studied it to answer questions relevant to their own times; he thus stressed the importance of the fact that history takes place in the present. As a leading American historian, Carl Becker, summarized Croce's argument, "all *living* history. . . is contemporaneous: in so far as we think the past (and otherwise the past, however fully related in documents, is nothing to us) it becomes an integral and living part of our present world." The English historian and philosopher R. G. Collingwood developed Croce's ideas in *The Idea of History* (1946), a work still frequently assigned in historiography classes. To understand the past, Collingwood argued, "the historian must reenact the past in his own mind . . . only in so far as he does this has he any historical knowledge."[4] Critics asserted that this encouraged historians to confuse their own thoughts with those of their historical subjects, but Collingwood maintained that there was no other possible basis for knowledge of the past.

Whereas Dilthey and Croce argued that history was an inherently subjective form of knowledge, the German philosopher Wilhelm Windelband tried to reconnect it with the natural sciences by distinguishing between what he called "nomothetic" disciplines, such as the natural sciences of chemistry and physics, which sought to discover general laws behind phenomena, and what he called "idiographic" fields of knowledge that sought to explain unique individual events, a category that included history but also "historical" natural sciences like astronomy and geology, which study events that have only occurred once and cannot be reproduced, such as the creation of the universe and the formation of the earth. This distinction preserved the notion of history as a science, but at the price of qualifying the claims Ranke had made for history's autonomy and acknowledging that history would never achieve the mathematical precision and ability to make predictions characteristic of physics and chemistry. Another important German thinker in the period around the beginning of the twentieth century, the sociologist Max Weber, defended the use of social-scientific methods in historical research, but denied that scholarship could ever provide a basis for choosing between competing ideological values. His distinction between science and politics implied that history could not provide a meaningful justification for the nation-state, as most German historians insisted it did. Weber also challenged the notion that history could actually demonstrate the causes of past events purely through the analysis of empirical data. Historians needed to construct "ideal types," mental models of past societies, that did not correspond exactly to any past reality, but that allowed thought experiments that would explain historical outcomes. The most famous example of Weber's procedure was his argument, in his classic essay *The Protestant Ethic and the Spirit of Capitalism* (1905), that Calvinist beliefs inculcated an entrepreneurial spirit that explained the rise of capitalism in northern Europe. Rather than seeking empirical evidence about the motivations of Protestant entrepreneurs, Weber argued that certain consequences logically followed from their religious doctrines.

These philosophical debates about the nature and meaning of history, which continued to occupy scholars well into the twentieth century, were conducted mostly among academic specialists, who also formed most of the audience for the new history produced by university-trained scholars. By the early twentieth century, these professionals were beginning to take over the historical associations formed in the nineteenth century, pushing out the public figures and nonacademic writers who had made up an important part of their original membership. A celebrated exchange between two English historians, J. B. Bury and G. W. Trevelyan, in 1902 and 1903, underlined some of the consequences of this trend. When he gave his inaugural lecture as Regius Professor of History at Cambridge University in 1902, Bury, a disciple of Ranke and Ranke's leading British follower, Lord Acton, sternly insisted that "history is a science, no less and no more." Arguing that the scientific study of the past was still in its infancy, he called on scholars to see themselves as "heaping up material and arranging it, according to the best methods we know," but with the awareness that it might take generations before the significance of their findings was really understood.[5] Trevelyan, in an essay entitled "Clio: A Muse," published in 1903, responded directly to Bury, warning that the attempt to make history into a science on the German model and the refusal to suggest conclusions on the grounds that historians had not done enough research was cutting them off from the broader public. "Until quite recent times," he wrote, "historical writing was not merely the mutual conversation of scholars with one another, but was the means of spreading far and wide throughout all the reading classes a love and knowledge of history, an elevated and critical patriotism and certain qualities of mind and heart."[6] Whereas German historians largely rejected calls for a more socially oriented history along the lines suggested by Lamprecht, historians sympathetic to movements for social reform in other countries took up the cause; this was one way of reconnecting historical writing with the nonacademic public. The English husband-and-wife team of Sidney and Beatrice Webb published their *History of Trade Unionism* (1894), and a number of French historians contributed to the collectively written *Histoire socialiste de la Révolution française*, whose editor, Jean Jaurès, was a leading member of the French socialist movement who also held a university degree. This was one of the first attempts to combine academic scholarship with a Marxist approach.

France also saw efforts to bring history together with the ideas of the period's leading sociologist, Emile Durkheim. His ideas inspired Henri Berr (1863–1954), an influential French teacher, who called for an interdisciplinary approach to the study of the past and insisted that "society is a factor in the interpretation of history."[7] The journal Berr founded, the *Revue de synthèse historique*, and the publishing series he established, *L'Evolution de l'humanité*, encouraged publications that looked beyond the borders of the nation-state as well as beyond the boundaries of the historical discipline. In 1903, the *Revue de synthèse historique* carried an article by a sociologist, François Simiand, that formulated a sweeping critique of academic history as it had developed under the influence of Ranke. The "tribe of historians," Simiand complained, had become devoted to three "idols": an exaggerated focus on politics, "the ingrained habit of conceiving of history as a history of individuals and not a study of facts," and an excessive concern with the chronological development of institutions rather than with their significance.[8] Among those inspired by Berr's program and Simiand's critique were two younger historians, Marc Bloch and Lucien Febvre, who would go on after World War I to found what has come to be known as the *Annales* school, the most significant movement in twentieth-century historiography.

Early twentieth-century historians in the United States also made significant contributions to the development of a history open to social concerns. Many of these scholars were influenced by pragmatism, the first philosophical movement to develop on American soil. Pragmatist philosophers, such as Charles Peirce and William James, argued that truth should be defined in terms of what was useful, rather than measured by an absolute standard. Applied to historical research, this attitude favored writings that helped explain the unique characteristics of American society and pointed the way to social reforms. Frederick Jackson Turner's celebrated essay, "The Significance of the Frontier in American History," inspired by the 1890 census, which showed that there was no longer a distinct line between settled and unsettled regions of the country, argued that "this fluidity of American life, this expansion westward with its new opportunities," had shaped the national character and that the closing of the frontier would necessarily mark the beginning of a new historical era.[9] Just as Turner insisted that it was the experience of ordinary individuals along the frontier, rather than of political elites, that defined American history, James Harvey Robinson, in arguing for what he called "the New History," called for scholarship that would deal with all aspects of society and prepare its audience for "intelligent social activity." For this purpose, he maintained, students needed to learn not obscure facts but rather the processes that had created the world in which they lived. Such historical education, he predicted, "will promote rational progress as nothing else can do."[10]

As they debated the nature of historical knowledge and its relationship to political ideals, few academic historians at the beginning of the twentieth century paid much attention to the new ways in which history was reaching a growing general public, other than to denounce what they saw as the unscientific nature of popular publications. The spread of literacy during the nineteenth century had greatly enlarged the reading audience, and popular history was one of the genres that enjoyed the greatest success. Women authors, unable to make careers as university scholars, often wrote for more general audiences. Elizabeth O'Neill's *Nursery History of England*, first published in 1912, was one of the most successful history books written specifically for children and continues to be reprinted even in recent years. Its colorful illustrations, made possible thanks to advances in printing technology, stimulated the imaginations of generations of children, including the author of this book. At the end of the century, the invention of "moving pictures" provided a new way of giving spectators the sense of being plunged into the world of the past, even if they were really watching actors recreating events. As early as 1899, the French cinema pioneer Georges Méliès produced a silent film recreating high points of the controversial Dreyfus Affair, the trial of a French Jewish army officer accused of treason that had convulsed French society. D. W. Griffiths's artistically innovative but overtly racist depiction of the Reconstruction era in the United States, *Birth of a Nation*, released in 1915, demonstrated both the power and the perils of this new medium. A deeply impressed President Woodrow Wilson, who shared the period's prejudices against blacks, said "It is like writing history with lightning." African American groups such as the recently formed National Association for the Advancement of Colored People protested against the distorted vision of the past the film conveyed, but were unable to counter its influence on white audiences.

World War I and the Understanding of History

With a few exceptions, until the outbreak of World War I in 1914, historians were just as confident about the future of Western civilization as they were about the development of their discipline. In all the combatant countries, historians eagerly endorsed the war effort and seized the opportunity to demonstrate their usefulness and patriotism by writing books and articles showing how the triumph of their side was essential to human progress and how the conduct of their enemies revealed their backwardness and barbarism. After the United States entered the war in 1917, for example, the first survey courses on the history of Western civilization in American universities were developed to teach students that they were fighting to defend the progressive values supposedly embodied in British and French history and contradicted by German institutions.[11] Unless they actually served at the front, like the French historian Marc Bloch, scholars were often slow to grasp the realities of a war that was far more brutal and destructive than any previous armed conflict. As late as October 1918, at a time when the German high command had already informed its government that the army was on the point of collapse, Friedrich Meinecke, the most sophisticated of the prewar German nationalist historians and a man with good political connections, still believed that his country could obtain favorable peace terms that would leave it with territorial gains.[12]

By the time the guns finally fell silent in November 1918, the entire world had been profoundly changed. The general faith in human progress that had underlain the development of academic history in the nineteenth century was shattered: the technological achievements of modern civilization had been used to cause devastation on an unprecedented scale, and the most "advanced" countries had fought each other with a shocking disregard for the human cost of the struggle. Postwar Western culture would be dominated by thinkers who questioned the power of human reason, such as the psychologist Sigmund Freud, who suggested that the war had shown instead the existence of an innate "death instinct" in the human psyche. The war also remade the political world. Centuries-old historic institutions such as the Austro-Hungarian and Ottoman empires disappeared from the map, replaced by new nation-states determined to legitimate themselves by producing their own versions of the past. Russia's imperial government was overthrown in 1917, its place taken by a revolutionary Communist dictatorship inspired by the ideas of Karl Marx that claimed to be opening a new era of human history. The authoritarian German monarchy was replaced by the democratic Weimar Republic, a regime that many Germans regarded as an unacceptable symbol of their defeat. In East Asia, Japan, which fought on the side of the Allies, established itself as a major military power bent on establishing an empire of its own, particularly at the expense of China, whereas China, where the imperial dynasty, the heir to more than two thousand years of history, had already been overthrown in 1911, was in the throes of ever-intensifying internal conflicts that would continue until the Communist victory in 1949. In some of the victor countries, particularly France, Britain, and the United States, the postwar period brought a reaction against the nationalism of wartime propaganda, and the victorious Communists in Russia proclaimed a new era of international solidarity. Elsewhere, in countries that had been on the losing side, in most of the new "successor states" carved out of the Austrian, Russian, and Ottoman empires, and in many European colonies, the war resulted instead in more intense national sentiments.

Historians reacted to the challenge of making sense of the war and its aftermath in different ways. Some historians concluded that the war, with its immense destruction, foreshadowed the end of Western civilization. The German author Oswald Spengler's *Decline of the West*, published just at the end of the war in 1918, depicted world history as a succession of civilizations, each of which had followed a cycle of growth and decay. Like biological organisms, Spengler argued, civilizations inevitably aged and lost their vitality. Spengler's gloomy prognosis for the future of the Western world resonated with the mood in defeated Germany, but it also impressed readers in many other countries. His attempt to fit the entire course of human history into a single pattern inspired a few successors, most notably the British scholar Arnold Toynbee, whose *A Study of History*, completed in 1939, at the beginning of a new world war, was somewhat more optimistic. The challenge of finding overarching patterns in the entire course of human history without resorting to assumptions that cannot be proved on the basis of historical evidence remains a daunting one, however, and there have been few attempts to emulate Spengler and Toynbee in recent decades.

Rather than attempting to find an overall pattern in human experience, most historians after World War I dealt with more limited questions. The inclusion in the Versailles peace treaty of 1919 of a "war guilt clause" affirming "the responsibility of Germany and her allies for causing all the loss and damage" resulting from the war provoked an immense controversy that still echoes today. Even many historians in the victor nations soon became convinced that this conclusion was contradicted by the documentary record, particularly the evidence contained in previously secret archives published by the postwar regimes in Germany, Austria, and Russia after 1919. The seemingly endless "revisionist" controversy about the origins of the war shook readers' and historians' confidence that the research methods developed in the nineteenth century could determine the truth about the past. "A writer by centering attention on the acts of any one man or country, and by picking out passages in the documents to support his contention, can easily make a seemingly convincing argument," the American historian Sidney Fay wrote in 1928.[13]

The war guilt controversy was just one of the challenges to the ideal of historical objectivity during the interwar period that led the most famous American historian of those decades, Charles Beard, to write that "historians were not so sure of themselves after 1918" and to argue that "whatever acts of purification the historian may perform he yet remains human, a creature of time, place, circumstance, interests, predilections, culture," and therefore incapable of complete objectivity.[14] Even before the war, Beard himself had challenged the standard picture of American history with his *Economic Interpretation of the Constitution of the United States*, in which he claimed to have shown that the provisions of the Constitution reflected the economic interests of its drafters more than any commitment to ideals of liberty. Beard was the leading voice of what came to be known as the "progressive school" of American history, which taught that economic conflicts had shaped the country's development and cast doubt on the notion that a historian could truly adopt a neutral stance on such questions. Beard's relativist perspective was shared by Carl Becker, whose 1931 presidential address to the American Historical Association, "Everyman His Own Historian," put forward a pragmatist vision of history as something always necessarily changing to meet the changing needs of the present. "It must then be obvious that living history, the ideal series of events that we affirm and hold in memory, since it is so intimately associated with what we are doing and with what we hope to do, cannot be precisely the same for all at any given time, or the same for one generation as for another," Becker concluded.[15]

A challenge to the notion that there could be a unified and objective interpretation of American history came from black historians. W. E. B. Du Bois, the author of the classic *The Souls of Black Folk* (1903), was the first African American to receive a doctorate in history. In 1915, he published a pioneering survey of the history of black people in Africa and America. The African American historian Carter G. Woodson founded the Association for the Study of Negro Life and History (now the Association for the Study of African American Life and History) and the *Journal of Negro History* in 1915–1916. Woodson's initiative was meant to counter racist representations of history such as "Birth of a Nation" by showing that black people in America had a history of their own and had made important contributions to the growth of the nation. Until the middle of the twentieth century, however, African American history remained on the margins of academic scholarship on the history of the United States and African Americans were excluded from teaching at most research universities. White Southern historians such as Ulrich B. Phillips, whose *American Negro Slavery* (1918) and *Life and Labor in the Old South* (1929) were regarded as standard references, painted a picture of slavery as a benevolent system. Outside of the United States, black authors such as the Haitian Jean Price-Mars joined Du Bois in showing that Africans had made major but unrecognized historical contributions to the development of world civilization. During the interwar period, such ideas bore fruit in the development of the *Négritude* movement, exemplified in the works of the French-speaking Senegalese author Léopold Senghor.

The challenge to the ideal of objective historical knowledge posed by developments such as the war-guilt controversy led some interwar historians to conclude that since historical writing was inherently biased in one direction or another, they should write history to support the causes they believed in. This tendency was elevated to a principle in the Soviet Union, where the Communist government established after the Russian Revolution of 1917 called on historians to follow Marx's ideas and write history to combat "bourgeois" critics. "Only he who fights in history for the interests of the proletariat . . . is a genuine Leninist historian," one official spokesman for the new regime wrote.[16] The most influential example of Marxist historiography from this period was Leon Trotsky's *Russian Revolution* (1932). Trotsky had himself been one of the leaders of the revolutionary movement, before he was ousted and forced into exile by his rival Joseph Stalin. For Trotsky, there was no contradiction between the idea of a history committed to the cause of the masses and one written according to scientific procedures, since "the natural laws . . . of the historic process itself" demonstrated the necessity of the proletariat's triumph. Trotsky did modify Marx's doctrines to explain how the working class could have come to power, not in one of Europe's most economically developed countries, as Marx himself had expected, but instead in one of its most backward societies. "The privilege of historical backwardness," Trotsky argued, was that such countries could learn from the experience of others and thus skip certain stages of historical development.[17]

Beneath the veneer of Trotsky's supposedly scientific approach was a romantic impulse to tell the story of the Russian Revolution as a heroic saga, in which farseeing leaders such as Lenin and Trotsky himself enabled the masses to defeat their foes. In this respect, the history promoted in the Soviet Union had some elements in common with the more openly nationalistic history written in some of the new countries established after the war. In Turkey, the new national state carved out of the ruins of the Ottoman Empire, the postwar leader Kemal Atatürk promoted scholarship guided by a "Turkish historical thesis" that posited the unique role of the Turkish people in spreading civilization and saw the Islamic faith that had long linked Turks to the Arab world as an obstacle to the country's progress.[18] The way in which the Soviet regime imposed "proletarian" history also resembled the Nazis' promotion of a version of the past based on their "Volkish" racial ideas. Once Hitler came to power in 1933, historians in Germany had to conform to an ideological line that made race the dominant factor in shaping events. Scholars of Jewish descent had to flee the country, and those who resisted Nazi pressure were forced out of their jobs.

In the United States, government involvement with history also reached a high point during the Depression years of the 1930s, but in different ways than under the dictatorial regimes in Europe. The governmental initiatives taken in the 1930s were in line with the ideas of the "Progressive school" about creating a history that reflected the contributions of common people that dominated the profession during this period. As part of the New Deal program to reduce unemployment launched by President Franklin Roosevelt, hundreds of historians were hired to make an inventory of the country's historical sites. This represented an enormous increase in the government's engagement on behalf of historical preservation, which had previously been left to private philanthropists like Henry Ford and John D. Rockefeller Jr., the founders of the historical theme parks of Deerfield Village in Michigan and Colonial Williamsburg in Virginia, and to local initiatives, such as the creation of the country's first "historic district" in Charleston, South Carolina, in 1931. According to Verne Chatelain, head of the National Park Service's history office, the demand for competent workers created by the New Deal initiative was so intense that "we almost had to invent historians, the pressures became so great."[19] Another government agency, the Works Progress Administration, employed numerous scholars to survey the historical records held by state and local archives. The Federal Writers' Project collected the reminiscences of surviving former slaves, a pioneering venture in oral history.

The Founding of the "Annales" School

By the end of the 1920s, professional academic historians had lost much of the confidence that had inspired their predecessors in the late nineteenth century. The value and the scientific status of their work had been called into question by critics as diverse as Nietzsche, Becker, and Croce. Many of them had abandoned the value of scholarly neutrality to embrace the cause of their nations during World War I, and those who lived under authoritarian regimes after the conflict found themselves under pressure to conform to state-imposed guidelines in their work.

In democratic countries, they were regularly accused of neglecting the general public. University historians continued to research, write, and teach during these years, but it was not clear where the profession was headed.

The most significant effort to reinvigorate scholarly historical research during the interwar years, one that was eventually destined to have an impact on professional historians' work throughout the world, emerged from the so-called "Annales" school, a scholarly movement that took shape in interwar France. The name Annales school comes from the scholarly journal, *Annales d'histoire économique et sociale* (*Annals of Economic and Social History*) founded by Marc Bloch and Lucien Febvre, two professors at the University of Strasbourg, in 1929. As its title indicated, the new journal privileged economic and social history, rather than political history, and from the start its contributors strove to liberate themselves from the national framework in which most historical research remained confined. Bloch and Febvre drew some of their inspiration from Henri Berr's call for an interdisciplinary history of human civilization and from François Simiand's denunciation of historians' excessive concentration on politics, individuals, and origins, formulated a generation earlier. They also found allies among historians in other countries who had independently moved away from political history, such as the Belgian Henri Pirenne, whose thesis about the economic impact of the expansion of Islam in the early Middle Ages directed attention to the interaction of civilizations, and the Dutch scholar Johan Huizinga, whose *Autumn of the Middle Ages* revived the cultural history approach of Carl Burckhardt and whose essay on the reasons why humans engage in play, *Homo Ludens* (1938), remains essential reading for anyone interested in the history of sport. Bloch and Febvre consciously reached out to the other social sciences, including not only economics and sociology but also geography, psychology, anthropology, and linguistics. Their own writings ranged widely and offered many fresh approaches to the study of the past. Febvre's first book, a close study of one French province, demonstrated the possibilities of a regional study, an approach that came to be closely associated with the Annales school in later decades, whereas Bloch's monograph on the healing powers supposedly possessed by the kings of France and England showed the insights into collective psychology that could be gained by taking an apparently irrational phenomenon seriously.

The Annales school would come to influence historians all over the world because of its open and flexible approach, which contrasted sharply with the rigid guidelines dictated by the "scientific" scholarship of the nineteenth century. All aspects of human existence were potentially worthy of study, the Annalistes asserted; the goal of historical research should be to produce a "total" history that would take in every aspect of the past. "The good historian is like the giant of the fairy tale. He knows that wherever he catches the scent of human flesh, there his quarry lies," Bloch wrote.[20] Although Bloch and Febvre insisted on the importance of the rigorous scholarly standards for the interpretation of documents, they urged historians to greatly broaden the sorts of evidence they drew on. In addition to written documents, historians could learn from physical artifacts, from the study of language, from the study of customs and rituals, and many other sources. Whereas historians trained in the Rankean tradition had been primarily concerned with the articulate members of political and intellectual elites, the Annalistes showed that the records of the past could be used to illuminate the lives of the poor and the illiterate. Bloch's *French Rural History*, for example, recreated the world of medieval and early modern French peasant farmers, hardly any of whom had been capable of writing, by combining physical evidence about farming practices with documents about tax payments, land disputes, and the vocabulary of the period.

Part of the attraction of the Annales approach came from its nondogmatic character. Although Bloch and Febvre and their followers shared Marxist historians' interest in the connections between economic and social change, they did not feel obliged to fit their research into an ideological framework. The fact that they tended to focus on historical periods remote from the present helped them avoid entanglement in political controversies and distanced them from nationalist crusades. As willing as they were to broaden the scope of historical inquiry, the Annales school founders did have their blind spots. They showed no interest, for example, in possible differences between the historical experiences of men and women: there was no Annales school equivalent to the American Mary Beard, who worked valiantly during this period to insinuate a recognition of the importance of women's history into the works she collaborated on with her husband, Charles Beard. In liberating themselves from what they saw as the excessive concentration on politics and wars, or what they stigmatized as "the history of events" ("*histoire événementielle*"), the "Annalistes" downplayed an aspect of human experience whose drastic impact on ordinary lives became painfully obvious when the school's co-founder, Marc Bloch, was arrested and executed by the Germans for his efforts to free his country from occupation during World War II.

History and World War II

Marc Bloch was only one of many historians whose personal destiny was affected by the conflict that swept the world from 1937 to 1945. The war also had far-reaching effects on the discipline of history. The conflict itself was a dramatic historical story, and two of the main war leaders, British prime minister Winston Churchill and French Resistance leader Charles de Gaulle, profited from their personal role in events to write best-selling accounts from their own points of view.[21] In the United States and Western Europe, the defeat of Nazi Germany and Japan reaffirmed the basic values of democracy and progress that had been shaken during the interwar period. The claim that the totalitarian regimes in Germany and the Soviet Union had frequently twisted the truth about history for propagandistic purposes lent a new importance to historical honesty and objectivity. The hero of George Orwell's dystopian novel *1984*, published in 1948 and set in an imagined world ruled by such dictatorships, rebels against his cynical bosses at the "Ministry of Truth," where his job is to destroy documents that contradict the government's newest version of the past, in accordance with the slogan, "He who controls the past controls the future. He who controls the present controls the past." The implication of Orwell's story was that the defense of historical truth was directly linked to the defense of freedom and democracy.

By the end of the war, Germany's long-held position as the acknowledged leader in historical scholarship was ended, first by the Nazi regime's imposition of its racist ideology and then by the destruction of many of its universities. By contrast, the historical profession in the United States and, to some extent, in Britain and France, enjoyed an unprecedented boom. Service in the military had taken many young people to distant parts of the globe and inspired them with an interest in the historical roots of the war they had served in. Some, like the Japanese history specialist Edwin Reischauer, had served in American intelligence agencies and been able to follow the making of historical decisions as they were made. The experience "taught me much about the workings of government and the realities of the world situation which would be of great help to me in the future," Reischauer wrote in his memoir.[22] In the United States, the GI Bill, which paid for war veterans to attend college, transformed higher education from a privilege of the wealthy into an opportunity for students from all social classes. The flood of new students created a demand for professors to teach them, a reversal of the situation during the prewar years of the Great Depression when academic jobs had been difficult to obtain.

One result of the expansion of higher education in the United States after the war was that the barriers that had kept Jews from obtaining academic positions in the humanities were swept away, the first step toward an opening up of participation in university scholarship for previously excluded groups that would eventually extend to women and members of other ethnic minorities. Among the historians of Jewish origin who benefitted from these new opportunities were a number of refugees who had fled Hitler's Germany, bringing with them an acute awareness of the drastic ways in which historical events could affect ordinary people's lives and a willingness to use unconventional methods to study the past. Included in this group were such figures as George Mosse, a pioneer in the history of the Nazi regime and later in the history of sexuality, the psychohistorian Peter Gay, Raul Hilberg, the founder of academic historical scholarship on the Holocaust, Gerda Lerner, one of the pioneers of women's history, and the historiography specialist Georg Iggers. After a century during which Americans had gone to Germany to learn the most advanced historical approaches, the situation was reversed by another German refugee, Hans Rosenberg. On visits to his former homeland, Rosenberg introduced a younger generation of German history students to the new social science–oriented history that had developed in his adopted country.

The war had greatly increased the prestige of scientific research in both the natural sciences, where prewar scholarly findings had led to striking developments ranging from the atomic bomb to the first antibiotic drugs, and the social sciences. In organizing to fight the conflict, governments had called on economists to plan the use of resources, psychologists to design propaganda campaigns, and sociologists, anthropologists, and historians to explain the nature of the societies involved and to help plan programs for postwar reconstruction. The doubts about the possibility of achieving objective historical knowledge that had been voiced by figures such as Charles Beard between the wars gave way to greater optimism about the possibility of making history a rigorous scientific discipline. In 1942, the philosopher Carl Hempel firmly rejected the arguments first formulated by Dilthey and others in the late nineteenth century that had sought to separate historical methods from those of the natural sciences. According to Hempel, historians could and should seek to discover general laws like those in the other sciences. "Historical explanation, too, aims at showing that the event in question was not 'a matter of chance,' but was to be expected in view of certain antecedent or simultaneous conditions," he wrote.[23] Hempel's article initiated a long-running debate among American philosophers about the scientific status of history, although few historians ventured into what they saw as an abstract discussion with little relationship to their actual research practices. In the United States, historians more often cooperated with colleagues from other social science disciplines in area-studies programs that were designed not only to advance knowledge about the regions they covered but also to provide practical policy advice, both for American leaders and for the countries in those parts of the world.

The fact that the United States had survived the ordeals of the two world wars and the Great Depression without succumbing either to fascism or to Communism, as so many European countries had, raised questions about the prewar "progressive" school's emphasis on the importance of social conflict in the country's past. Postwar historians, such as Richard Hofstadter and Louis Hartz, argued instead that American history reflected the existence of a broad consensus on the liberal values incorporated in the nation's founding documents. The intellectual historian Perry Miller's emphasis on the ways in which New England's religious Puritanism had shaped subsequent American thought shifted attention from economic to cultural issues and emphasized the unique qualities of American civilization.

The major challenge to the notion of American history as the expression of a broad consensus shaped by shared cultural values was the history of race and slavery. Black historians, notably John Hope Franklin, participated in the legal research that prepared the way for the successful lawsuit against segregation in public schools that led to the Supreme Court's 1954 decision, *Brown v. Board of Education*, outlawing the practice. The southern-born historian C. Vann Woodward's *The Strange Career of Jim Crow*, first published in 1955, argued that segregation in the American South was not the reflection of a "natural" difference between the races, but rather the result of deliberate political decisions taken after the Reconstruction period. Civil rights activists seized on Woodward's book as a powerful argument for the idea that the laws on segregation were historical artifacts that could and should be changed to reflect changed circumstances. Behind the scenes, Woodward had played a role in arranging for Franklin to become the first black scholar to speak at the Southern Historical Association, one of the country's major professional organizations. To gain the approval of established white historians, however, black academics had to conform to prevailing norms. Woodward himself praised Franklin because his writings were "freer of race-consciousness and propaganda than preceding works of the kind."[24]

Even as university-based history achieved a new level of prosperity and reached an unprecedented number of students in postwar America, history also constituted an important aspect of popular culture. Both university-based historians, such as Arthur Schlesinger Jr., who won the Pulitzer Prize for his *Age of Jackson* in 1945 and whose three volumes on the history of Franklin Roosevelt's New Deal also enjoyed great success, and independent authors like Bruce Catton, a specialist on the Civil War, and Barbara Tuchman, author of a best-selling volume on World War I, *The Guns of August* (1962), reached wide audiences. The stark cover of journalist William Shirer's *Rise and Fall of the Third Reich* (1960), featuring a swastika, stood out on bookshelves and coffee tables in many American homes. The Civil War historian Catton was also the first editor of *American Heritage* magazine, whose lavishly illustrated issues made it a cultural icon for many decades.

A new medium, television, brought dramatic reenactments of famous historical episodes into American homes. For nearly twenty years, the gravelly-voiced journalist Walter Cronkite narrated "You Are There," a weekly program, ending each emission with his trademark line, "What sort of a day was it? A day like all days, filled with those events that alter and illuminate our times." The program's formula, in which a present-day reporter was projected back into the past and interviewed actors playing historical personages, now seems contrived, but the show attracted a wide audience. World War II and the Korean War of 1950–1953 provided endless material for comic-book authors, who were now seeking to educate as well as to entertain. More serious young readers, like this author, devoured the volumes of the Landmark Books series, many of them written by well-known adult authors, which covered a wide range of topics in both American and world history. In a period when academic jobs in history were still largely closed to women, the Landmark series featured works by a number of woman authors. Several of the volumes also dealt with female historical figures, including Betsy Ross, Catherine the Great, Clara Barton, and Marie Antoinette, whereas others were devoted to African American and Native American topics. The general public's interest in serious historical topics indicated a certain consensus, shared by academic scholars and popular authors, on the meaning of history and the ways in which it should be portrayed.

Social History in the Postwar Period

The postwar period was a dynamic one for American historians, but the most important theoretical developments in historiography continued to take place in Europe. Among the most important was the growing impact of the Annales school founded in France between the wars by Lucien Febvre and Marc Bloch. Bloch had died heroically during the war, but his colleague Febvre survived and in 1947 he was named the first president of what was then called the 6th section of the Ecole Pratique des Hautes Etudes in Paris, giving the Annales school an institutional base it had not had in the 1930s. (In 1975, the institution was renamed the Ecole des Hautes Etudes en sciences sociales ("School for Advanced Studies in the Social Sciences")). Under Febvre's successor, Fernand Braudel, the Ecole developed into an international center for research in the social sciences, along the lines suggested in Bloch's and Febvre's earlier work. Braudel raised funds for the construction of the Ecole's building at 54 boulevard Raspail in Paris, a structure whose glass-and-steel exterior, devoid of any historical references, reflected mid-twentieth-century historians' ambitions to emphasize their association with modernity and progress.

The impact of the Annales school on historical scholarship has been so broad that the school itself has become the subject of numerous historical studies, which separate its leading members into distinctive "generations." Braudel was certainly the dominant member of the group's "second generation." His best-known book, *The Mediterranean and the Mediterranean World in the Age of Philip II*, largely composed during his time in a German prisoner-of-war camp after 1940, exemplified the "total history" that the Annales school founders Bloch and Febvre had advocated. Transcending national and civilizational boundaries, Braudel took the entire region of the Mediterranean as his subject, showing how its distinctive climate and geography had shaped the history of all the peoples living around it, compelling them to develop systems of agriculture and settlement patterns adapted to their natural environment. These fundamental features of life in the past did change, Braudel claimed, but at a glacially slow pace that required historians to take the perspective of the *longue durée*, the "long term," and to recognize that for those living at the time, these constraints would have seemed permanent or structural. Interacting with this level of slow-motion development were events that moved at a somewhat faster pace, such as economic cycles of prosperity and decline and cultural movements, which might unfold over a period of a human generation or more. Braudel did not entirely neglect the faster-paced events of war and politics, such as the battle of Lepanto in 1571 that ended Turkish supremacy in the eastern Mediterranean, but in his narrative, he treated them like "delusive smoke" that, he wrote, "fills the minds of its contemporaries," but should not preoccupy historians, because "it does not last."[25]

Braudel's vast panorama, integrating history with economics, demography, and geography and sweeping across centuries and the frontiers between civilizations, had an undeniable power to it. His second major work, *Civilization and Capitalism* (1967–1979), was even broader in scope, providing an interdisciplinary account of the economic and social history of the world over a period of some three centuries. Impressive as Braudel's example was, his insistence on the dominant influence of long-lasting structures in shaping human life seemed to leave little room for human agency and for the world of ideas and culture that had been one of the main concerns of the Annales school founders Bloch and Febvre. The other main figure of the Annales school's "second generation," Robert Mandrou, pursued what he called "historical psychology," which later came to be known as "the history of mentalities," in his *Introduction to Modern France* (1961), but Braudel's dominating personality kept Mandrou from having much influence on the direction of the "school" as a whole until after his death.

Although the leading figures of the Annales school were not Marxists, they shared the Marxist tradition's concern for social and economic history. This gave the Annales school's work much in common with that of another influential group of historians that formed in the

1950s, the cluster of British Marxist scholars associated with the social history journal *Past and Present*, founded in 1952 by a group that included Christopher Hill, Eric Hobsbawm, and E. P. Thompson, along with some non-Marxist social historians such as Lawrence Stone. Less tied to Marxist dogma than their counterparts in other parts of the world, the members of the *Past and Present* group brought fresh insights to the study of such topics as the dissenting religious movements during the English Revolution of the seventeenth century, the development of the working class during the early industrial revolution, and the role of "primitive rebels" who resisted modernization. In contrast to the French Annales historians, the members of the *Past and Present* group were more open about the connection they saw between historical research and social justice. Perhaps the most influential single volume published by a member of the group was Thompson's *Making of the English Working Class* (1963), with its call for a history that would "rescue the poor stockinger, the Luddite cropper, the 'obsolete' hand-loom weaver, the 'utopian' artisan, and even the deluded follower of Joanna Southcott, from the enormous condescension of posterity."[26] Thompson expanded the bounds of traditional Marxism by defining social class more in terms of consciousness and culture than by reference to economic structures and by paying serious attention to the role that religion played in the lives of the poorer classes, instead of treating it simply as a mechanism of social control. Thompson's passionate commitment to social justice contrasted sharply with that of more mainstream historians of the Industrial Revolution, who treated the sufferings of early-nineteenth-century workers as the unavoidable price of technological progress. For more than fifty years, his work has continued to inspire historians of other oppressed and marginalized groups.

History in the Cold War World

By the early 1960s, the postwar world had taken on a shape that seemed to promise a certain amount of stability. Politically, the United States and its allies in Western Europe confronted the Soviet Union and its satellite states, with neither side able to alter the equilibrium between them. East Asia was similarly divided between Communist regimes in China, North Vietnam, and North Korea and Western-backed governments in Japan, South Korea, and South Vietnam. The era of overseas European imperialism had come to a remarkably rapid end, with the achievement of independence in almost all the former colonial territories of South Asia, the Middle East, and Africa. In general, historians' viewpoints corresponded to the political systems of the countries they lived in. Most historians in the Western world saw history as a long story of progressive development, despite some spectacular interruptions, that culminated in prosperous democratic societies; for the most part, despite the example of the Annales school, they also continued to write history within national frameworks. In the Soviet bloc, historians were constrained to adhere to an increasingly stultified version of Marxist dogma, particularly when they dealt with the modern world, and there was little real dialogue across the Iron Curtain that separated them from scholars in the West. In the "Third World" of newly independent former colonial countries, the model of national history exercised a strong influence as scholars tried to create academic institutions modeled after those in the West and to provide new societies with unifying narratives of their past.

As the colonies of the European overseas empires began to achieve national independence after 1945, they were determined to assert control over the definition of their own history; at the same time, scholars from these areas were eager to demonstrate that they could meet the standards of historical scholarship inherited from the West. After India achieved its independence in 1947, the new government encouraged histories of the struggle that had culminated in that result, emphasizing the importance of the state and of the political leaders, such as Mohandas Gandhi, who had led the national movement. Like nationalist histories in Europe, this approach tended to assume that there had always been a clear national identity, and it gave more attention to political and intellectual elites than to the mass of the population. Indian historians were seriously divided about the question of whether the country's identity was essentially bound up with Hinduism, the religion of the majority of the population, or whether it had room for other groups, most significantly the Muslims who had dominated most of the subcontinent for several centuries before the arrival of the British. Impressive as the achievements of Indian scholars were in the first decades after independence, the "nationalist" history written in this period would generate a powerful backlash within India itself by the late 1970s. The development of professional history-writing in the newly independent countries of the postcolonial world also depended on the creation of universities modeled after those in the Western world, such as the

University of the West Indies, whose main campus in Kingston, Jamaica, opened in 1962. The University of the West Indies became the main producer of Ph.D.'s in the history of the English-speaking Caribbean and sponsored the publication of *The Journal of Caribbean History*, which provided an important outlet for their work.[27]

The challenges of writing the history of sub-Saharan Africa, where anticolonialist movements were gaining strength after 1945, were particularly daunting. In most of the continent, written documents of the sort that historians could rely on elsewhere did not exist for the precolonial period, and university-level instruction in history was only beginning to develop. Outsiders doubted the very possibility of writing a history of Africa. In 1963, when most of the former European colonies in Africa had already achieved their independence, Hugh Trevor-Roper, a leading British scholar, condescendingly announced, "Perhaps in the future there will be some African history to teach. But, at present there is none: there is only the history of the Europeans in Africa. The rest is darkness."[28] In response, historians such as the Belgian-born Jan Vansina, the British scholar Roland Oliver, and the Nigerian Kenneth Onwuka Dike turned to oral history, arguing that, through the application of proper methods, such testimonies could provide significant information about the continent's precolonial past. Vansina devoted an entire book to explicating the value of oral traditions as historical sources, contending that they "are not just a source about the past, but a historiology (one dare not write historiography!) of the past, an account of how people have interpreted it." Like all evidence, they need to be interpreted critically, but, Vansina asserted, this did not make them different from written documents. "Such sources are irreplaceable," he continued; "without oral traditions we would know very little about the past of large parts of the world, and we would not know them from the inside."[29] The UNESCO *General History of Africa*, a project launched in 1964 by a committee composed primarily of historians from the continent, aimed to put the history of Africa on par with that of the other parts of the world that had longer traditions of written historical scholarship. As in India, however, the history that resulted was criticized for its emphasis on political elites and its tendency to celebrate the political parties and leaders who had gained power after independence.

By the 1960s, the writing of history appeared to have achieved a status of solid respectability around the world. As an academic discipline, it had time-tested methods that could be applied, so it seemed, to a wide range of questions about the human past. If history did not have the prestige of some of the "hard" social sciences, such as economics and political science, which seemed to offer more in terms of lessons for the solution of practical problems, it nevertheless had a respectable place in public life. The division between Marxist scholarship in the Communist world and the variety of ideological approaches represented elsewhere, a product of the Cold War, was a reminder that historians were sometimes divided about fundamental methodological issues, but the dogmatic restrictions imposed on scholars in the Soviet world limited the interest of their work. In 1961, it is true, a British historian, E. H. Carr, published a highly readable assault on the notion of historical objectivity, reviving arguments for the subjective nature of historical knowledge similar to those made by figures such as Carl Becker between the wars and urging readers to "study the historian before you study the facts."[30] Carr's book is still frequently assigned in historiography classes, but it hardly represented the common wisdom of academic historians. J. H. Hexter, a British-born immigrant to the United States, wrote a stinging reply arguing that the ideological preferences of historians were less important than their adherence to professional standards. "Evidence and proof are never radical or conservative," Hexter asserted.[31] Another British scholar, G. R. Elton, responded to Carr with *The Practice of History* (1967), a ringing defense of the search for historical objectivity that is also still widely read. Neither Carr, Hexter, nor Elton, however, could have imagined how radically historical practice was going to change in the decades to come.

Notes

1. John Franklin Jameson, *The History of Historical Writing in America* (1891), cited in Robert B. Townsend, *History's Babel: Scholarship, Professionalization, and the Historical Enterprise in the United States, 1880–1940* (Chicago: University of Chicago Press, 2014), 19.
2. Friedrich Nietzsche, "The Utility and Liability of History," in Nietzsche, *Unfashionable Observations*, trans. Richard T. Gray (Stanford, CA: Stanford University Press, 1995), 85, 107, 93.
3. Wilhelm Dilthey, *Gesammelte Schriften* (Stuttgart: Teubner, 1914), 7:278.

4. Carl L. Becker, "Everyman His Own Historian," 1931 American Historical Association presidential address, in Stephen Vaughn, ed., *The Vital Past: Writings on the Uses of History* (Athens, GA: University of Georgia Press, 1985), 27; R. G. Collingwood, *The Idea of History* (New York: Oxford University Press, 1956), 282, 283.

5. Cited in Stern, *Varieties of History*, 210, 220.

6. Cited in Stern, *Varieties of History*, 229.

7. Cited in Stern, *Varieties of History*, 251–52.

8. François Simiand, "Méthode historique et science sociale," pt. ii, *Revue de Synthèse historique* (1903).

9. Frederick Jackson Turner, "The Significance of the Frontier in American History," cited in Caroline Hoefferle, *The Essential Historiography Reader* (Upper Saddle River, NJ: Pearson Education, 2011), 102.

10. James Harvey Robinson, "The New History," cited in Stern, *Varieties of History*, 265.

11. See Gilbert Allardyce, "The Rise and Fall of the Western Civilization Course," *American Historical Review* 87 (1982), 695–725.

12. Friedrich Meinecke, *Strassburg, Freiburg, Berlin 1901–1919. Erinnerungen* (Stuttgart: Koehler, 1949), 266.

13. Sidney Bradshaw Fay, *The Origins of the World War* (New York: Macmillan, 1928), 1:vi.

14. Cited in Peter Novick, *That Noble Dream: The 'Objectivity Question' and the American Historical Profession* (Cambridge, UK: Cambridge University Press, 1988), 186; Beard, "That Noble Dream," cited in Stern, *Varieties of History*, 324.

15. Becker, "Everyman His Own Historian," in Vaughn, *Vital Past*, 27.

16. M. N. Pokrovsky, "The Tasks of Marxist Historical Science in the Reconstruction Period" (1931), cited in Stern, *Varieties of History*, 340.

17. Leon Trotsky, *The Russian Revolution*, trans. Max Eastman, ed. F. W. Dupee (New York: Doubleday, 1959), xiii, 3.

18. Iggers and Wang, *Global History*, 199–200.

19. Cited in Ian Tyrrell, *Historians in Public: The Practice of American History, 1890–1970* (Chicago: University of Chicago Press, 2005).

20. Marc Bloch, *The Historian's Craft*, trans. Peter Putnam (New York: Knopf, 1953), 26.

21. Winston Churchill, *The Second World War*, 6 vols. (Boston: Houghton Mifflin, 1948–53); Charles de Gaulle, *War Memoirs*, trans. Jonathan Griffin, 3 vols. (London: Collins, 1955).
22. Edwin Reischauer, *My Life between Japan and America* (New York: Harper & Row, 1986), 109.
23. Carl G. Hempel, "The Function of General Laws in History," *Journal of Philosophy* 39 (1942), 35–48, cit. p. 39.
24. C. Vann Woodward, letter to Guggenheim Foundation, November 1949, in Michael O'Brien, ed., *The Letters of C. Vann Woodward* (New Haven, CT: Yale University Press, 2013), 124..
25. Fernand Braudel, "History and the Social Sciences: The *Longue Durée*," in Fernand Braudel, *On History*, trans. Sarah Matthews (Chicago: University of Chicago Press, 1980), 27.
26. E. P. Thompson, *The Making of the English Working Class* (New York: Vintage Books, 1966 (orig. 1963)), 12. The Luddites were workers who protested against the introduction of machinery in factories at the beginning of the nineteenth century. Joanna Southcott was a self-proclaimed prophet who attracted a large following among the poor around the same time.
27. See B. W. Higman, *Writing West Indian Histories* (London: Macmillan, 1999), ch. 5.
28. Cited in Kwame Anthony Appiah, "Africa: The Hidden History," *New York Review of Books*, Dec. 17, 1998.
29. Jan Vansina, *Oral Tradition as History* (Madison: University of Wisconsin Press, 1985 (original edition 1959)), 196, 197, 198.
30. E. H. Carr, *What Is History?* (New York: Vintage Books, 1961), 26.
31. J. H. Hexter, "The Historian and His Society: A Sociological Inquiry—Perhaps," in J. H. Hexter, *Doing History* (London: Allen & Unwin, 1971), 100.

PART TWO

Historiography in the Contemporary World

CHAPTER 6

Glorious Confusion: Historiography from the 1960s to the End of the Millennium

Viewed in retrospect, the decade of the 1960s appears both as the high point of a certain kind of confidence about the prospects for historical scholarship and as the moment when new historical questions and new methodological approaches began to challenge the unity of the discipline. In the United States and Western Europe, academic historians lived in societies that were investing unprecedented resources in higher education, and they largely shared a consensus about the proper methods for historical research. Universities were growing rapidly to accommodate the rising number of students, a reflection of the "baby boom" that had taken off after the end of World War II, and the employment prospects for would-be historians had never been better. The newly independent countries in the former colonial world seemed eager to adopt Western models of scholarly inquiry, including those of historical research. Historians living in the countries in the Communist bloc operated under different conditions, constrained to make their findings conform to a rigid Marxist orthodoxy, but the contrast between their situation and the greater freedom of scholars in the West only seemed to underline the possibilities for the latter.

The Challenges of the 1960s

To be sure, historians in the 1960s were aware that they still lived in a world beset with problems. The tensions of the Cold War reached a peak during the Cuban missile crisis of October 1962, when a nuclear conflict between the United States and the Soviet Union was narrowly averted. When France recognized the independence of Algeria in 1962, after nearly all the other European colonies in Africa and Asia had become self-governing nations, the era of colonialism seemed to have ended, but the growing civil rights movement in the United States and the increasingly repressive apartheid policies of the white government in South Africa were reminders that racial equality was still a distant goal. By the mid-1960s, protests against the American military intervention in Vietnam had spread to college campuses in many countries. In their dress and behavior, the students who filled their overwhelmingly male history professors' classrooms signaled that they were increasingly willing to challenge their teachers' certainties about how the world worked. In France in May 1968, the largest student protest movement in history brought universities across the country to a standstill and set off a national strike wave that nearly toppled the government. In China, the "Cultural Revolution" unleashed in 1966 by radical followers of Mao Zedong targeted the "Four Olds," including anything reflective of the country's prerevolutionary past, and threatened the very notion that history had any value.

Some members of the historical profession were ready to show that the discipline could reshape itself to meet demands for a new understanding of the past. The works of the British Marxist historians, such as E. P. Thompson's *Making of the English Working Class* and Eric Hobsbawm's *Primitive Rebels* (1959), became cult classics, inspiring interest in labor movements and popular revolts in many different historical contexts. In the United States, C. Vann Woodward's *The Strange Career of Jim Crow* (1955) and the publications of a new generation of "revisionist" historians of slavery and the Reconstruction era, such as Kenneth Stampp, provided historical ammunition for supporters of the civil rights crusade. The re-publication in 1963 of C. L. R. James's *The Black Jacobins*, a pioneering account of the Haitian uprising of the 1790s, gave historians interested in Third World liberation movements a powerful model. But the unrest of the 1960s created a demand for a "new history" that went beyond the boundaries of these earlier versions of radical scholarship. Recovering the reality of the lives of the poor and the oppressed seemed to require not only a new perspective but also new methods. The urgency of the causes with which many students of history now came to identify challenged the values of objectivity that had come to dominate the profession after 1945.

Even the traditional methods of pedagogy handed down from Ranke now came under criticism as devices for stifling subversive questions and maintaining traditional structures of authority. On many campuses, history students in the 1960s demanded courses that were "relevant" because they spoke directly to the concerns of their own lives: classes on the history of Vietnam, to explain the origins of the war there, courses on the history of radical movements in the past, on the history of blacks and other minorities in the United States, and on Africa and Latin America. Sometimes, students put together their own classes and pressured universities to grant credit for them; in other places, sympathetic professors worked with students to open up the curriculum, as Natalie Zemon Davis and Jill Ker Conway did when they offered a pioneering course on women's history at the University of Toronto in 1971. At Berkeley, the intellectual historian Carl Schorske combined his large lecture class with student-led "satellite seminars" that offered students a choice of perspectives on the material, challenging the idea that there was only one correct way to interpret his subject; at Princeton, Martin Duberman co-taught a seminar with a psychoanalyst in hopes that students would learn to recognize the unconscious motives for their reactions to the material they were studying. In Britain, the veteran Marxist historian Raphael Samuel took the discipline off campus, founding the History Workshop in 1967, bringing together students, academics, and workers, many of them trade unionists, with the aim of generating a "people's history." Older professors often objected that such experiments devalued the authority that came from having studied a body of knowledge and learned time-tested methods, and many of the more radical attempts to change traditional patterns of history teaching petered out as the movements of the 1960s dissipated in the harsher economic climate of the 1970s. Nevertheless, the innovations of the period did result in a permanent diversification of history curricula and, often, in the institutionalization of student evaluations of courses and student representation on departmental committees.

Although the student radicalism of the 1960s soon faded, the highly vocal challenges to historical norms that exploded in the 1960s opened a new era in historiography, one in which we are still living and that shows no signs of coming to a close. Not all professional historians welcomed these challenges: in 1970, David Hackett Fischer published a manifesto, *Historians' Fallacies*, in which he argued that much of the argumentation in the historical works of the period did not stand up to serious examination. Although Fischer's book is still assigned in many historiography courses, it did little to reduce the enthusiasm for new approaches to the subject. One of the surest signs of the ferment in history that started in these years was the multiplicity of new scholarly journals created to publish work in new fields or using new approaches. These included the *Journal of African History* and *History and Theory*, the first journal devoted exclusively to historiography, in 1960, the *Journal of Social History* in 1967, and the *Journal of Interdisciplinary History* in 1969. To some historians, the heated debates and the repeated rise of new perspectives and fields of interest that have characterized this period are signs that the discipline is alive and well, able to respond to new questions and even to help show how society needs to evolve. What looks like healthy diversity to some historians, however, strikes others as anarchistic cacophony, in which scholarly standards have been abandoned and any hope of determining the truth about the past has disappeared. Optimists cite the new attention given to groups largely excluded from earlier historical narratives, such as women and racial and ethnic minorities; pessimists warn that the redefining of history has provided openings for those who would deny that the Holocaust ever occurred or who would impose an oppressive "political correctness" on scholars and teachers. In some ways, these debates can be read as renewals of older controversies; one can imagine Herodotus taking the side of today's optimists and Thucydides warning against the hazards of innovation. In other ways, however, the issues that divide historians today really are new and require new responses.

Searching for a New History

In the 1960s and early 1970s, radical historians such as Jesse Lemisch, a scholar of the American revolutionary period, called for a history "from the bottom up" that would concentrate on "the powerless, the inarticulate, the poor."[1] The radicals drew inspiration from the Marxist tradition and from the Progressive school of American history, which had been overshadowed by the "consensus" interpretation for several decades. Few fields were more thoroughly transformed by the drive to recover the experience of marginalized groups than that of the history of slavery in the United States. A new generation of historians, both black and white, many of them inspired by the "Black Power" movement that was challenging more moderate civil rights leaders such as Martin

Luther King, turned to nontraditional sources, such as the words of the spirituals sung by slaves and oral interviews with survivors of slavery that had been compiled in the 1930s but generally neglected by scholars, to show that blacks had never accepted the hegemony of their masters and had developed a meaningful culture of their own. Books such as Eugene Genovese's *Roll, Jordan, Roll: The World the Slaves Made* (1973) summed up this new research and demonstrated "the beauty and power of the human spirit under conditions of extreme oppression," as Genovese put it.[2] The intense interest in African American history resulted in the creation of courses on the subject at campuses across the country, although there were often heated disputes about whether the subject should be taught as part of the history curriculum or in interdisciplinary programs devoted to black or African American studies and about whether white scholars such as Genovese were capable of understanding the experience of blacks.

Attempts to create a "new social history" more attentive to the experience of the lower classes often went together with efforts to link history more closely with the "hard" social sciences of economics, sociology, and demography, as the Annales school historians of France had advocated. Many scholars saw particular promise for historical research in the use of quantitative data, which would give the discipline a more scientific character. Individual members of the lower classes in the past rarely left much documentation about their lives, but by accumulating information on hundreds or thousands of people, historians could construct a group portrait that would offer insights into their experiences. The development of computing technology, which began to be accessible to historians during these years, made it possible to analyze large amounts of quantitative data that would have been difficult to handle in earlier times.

The flourishing of statistically based demographic history, the study of the movement of population in the past, demonstrates both the important contributions made by what came to be known as "cliometrics" and the reasons why most historians eventually turned away from this approach. Studying such basic features of life in the past as life expectancy, birth rates, and the impact of disease was clearly one way of probing the experience of ordinary people in the past. For recent centuries, census data were available from many countries. In France, a "third generation" of Annales school historians, such as Emmanuel Le Roy Ladurie, abandoned Fernand Braudel's broad approach and undertook intensive regional studies using sources like church records of baptisms, marriages, and burials to answer questions about how long people lived, how many children married couples had, and what the leading causes of death were in earlier centuries. The study of demography lent itself to a social science approach and even linked history to the natural science of biology. The heyday of historical demography coincided with the introduction of the first birth control pills in the mid-1960s and the intense interest in the threat of overpopulation generated by Paul Ehrlich's best-selling book, *The Population Bomb* (1968), developments that made the question of population trends in the past appear vital to understanding major present-day issues.

The historical research on demography initially produced impressive results. When earlier historians had touched on these topics, they had relied on evidence from literary texts, assuming, for instance, that when Shakespeare made his ill-fated lovers Romeo and Juliet young teenagers, he was reflecting the reality of the world around him. The statistics produced by demographic historians convincingly demonstrated, however, that the average age of marriage for ordinary people in the Europe of Shakespeare's day was actually much higher: most peasant couples were in their mid-twenties when they married and began having children. Although no methods of artificial birth control existed in this period, population levels remained stable because of the high rate of infant mortality and the fact that the interval between births for most married women turned out to be much longer than had been assumed. Correlations of data about deaths with figures for prices for staple foods, particularly grain, left no doubt about the connection between famine years and peaks in mortality. From the patterns that emerged from this painstakingly acquired statistical data emerged a new picture of the harshness of ordinary people's lives in the early modern period, one that contrasted strongly with a vision of the period derived from documents about rulers, artists, and religious reformers. The insights produced by statistically based demographic history were not confined to the study of early modern Europe. In the United States, Herbert Gutman's *The Black Family in Slavery and Freedom* argued that blacks had been able to form family units even under slavery and that the breakdown of the family in impoverished urban ghettoes was a recent development, not the inevitable consequence of slavery.

Studies of historical demography proved the value of cliometrics, but they also demonstrated some of its shortcomings. Even scholars who had initially turned to quantification to elucidate the experience of the masses often became frustrated that their own methods reduced the people they wanted to study to a collection of numbers. Noting the high death rate for small children in seventeenth-century France, Annales school historian Pierre Goubert wrote that it was nevertheless impossible to tell from the data whether parents mourned deeply for their losses or protected themselves from grief by avoiding emotional attachment to their babies. Quantitative history also required a tremendous commitment of effort and, frequently, money, to piece together data from sources that were often not, in themselves, especially interesting to work with. Presenting the results of such research also posed problems: most readers did not have the patience to wade through detailed discussions of the problems of source interpretation that beset cliometricians, whereas other specialists in the field were quick to pounce on arcane methodological shortcomings.

The reputation of the cliometric approach in general was shaken by the highly publicized controversy set off in 1974 when two economic historians, Robert Fogel and Stanley Engerman, published a quantitative study of American slavery, *Time on the Cross*, which one reviewer called "probably the largest and most costly enterprise in historical scholarship ever undertaken." The work's conclusions, which suggested that physical punishment of slaves was relatively infrequent and that slave laborers had embraced the value of hard work propagated by their masters, were almost unanimously rejected by scholars in the field. Other cliometricians denounced the authors' reliance on what they claimed was flimsy evidence, underlining the fact that statistics about the past are often based on small and possibly unrepresentative samples of data; nonquantitative historians of slavery insisted that numbers could not measure the traumatic effect of the whippings and other cruelties that slaves suffered. The attacks on *Time on the Cross* shook historians' faith even in other examples of quantitative history that did not have the same flaws.[3]

New Paradigms for History

In 1984, Lynn Hunt, a young American historian, published a book, *Politics, Culture, and Class in the French Revolution*, that illustrates how approaches to history were transformed as a result of the so-called linguistic and cultural turns that swept the humanities and social sciences in the decade after the publication of *Time on the Cross*. It is not unusual for historians to alter their approach over the course of their career, but Hunt's book is an unusual instance of a historian letting readers watch her change methodological gears in "real time." As Hunt explained to her readers, she had begun the book in the 1970s, planning to use the tools of cliometric quantitative social science to study which population groups and which regions of France most enthusiastically embraced the new ideas of the Revolution and which resisted them. The chapters in the second half of her book, which were actually written before those in the first half, were classic examples of social science history, filled with statistics on the social status of local officials in French cities and voting patterns in elections and making reference to scholarly literature in disciplines such as political science and geography. In the course of writing the book, however, Hunt herself became converted to a different historical approach. The chapters that became the first half of her book abandoned quantification and turned instead to analysis of the language and rhetoric employed by revolutionary activists, the visual symbols they created, and even the clothing they wore. In these chapters, Hunt drew inspiration from scholarship in literature, art history, and anthropology, and readers could sense her excitement about the new insights their viewpoints allowed her to formulate. The question, as Hunt herself admitted, was whether the two halves of the book fit together or whether they represented two incompatible ways of trying to understand the past.

The new approaches Hunt adopted in the course of writing her book were evidence of a "paradigm shift" that affected both history and academia in general. A historian—the historian of science Thomas Kuhn—coined the phrase paradigm shift in his *The Structure of Scientific Revolutions*, which appeared in 1962 but only achieved its full impact some years later. Kuhn's work challenged the fundamental notion that scientific knowledge increased gradually but steadily over time, through the accumulation of new data. Instead, Kuhn argued, the history of science reflected a succession of entirely different models about how the universe worked, and shifts such as that from Isaac Newton's picture of a stable universe to Albert Einstein's theory of relativity were not responses to more accurate information, but rather reflections of sudden and somewhat inexplicable changes in ways in which scientists formulated problems. In Kuhn's view, new theories did not necessarily prevail because they were "truer" than those they replaced, but because they were adopted by a majority of the professionals in a given discipline. Translated into historiographical terms, Kuhn's theory of paradigms suggested that knowledge about the past was not a matter of the steady perfection of research methods and the piling up of ever more information. Instead, new ways of thinking about the past resulted from changes in historians' notions of how individuals and societies worked, and there might not be any single criterion by which historical truth could be defined.

Lynn Hunt's book was evidence of the paradigm shift that came to be called "the linguistic turn," which posited that the understanding of language was the key to the comprehension of human experience. The linguistic turn was closely associated with the rise of what came to be called "the new cultural history." The new cultural historians were inspired by the American anthropologist Clifford Geertz, who wrote in 1973 that the study of human societies is "not an experimental science in search of law but an interpretive one in search of meaning." Geertz's approach was linked to the linguistic turn by his definition of "the culture of a people" as "an ensemble of texts . . . which the anthropologist strains to read over the shoulders of those to whom they properly belong."[4] Among other things, the linguistic and cultural turns raised major questions about the relevance of the boundaries between academic disciplines. At the same time, the humanities and social sciences were profoundly affected by other challenges to long-held assumptions. One was the rise of feminism, which questioned basic assumptions about gender relations. Another fundamental challenge came from scholars who questioned whether intellectual frameworks originally developed in Western societies could comprehend the experience of peoples from other parts of the globe. Advocates of a "postcolonial" approach denounced the "Eurocentrism" of scholarship that treated the culture of Europe and the United States, including its approach to the study of the past, as a model to which other parts of the world needed to conform.

What was at stake for historians in this shift in the academic atmosphere was dramatized in Hayden White's *Metahistory: The Historical Imagination in Nineteenth-Century Europe*, which appeared in 1973 and generated controversy as heated as that which surrounded *Time on the Cross*, published only a few months later. White intransigently announced that "I will consider the historical work as what it most manifestly is—that is to say, a verbal structure in the form of a narrative prose discourse that purports to be a model, or icon, of past structures and processes in the interest of *explaining what they were by representing* them." Drawing heavily on the literary theorist Norbert Frye, White analyzed many of the major historians and historically minded philosophers of the nineteenth century, including Hegel, von Ranke, Tocqueville, Michelet, Marx, and Burckhardt, to bolster his argument that historical works are not transparent reflections of the facts about the past but are instead literary texts, not easily distinguishable from fiction, and that the way in which historians "emplot" their stories—as comedies, tragedies, romances, or examples of irony—reflects their own presuppositions rather than being dictated by the evidence they rely on. Historians disagree with one another, White concluded, not because some of them have done a better job of gathering the data: "When it is a matter of choosing among these alternative visions of history, the only grounds for preferring one over another are *moral* or *aesthetic* ones."[5]

White's insistence on the discrepancy between historical documentation and historical narrative and his insistence on calling historical narratives "fictions" struck most of his colleagues as extreme and even dangerous. Even one favorably inclined reviewer commented that White's theory "may be construed to be the most damaging undertaking ever performed by a historian on his profession."[6] Nevertheless, *Metahistory* has had an impact even on historians who have not read it. White's emphasis on the literary character of historical narrative and his insistence that historians represent events rather than simply letting the facts speak for themselves has made members of the discipline more self-conscious about how they use language and shape their accounts. In one way or another, the issues raised in *Metahistory* still remain central to major debates about the nature of historical knowledge. Self-proclaimed disciples such as Keith Jenkins and Frank Ankersmit continue to elaborate on White's ideas. Others, such as the philosopher Paul Ricoeur, acknowledge that White has inspired them to attempt to define the nature of history in ways more concordant with mainstream historical practice. In his *Time and Narrative* (1984), Ricoeur proposed a theoretical basis for distinguishing between fictional and historical narratives by insisting that the latter must be based on "traces" or evidence that can be dated, that historical narratives must be able to be fitted into a common temporal framework in such a way that they can be coordinated with one another to build a comprehensive picture of the human past, and that historians' narratives must acknowledge the "chain of generations," or in other words, that they need to realize that human beings have seen the world differently depending on the time in which they have lived.[7] Ricoeur's work suggests a way in which some of White's insights can be incorporated into history without dissolving the distinction between history and fiction.

White and Ricoeur directed attention to the linguistic nature of historical narratives and their status as cultural constructs, but both of them focused on a strictly historiographical issue: the nature of the texts created by historians. In his influential 1979 essay, *The Post-Modern Condition*, the French philosopher Jean-François Lyotard added an additional dimension to the critique of traditional forms of history-writing with his contention that cultural and economic changes in the world had made it impossible to cast history in the form of a "grand narrative," in which all developments were fitted into a coherent overall framework. Examples of such grand narratives, including the Enlightenment claim that history reflected an evolution toward higher levels of civilization, nationalist stories of the inevitable rise of particular states, and the Marxist vision of history culminating in the triumph of an emancipated proletarian class, were no longer persuasive, Lyotard insisted. "The grand narrative has lost its credibility, regardless of what mode of unification it uses, regardless of whether it is a speculative narrative or a narrative of emancipation," he wrote.[8] In this "postmodern" era, historians would have to find new ways to justify their arguments and the value of their discipline.

The French philosopher-historian Michel Foucault offered an exceptionally influential demonstration of how these new ideas about the influence of language and the bankruptcy of grand narratives could be applied to the understanding of the past in general. In one of his early works, *Madness and Civilization* (1961), Foucault argued that the phenomenon of insanity was fundamentally defined or constructed by the language used to describe certain kinds of behavior. In the Middle Ages, he claimed, individuals who would later be classified as mentally ill were instead regarded as religious visionaries. Like Kuhn, Foucault argued that changes in frameworks of discourse were not the result of gradual evolution; indeed, Foucault's failure to address the question of what causes such shifts is one of the main points on which historians have criticized him. Nevertheless, Foucault's notion of discourse as the mechanism by which members of any society are shaped or "disciplined," to use a term from the title of his book *Discipline and Punish* (1975), has had far-reaching impact on historians.

Foucault's concept of discourse was only one of his many contributions to historians' thinking. Equally influential has been his analysis of the ways in which power relations structure every level of human interaction. For Foucault, politics is not just exercised by governments and leaders; it also exists in the form of a "micropolitics" or "biopolitics" at the level of everyday life, involving control of the behavior of human bodies. Foucault's analysis thus challenged the separation between social history, long defined as "history with the politics left out," and political history. Historians themselves are engaged in the exercise of power, Foucault argued. Claims to knowledge, including the knowledge that historians claim to possess by virtue of their research, are claims to power and authority, he insisted, and even the structure of the historian's "archive" or selection of sources is the result of an exercise of the power to decide what counts as evidence and what is excluded. Foucault thus challenged historians to be much more self-conscious about the implications of their work. His final project, left unfinished at his death in 1984, was a multivolume *History of Sexuality*, in which he argued that the discourses that created categories of gender identification were not fixed but had differed widely over the course of history and that they functioned to shape identities. Foucault's work was fundamental in encouraging attention to the history of gender relations.

The impact of authors such as Lyotard and Foucault has often led critics to see the historical discipline's linguistic and cultural turn as a product of the abstruse postmodernist theory that was a French specialty in the 1970s, but notions of the structuring importance of language were also put forward around the same time by several prominent historical scholars from other countries, such as J. G. A. Pocock and Quentin Skinner in the English-speaking world and Reinhart Koselleck in Germany. Pocock's study of the language of "civic republicanism" as it moved from Renaissance Italy to seventeenth- and eighteenth-century England and then to North America has shaped several decades of research on the origins of American political thought and institutions, and Skinner's insistence that texts such as the writings of the political theorists Thomas Hobbes and John Locke can only be understood by situating them in the context of the debates of their own time has transformed the history of early modern political and religious thought. Koselleck promoted *Begriffsgeschichte*, the systematic study of the changing meaning of key concepts in philosophy and political and social theory. His observation, for example, that the eighteenth century saw a shift from references to "histories" in the plural to the notion of a single "history" involving all of mankind led him to argue that that period saw a fundamental shift in the way in which people understood the relationship between the past, the present, and the future.[9] Pocock, Skinner, and Koselleck did much to help the subdiscipline of intellectual history, which had suffered in the 1960s because of its association with the study of "elite" thinkers, adapt to a new historical climate created by the linguistic turn, which rejected the notion of the "great mind."

Michel Foucault's work was initially welcomed by many French scholars associated with the celebrated Annales school originally founded by Marc Bloch and Lucien Febvre. Bloch and Febvre had anticipated important aspects of the "cultural turn," such as the adoption of insights from anthropology, in Bloch's study of beliefs about kings' magical healing powers, and the emphasis on language, in Febvre's book on the emergence of atheism in early modern Europe, but under the leadership of their successor Fernand Braudel and the school's "third generation" of younger scholars, the Annales tradition had come to be identified with heavy reliance on quantitative data and an emphasis on long-term historical processes. Nevertheless, Annales historians had often talked of cultural phenomena as a "third level" of historical reality, connected to a basic foundation defined by demographic and economic conditions and an intermediate stratum of social institutions. By the 1970s, however, the third level was coming to take precedence over the others, as the school's third generation began to free themselves from Braudel's emphasis on social and economic structures and to pay more attention to the notion of "mentalities" associated with Braudel's rival, Robert Mandrou. The medieval historian Georges Duby's widely read study of the historical memory of the battle of Bouvines, published in France in 1973, was devoted to precisely the kind of short-term military and political event that Braudel had dismissed as irrelevant "smoke" concealing more fundamental structural realities. Another leading Annales scholar, Emmanuel Le Roy Ladurie, caused a similar sensation in 1975 when he turned away from his earlier, heavily quantitative work and wrote a dramatic study of heresy in a medieval village, *Montaillou*. Both books were seen as acts of defiance against Braudel's social science–oriented approach.

Annales school historians who converted to what they called "the history of mentalities" found an ally in the unconventional Philippe Ariès, an independent scholar who called himself "a Sunday historian" because he had written his historical works in his spare time while pursuing a nonacademic career. Ariès's *Centuries of Childhood*, a pioneering essay on the changing treatment of children over the course of history, had originally appeared in 1960, but only attracted scholarly attention a decade later. Based on visual and literary sources rather than demographic statistics, the book, together with Ariès's subsequent publications on attitudes toward death, showed how imaginative historians could attempt to reconstruct the psychological realities of everyday life, rather than limiting themselves to measuring quantitative trends. Ariès's appointment to a teaching position at the Ecole des Hautes Etudes in 1977 marked the full acceptance of the "history of mentalities" there. He became the principal inspiration for the multivolume *History of Everyday Life*, a five-volume collaborative work that appeared in the mid-1980s, featuring essays on almost every aspect of ordinary life, including food, clothing, and family relations. The history of everyday life extended the Annales school's impulse to elevate the personal sphere of life in which all human beings participate over the more elitist concerns of politics and intellectual activity to its ultimate limit.

The history of everyday life was closely linked to a new genre that developed out of the movement to cultural history and came to be known as "microhistory." Microhistory, a genre developed originally by a group of scholars from Italy, such as Carlo Ginzburg, whose study of a sixteenth-century village miller who became a self-taught religious heretic, *The Cheese and the Worms* (1976), was defined by a concentration on specific incidents, narrowly limited in time and space, and usually involving otherwise unknown minor figures. Microhistorians use these small-scale stories to construct a kind of "total history" different from the grand tableaux of social historians such as Fernand Braudel, bringing together the different aspects of their subjects' lives to show how a single incident can illuminate much broader aspects of the culture and society of the past. Microhistory has also allowed historians to argue for the agency of ordinary people, rather than seeing them as prisoners of the large social structures that had figured in the work of Fernand Braudel. In Ginzburg's hands, for example, the trial of the heretical sixteenth-century Italian miller Menocchio became the basis for discussions of the structure of village society, the spread of atheistic and materialistic ideas about the universe, the impact of printing, and concepts of justice and social order. Skilled microhistorians are able to present their stories in ways that appeal to general audiences as well as to specialists and students; microhistory, as in Natalie Zemon Davis's *The Return of Martin Guerre* (1976), the story of a peasant woman's life with an imposter who claimed to be her long-lost husband showed, has some of the attractions of the novel. Davis even collaborated with two French filmmakers to produce a film of the same name that successfully attracted commercial audiences and remains a classic of historical reenactment on the screen.

The successes of the new cultural history were striking, especially in contrast to the intellectual difficulties that beset some rival approaches to the study of the past during the 1970s and 1980s. The Marxist approach to history, which had enjoyed a striking revival in the 1960s, encountered mounting criticism as the radical protest movements of that era dissipated. The publication, in 1974, of the exiled Russian novelist Alexander Solzhenitsyn's devastating exposé of the horrors of the Soviet prison system, *The Gulag Archipelago*, discredited the regime established by the 1917 Russian Revolution and, by implication, the ideological system associated with it. A school of "revisionist" historians in France, led by the ex-Communist François Furet, undermined the long-held argument that the French Revolution of 1789 had been a "bourgeois" revolution, the result of changes in the country's economic and social structure. In Britain, Gareth Stedman Jones challenged the premises of E. P. Thompson's *Making of the English Working Class* in the name of the new perspectives generated by the "linguistic turn." Whereas Thompson had insisted that there was an objectively identifiable "working class," Stedman Jones contended that "class" was a linguistic construct, not a measurable reality.

The optimistic "modernization thesis" that underlay many social science–oriented studies of the history of economic development written in the 1960s and early 1970s, such as David Landes's *The Unbound Prometheus* (1969), came under fire from critics such as André Gunder Frank and Immanuel Wallerstein, who argued that development in the West came at the expense of the systematic exploitation and "underdevelopment" of the "peripheral" non-Western world. In place of the grand narrative of economic progress that had underlain much of the work in that field, pioneering environmental historians such as William Cronon offered analyses of that highlighted the damaging ecological consequences of economic exploitation. At the end of his history of early settlement in New England, Cronon concluded that, from the start of

American history, "ecological abundance and economic prodigality went hand in hand: the people of plenty were a people of waste." Although he warned against a facile countercultural assumption that the Indians had lived in harmony with their natural environment, the critical point of his conclusion was clear.[10]

As the new cultural history established its hegemony in the 1980s, it was subjected to criticism in its own right. Noting that thinkers such as Geertz and Foucault were better at describing patterns of meaning than at explaining historical change, some historians complained that the adoption of a cultural perspective meant abandoning historical scholarship's most distinctive feature, its emphasis on the causes of change. Political historians warned that the cultural turn was leading historians to neglect the impact of governments, leaders, and ideologies; in a widely read review of Lynn Hunt's book on the political culture of the French Revolution, Robert Darnton, a historian himself sympathetic in some ways to the new historical approach, asked how a book on the subject could say virtually nothing about figures such as Mirabeau and Robespierre or topics such as the Declaration of the Rights of Man and the Reign of Terror. "Is this what the Revolution was all about? None of the revolutionaries would have recognized it," Darnton complained.[11] Other historians noted that an excessive emphasis on the power of discourse to shape human lives could wind up generating a vision of history just as impersonal as the structural social history that some of the cultural historians were revolting against.

Women's History and the History of Gender Relations

The rise of linguistic and cultural history coincided chronologically with a dramatic increase in interest in the history of women and the subject of gender relations. Many pioneering women's historians had been influenced by reading the French philosopher Simone de Beauvoir's *The Second Sex*, a classic analysis of the situation of women originally published in 1949, and young historians in America often drew inspiration from Betty Friedan's best-selling *The Feminine Mystique* (1963), a challenge to the notion that women's place was only in the home. More than a reaction to the ideas of a few writers, however, the growth of women's history was a collective process, carried out by participants in the feminist movement that began to develop in the radical atmosphere of the 1960s. The developing interest in the study of women in the past was directly linked to a concern about the status of women in the present and especially to demands that women be given greater access to jobs in the academy and that women students be protected from harassment and sexual exploitation by professors. The rise of women's history thus affected not only the content of historical studies, but also the substance of historians' careers and the nature of interactions between students and teachers. Historians of women found resources in many of the new developments in historiography that were occurring at the same time as the women's history movement was taking off. Whereas women had traditionally been excluded from positions of power and therefore rarely appeared in works of political history, for example, they could more easily be featured in studies of cultural history and the history of everyday life. The techniques of microhistory could often be employed to highlight women's agency in past eras, as Natalie Davis's interpretation of the life of Bertrande de Rols, the wife of Martin Guerre, demonstrated.

The development of women's history from the 1960s to the 1980s was part of what is now commonly labeled the "second wave" of feminism, going beyond the "first wave" of the movement in the late nineteenth and early twentieth centuries that had concentrated on the political issue of women's suffrage and on obtaining access to higher education for women, but without seriously challenging the nature of institutions or the content of curricula, including those in history. Now, historians began insisting not only that women had the same right to study and teach history as men, but also that the definition of history had to be rethought in light of women's experiences, that "herstory" needed to be added to "history." Adopting the term popularized by Thomas Kuhn, one of the movement's leaders, Gerda Lerner, wrote that "Women's history asks for a paradigm shift."[12] What this meant was exemplified in the work of Joan Kelly-Gadol, Carroll Smith-Rosenberg, and many other scholars. Kelly-Gadol asked, "Did women have a Renaissance?" and concluded that although the Italian Renaissance had been a liberating experience for many elite men of the time, "women as a group ... experienced a contraction of social and personal options."[13] She suggested that similar questions could be asked about the consequences of other supposedly progressive events in world history, such as the French Revolution. Using the language of "separate spheres," Smith-Rosenberg sought to go beyond demonstrating women had been oppressed by patriarchal social systems and ideologies by showing that there were areas where women had been able to exercise agency in their lives. Her investigation of the bonds of friendship among nineteenth-century American women became a model for historical scholarship in many other areas.[14]

The sense of exploring virtually unknown territory was exhilarating for many of the scholars who helped develop the field of women's history. "Oh, the excitement of that decade among professors and students, as we sought primary sources in rare book libraries and archives and exchanged bibliographies and syllabi across North America," Natalie Zemon Davis later recalled.[15] Starting in 1973, the Berkshire Conference of Women's Historians provided a periodic opportunity for women scholars to meet and share ideas and experiences. Together with intellectual excitement, however, women in history experienced considerable frustration and often outright anger as they pushed to expand their career opportunities and gain recognition within the profession. When she served on a committee investigating the treatment of women at Harvard, the medieval historian Carolyn Bynum "received hate mail, even threats, and at one point had to seek police protection."[16] Women historians in the United States formed a Coordinating Committee on Women in the Historical Profession in 1969. In response to the group's demands, the American Historical Association appointed a committee headed by a prominent woman historian, Willie Lee Rose, whose report, issued in 1970, documented the underrepresentation of women on the faculties of leading universities and within the organization itself and called for attention to issues such as child care that created obstacles for women who wanted to pursue academic careers.

Thanks to pressure from the women's movement and, in the United States, legislation against hiring discrimination, career opportunities for women in universities have expanded greatly since the early 1970s. The consequences of the rise of feminism for the understanding of history are harder to define. Despite calls like Joan Kelly-Gadol's in the 1970s to reconsider fundamental issues such as the periodization of history in light of women's experiences, traditional labels such as "the Renaissance" and "the age of revolution" have continued to structure historical discussions, and women's history often remains a "supplement," to be added to historical narratives essentially shaped by other considerations. In her *The Gender of History* (1998), Bonnie Smith protested that the study of historiography itself continued to marginalize women and ignore the contribution they had made to the study of the past. "The historian of historiography, which is virtually all male, seldom shares the stage with a woman."[17] As the impact of the feminist movement has grown, it has also become more diffuse. Women historians never subscribed to a single point of view, and some, like the French historian Michelle Perrot, objected from the start to the notion of women's history as a separate branch of scholarship, fearing that it might become "a new ghetto in which women would close themselves off" and that the movement might generate a "feminist science" that would be as dogmatic and politicized as the "proletarian science" imposed on historians in Communist countries during the Soviet period.[18] Women's historians themselves critiqued the emphasis on an unchanging model of "patriarchy" that they often found in the work of feminist theorists from other disciplines. By making it seem that the situation of women had been essentially the same in all times and places, the concept of patriarchy disregarded the notion of historical change and ignored the basic insight of history, they warned.

From an early date, some scholars interested in women's history had insisted that any investigation of the importance of sexual identity in the past had to take into account not only women but also men and the relations between the sexes. Michel Foucault's last major work, his unfinished *History of Sexuality*, provided a framework for exploration of these issues, and Joan Scott underlined the significance of this insight in an influential article published in 1986, "Gender: A Useful Category of Historical Analysis." Gender identities, Foucault and Scott argued, are not a simple matter of biology but are culturally constructed, and these constructions affect men as much as women. These theoretical perspectives helped stimulate new research on the history of masculinity and the history of homosexuality, a subject brought into the limelight by the devastating AIDS epidemic that began in the early 1980s and claimed the life of Foucault himself. By the 1980s, a third wave was transforming feminism itself, raising questions about whether the placing of all women in a single category privileged the experience of middle-class white women and obscured the differences between women of different races, ethnic groups, social strata, and sexual orientations. Historians of lesbianism, for instance, sometimes complained that they were marginalized both by other women's historians and by the male scholars who dominated the fields of gay and queer studies. Even if the expansion of women's history into the domains of gender, masculinity, and the study of sexual minorities means that scholarship had moved a long way from the original concerns of the pioneering women's historians of the 1970s, however, there is no doubt that the new perspectives first generated by the interest in women's history have profoundly changed the historical profession and the content of scholarship.

Contesting Eurocentrism

A third challenge to established ways of thinking about history, linked in some ways to the linguistic turn and other developments of the 1970s, was the increasing demand for a way of thinking about the past that did not take the experience of Europe and the United States as the model for the rest of the world. The literary critic Edward Said's *Orientalism*, published in 1978, described European views of "Eastern" cultures, including academic historical scholarship, as "a Western style for dominating, restructuring, and having authority over the Orient." Said drew on Foucault's notion that claims to knowledge about a subject are a way of establishing power relations to associate "Orientalist" research with European imperialism and colonialism. Particularly important for historians was Said's assertion that Orientalism had denied non-European societies any real history of their own, positing instead that changes in them were "mere responses to the West."[19] The notion of non-European societies as static and unchanging until they were acted on by outside forces was a way of implying that the only proper focus of history was the development of European civilization. In *Islands of History* (1985), another work that has been influential in making historians more conscious of non-Western historical perspectives, the anthropologist Marshall Sahlins used his research on the island peoples of the Pacific to argue that "different cultural orders have their own modes of historical action, consciousness, and determination—their own historical practice."[20] Questioning European perspectives on the non-European past required a recognition that other peoples might have their own ways of experiencing the flow of time itself and that their ways of representing the past could be as valid as those developed in the West.

Said's sweeping indictment of Orientalism, which focused primarily on nineteenth-century authors and in which serious scholarship about non-European societies was conflated with literary representations and pro-imperialist propaganda, has not gone unchallenged. Said has been criticized for "adopting the approach that he himself had condemned" by lumping together a vast variety of scholarship on Asia, written at different times and from different perspectives.[21] His critics have argued that many European scholars had developed a genuine appreciation for the languages, the art, and the culture of the societies they studied and had made valuable contributions to their understanding. Historians of Latin America and Africa have questioned whether Said's approach, often extended to the entire non-European world, actually applies to the study of those regions. Sahlins, too, has been criticized, with some scholars contending that his claim that indigenous people had their own modes of historical thought amounted to saying that they were fundamentally irrational. Nevertheless, the debates opened by *Orientalism* and *Islands of History* have raised issues that cannot easily be dismissed. At the time when Said's book was published, the American historian William McNeill's 1963 volume, *The Rise of the West*, was regarded as perhaps the best synthesis available on modern world history. The book's very title seemed to exemplify the phenomenon Said was addressing; as a recent historian of writing about world history has put it, "McNeill assumed a cause-and-effect relationship between European history and world history and built it into his chronology."[22] Even efforts to highlight the exploitative nature of Europe's impact on the rest of the world, such as the economic historian Immanuel Wallerstein's *The Modern World-System* (1974), still defined Europe as a "core" whose development created a "periphery" in other parts of the world.

One issue raised by the effort to redress the imbalance between history centered around the West and the experience of the rest of the world involved the question of sources. Some non-Western cultures, such as China, had long written traditions of their own and even extensive historiographies, but others, such as sub-Saharan Africa, did not; in addition, the annals of some civilizations, such as that of India, largely excluded their own lower classes. African historians were pioneers in developing the use of oral history: many societies there had passed down stories about their own past that, as scholars like Jan Vansina showed, could be mined for information, provided that one understood how these narratives had been reshaped as they were retold. In one of the most extensive efforts to evaluate oral history testimony from a nonliterate culture, Richard Price has argued that the oral narratives handed down by members of the Saramaka people of Surinam, descendants of black slaves who successfully revolted against whites in the 1700s, reflect a distinctive vision of their history, which he has been able to compare with European settlers' written records from the period. In *Alabi's World*, one of several books he has devoted to the subject, Price prints excerpts from these competing historical accounts in different typefaces to encourage readers to compare their differing perspectives, while demonstrating that they do refer to the same set of events.[23] In India, the Subaltern Studies Group, which developed in the early 1980s, acknowledged the sparsity of written sources dealing with the majority of that country's population in the past and the necessity of relying on documents generated by ruling elites and the British colonial administration, while paying particular attention to the "silences" about the poor and about women that they contained. The study of subaltern experience "could not just be the Indian version of the 'history from below' approach," Gyan Prakash insisted, since even that was a Western construct. "It had to conceive the subaltern differently and write different histories."[24] Often, the Subaltern Studies scholars argued, it was what was not mentioned in the documents that provided the only available clues to the life of the poor and the marginalized. Through its insistence on foregrounding the difficulties in recovering the voices of such groups, the Subaltern Studies group has had a major influence on historians throughout the world.

An important contribution to the debate about the relationship between European and non-Western history is Dipesh Chakrabarty's *Provincializing Europe: Postcolonial Thought and Historical Difference* (2000). Chakrabarty, originally a member of the Subaltern Studies group, argued that historicist thinking, as it had developed in nineteenth-century Europe through the contributions of historians such as Ranke, "enabled European domination of the world in the nineteenth century ... Historicism is what made modernity or capitalism look not simply global but rather as something that became global *over time*, by originating in one place (Europe) and the spreading outside it." In addition to making Europe look like the origin of all the important historical developments that define modernity, the acceptance of European methods of historical inquiry as normative justified an "asymmetric ignorance" about the past: historians writing about any other part of the world are obliged to refer to models of historical research developed to deal with the European past, but historians of Europe and the United

States are not expected to pay any attention to the work of historians from other parts of the world. Chakrabarty did not maintain, however, that non-Western historians should simply reject the heritage of Western historiography. Instead, historians had to recognize the impact of Western modes of historical thought as a reality and to use its own methods to "write into the history of modernity the ambivalences, contradictions, the use of force, and the tragedies and ironies that attend it."[25] Despite criticism that he does not go far enough in recognizing the role of capitalism and the national state in imposing European influence on the rest of the world, Chakrabarty's book has become fundamental to discussions of the relationship between Western and non-Western history.[26]

The History of Memory

Women's and gender history and the challenge to "Eurocentrism" were historical movements with obvious political implications. The political significance of the history of memory, another of the historiographical consequences of the turn to cultural or interpretive history during the 1970s and 1980s, was less obvious until this new approach became caught up in the noisy "history wars" that exploded in the later 1980s and continued through the following decade. The idea that there is such a thing as a collective memory, shared by the members of a given society, and that this memory alters over time—in other words, that is has its own history—had been put forward in 1925 by a French sociologist, Maurice Halbwachs, but his work had little impact at the time. Rediscovered in the early 1980s, Halbwachs's ideas became a major inspiration for historians' growing interest in the subject of memory. A pioneer in the field was the literature scholar Paul Fussell, who used the literature written in Britain about World War I to argue that the way in which that traumatic conflict was remembered had shaped the forms of "political and social cognition in our time" or, in other words, that the memory of the war had to be understood as a historical force in its own right.[27]

The French historian Pierre Nora turned the history of memory into a historiographical industry by organizing a massive collective project, *Les lieux de mémoire* ("Sites of memory"), whose seven volumes began to appear in 1982. The history of memory, Nora argued, emerged because the changes associated with modernization had torn apart the connection between French society and its living sense of collective memory. At the same time, he claimed, historians had lost their confidence in their ability to reconstruct the past as it truly had been. "History in general has begun to question its own conceptual and material resources, its production processes and social means of distribution, its origins and tradition; it has thus entered the historiographic age, consummating its divorce from memory—which in turn has become a possible object of history," Nora announced.[28] By "sites of memory," Nora and his collaborators meant all the various cultural objects that evoked collective memory and helped build French identity. Sites of memory could be physical objects, such as the palace of Versailles and the Eiffel Tower, but they could also be rituals, ranging from the celebration of Bastille Day to the Tour de France bicycle race, or texts, such as the fondly remembered school textbook *Le Tour de France par deux enfants*, from which several generations had learned their national history and geography. "Memory sites" could also be symbols, such as the tricolor French flag, and mental concepts, such as the French division of political movements into categories of "left" and "right." The elasticity—some critics called it the vagueness—of the concept of "memory sites" has undoubtedly been part of its attraction.

Most of the contributions to *Les Lieux de mémoire* were clearly exercises in cultural history, but Nora provided the nearly two hundred individual articles with an overall framework that isolated monographs in that genre often lacked. Indeed, one criticism of his project was that it amounted to a disguised return to the kind of nation-centered history that the founders of the French Annales school had so strongly criticized. Although the contents of the collection were quite varied, the definition of "French" was traditional: gender issues were barely mentioned, and the French overseas empire was virtually excluded, eliminating reference to such troublesome issues at the country's role in the Atlantic slave trade and the era of European colonialism. Despite the Nora project's exclusive focus on France, however, its demonstration of the possibilities of the "history of memory" had great impact on historians elsewhere. The terms in which Nora had cast the conflict between social memory and academic history helped make sense of controversies such as the history wars that developed in other countries toward the end of the twentieth century. More generally, as the British historian Jay Winter, one of the most important contributors to the history of memory, has argued, the history of memory helped provide critical perspective on the "memory boom" that seemed to be sweeping the world in general, marked by the growing interest in history museums, tours of historic sites, historical theme parks, and other forms of cultural consumption.

Awareness of the growing interest in historical memory has not been limited to professional historical scholars. The growth of the history of memory has coincided with increased attention to the testimony of witnesses and victims of historical events, whose personal stories are often accorded more attention than the work of professional historians. This phenomenon has been especially apparent in the field of Holocaust studies, where the first-person accounts of survivors such as Elie Wiesel and Primo Levi have had more impact in creating a collective memory than any of the works of trained historians. It was also raised by the widely publicized hearings of the Truth and Reconciliation Commission established in South Africa in 1995, after the end of the apartheid regime, to establish the truth about what had happened during the struggle against the racialist apartheid regime there. The highly emotional testimony given to the Commission had tremendous impact, but many important historical questions about the South African past were left aside in a process that concentrated on the experiences of individual victims and perpetrators. Such privileging of witness testimony has not always been happily accepted by historians: while acknowledging the attraction of the idea of giving history "back to its real authors," one Holocaust scholar has written of a "tension between the witness and the historian, . . . and, indeed, even a struggle for power."[29] Witnesses' authority to speak about the past is based on what they remember having experienced; they are often reluctant to concede that individual memory can be fallible or confused. Historians, on the other hand, are usually writing about events they did not experience, and they are accustomed to comparing evidence and preferring documentation created at the time rather than formulated later. It is, however, difficult for them to confront trauma survivors and tell them that their recollections are inaccurate.

The increased interest in memory and witness testimony did make historians more receptive to the value of oral history. Initially seen as valuable only when other forms of documentation were unavailable, as in the case of precolonial African history, oral history, in the form of interviews, now came to be employed as evidence even in writing about events for which copious printed sources existed. One of the most important practitioners of interviewing for historical purposes was Studs Terkel, a sometime actor and broadcaster with a gift for getting people to talk about their experiences. His most influential volume, *The Good War: An Oral History of World War Two*, appeared in 1985 and won the Pulitzer Prize. The way in which Terkel drew out of his subjects' words a composite depiction of a conflict that Americans had understood as brutal but morally necessary influenced even the work of academic historians; the title of the book serves to characterize what has become the prevailing interpretation of how the country saw the war. The Italian historian Alessandro Portelli provided oral history with a theoretical framework, arguing that interviews provided information about subjects' emotional experiences rather than just factual data. "The importance of oral testimony may lie not in its adherence to fact, but rather in its departure from it, as imagination, symbolism, and desire emerge," Portelli argued. "Therefore, there are no 'false' oral sources . . . 'wrong' statements are still psychologically 'true,' and . . . this truth may be equally as important as factually reliable accounts."[30]

Historian Jay Winter's own work, like that of the memory-history pioneer Paul Fussell, has centered on the memory of World War I, one of the major topics that has attracted historians of memory. "It is not just the injuries of war, but its drama, its earthquake-like character, which has fueled the memory boom," Winter has written.[31] Because of the strong public interest in past wars, historians studying how they are remembered have had the opportunity to communicate their research, not only in print, but also in ways that reach broader audiences. Winter himself has written about his role in helping to design a major museum dedicated to the World War I, the Historial at Péronne, France, in which he and his colleagues consciously tried to incorporate the multiple perspectives of the new cultural history and to represent the war in a way that would engage visitors without glorifying the horrors of the conflict. He also participated in making a television documentary on the subject that was shown in both the United States and Britain.

The many forms of ordinary people's involvement in keeping the memory of the Civil War alive in the United States are vividly chronicled in the journalist Tony Horwitz's entertaining *Confederates in the Attic*, a popular bestseller that is often assigned in college classes. Among other things, Horwitz's book is an object lesson in the differences between the research techniques of members of his profession and those of academic historians.[32] At the beginning of his story, Horwitz joins a band of Civil War reenactors, who try to experience a "period rush," the feeling of actually living what soldiers of the era went through, by wearing authentic uniforms and eating the indigestible food of the time, so that they can duplicate "soldierly misery."[33] He interviews Civil War fanatics, sometimes downing beers with them, probes the motives of those who put stars-and-bars flag decals on their cars and trucks, and notes with dismay the wide gap between what white and black Americans remember about the conflict. Professional historians might question how representative Horwitz's interviewees are of broader views on the subject and wonder whether he has not chosen to highlight the most colorful characters he encountered. By putting himself in the middle of the action, he has certainly taken to an extreme the counsel of some postmodernist historians to emphasize the subjective nature of his conclusions. Although much of the book is written in a serious tone, its frequent humorous passages are a reminder of an important element of human experience that is usually missing from what is accepted as history.

The "History Wars"

By the time *Confederates in the Attic* appeared in 1998, the dramatic changes in approaches to history that took place in the 1960s and 1970s had been stirring debates within the profession for several decades. Peter Novick's *That Noble Dream: The 'Objectivity Question' and the American Historical Profession*, the most significant and widely read work on historiography published in the United States in the 1980s, showed that debates about whether historical knowledge could be measured according to an objective standard or whether relativistic perspectives were inevitable in historical scholarship had a long history in the United States, but Novick's work also reflected a profound concern about the new challenges wrought by the linguistic turn and the rise of feminism and the history of minority groups. The titles of the chapters in his book's final section—"Objectivity in Crisis," "The Collapse of Comity," "Every Group Its Own Historian," "The Center Does Not Hold," and "There Was No King In Israel"—conveyed a sense of acute anxiety about the state of the historical profession. By the mid-1980s, Novick concluded, "As a broad community of discourse, as a community of scholars united by common aims, common standards, and common purposes, the discipline of history had ceased to exist."[34]

A similar sense of crisis enveloped the influential Annales school in France. In their eagerness to embrace the new perspectives of cultural history, the critic François Dosse charged in 1987, the Annalistes had abandoned any pretense that the study of history had a definable framework. "One detects an ever-stronger odor of decay from a school where everyone takes his own path to salvation, to the point where one can ask what links a history that has become historical anthropology to a quantitative demographic and economic history and a conceptual history," Dosse wrote.[35]

Whereas academic historians embraced or at least tolerated the new emphasis on the history of neglected groups and the shift from grand narratives to history as a form of cultural interpretation, the general public was slower to accept these new perspectives or in some cases reacted to them with hostility. In France, it is true, adepts of the new cultural history found an unusually warm welcome from the media and ordinary readers. Historians such as Emmanuel Le Roy Ladurie, the author of *Montaillou*, Georges Duby, and Philippe Ariès appeared regularly on French television in the 1970s and 1980s and their books became bestsellers. In his memoirs, Duby celebrated their success, writing, "A century after history withdrew from the marketplace and took refuge behind the opacities of erudition, it now showed renewed interest in the literary business and the possibility of reaching a wide audience."[36] Pierre Nora's seven-volume *Les Lieux de mémoire*, despite its lack of any overall narrative thread, was another popular success. In other countries, however, public enthusiasm for history often developed in directions quite different from those taken by academic specialists. In Britain, for example, university historians often criticized the enthusiasm for the restoration of aristocratic "stately homes" and the cult of "heritage sites" that attracted visitors by offering a vision of life in the past based on the experience of wealthy elites.

In the United States, public interest in the past was increasingly shaped by the popular media. The bicentennial of the American War of Independence, in 1976, was celebrated with lavish festivals and reenactments that often ignored the more critical views of academic scholars. Two television miniseries first broadcast in the late 1970s, the African American author Alex Haley's "Roots," which reconstructed the life of his own ancestors, from the time of their sales as slaves in Africa to the present, and Gerald Green's fictionalized miniseries, "Holocaust," had particular success in getting large audiences interested in history,

although both were also criticized for reducing large historical movements to dramatic stories about heroic individuals. *Roots* drew far
more Americans into the narrative of African American history than
any scholarly publication ever had; it also inspired Americans of all
ethnicities to take a new interest in their own family histories. Skeptics
wondered, however, whether the "griots" Haley found in Ghana, who
he claimed had told him stories handed down for generations about
his ancestor Kunta Kinte, had not in fact made up tales to please their
interviewer. Like "Roots," "Holocaust" had a real impact on viewers. In
the United States, it made the genocide of the Jews in World War II part
of the general culture; in Germany, this fictionalized depiction of the
Nazi period inspired a public debate about the past that serious works
of scholarship had been unable to initiate. The miniseries' implausible
plot led critics to complain that it trivialized its subject, but the interest
it generated did much to spur the growth of the academic field of
Holocaust studies.

Not all scholars condemned the forms that public interest in history
took. In *The Past Is a Foreign Country*, an ambitious analysis of the
motives for human interest in the past that he published in 1985, David
Lowenthal urged acceptance of the fact that all representations of the
past necessarily incorporated their share of distortions. Even physical
relics do not provide a direct, unmediated access to the past, Lowenthal
warned. If they are to be preserved and displayed, they must be altered
by restoration and framed, in signs and captions, in ways that impose
present-day meanings on them. Lowenthal was even prepared to express a certain tolerance for commercially motivated reconstructions
of the past, such as Disneyland's talking Abraham Lincoln: "Better a
misinformed enjoyment of history than none, a lighthearted dalliance
with the past than a wholesale rejection of it."[37] Although academic historians had often been critical of "Roots" and "Holocaust," many of them
were more appreciative of what they saw as serious efforts to use television and film to bring history to a mass audience. The American documentary filmmaker Ken Burns's ten-hour series, "The Civil War" (1990),
whose images were taken largely from photographs made at the time of
the conflict, was widely praised, although he was faulted for saying
little about the role of African Americans in the war. French filmmaker
Claude Lanzmann's equally lengthy "Shoah," released in 1986, presented
the history of the Holocaust in a different light than the popular television miniseries. Constructed out of interviews with surviving Jewish

victims, German perpetrators, and "bystanders" such as Polish peasants who had witnessed Jews being taken to their deaths, the film significantly influenced the direction of historical research, directing attention to neglected topics such as the role bystanders had played in these events.

Although professional historians sometimes acknowledged positive aspects of these popular versions of the past, they increasingly found themselves embroiled in controversies about how new historiographical approaches were challenging popularly accepted narratives about the past. The history wars that raged so fiercely in Germany and the United States in the late 1980s and early 1990s, as well as similar controversies that took place in France, focusing on the meaning of the French Revolution; in Australia, where the main issue was the treatment of the fate of the country's native Aboriginal population by the British colonists who settled there after 1788; and in Israel, where politically engaged scholars took aim at the claim that Arab governments were exclusively responsible for the flight of Palestinian refugees during the country's war of independence in 1948, all were in one way or another arguments about historical memory. Other enormously consequential debates about how to remember the past marked the post-Communist states that emerged in Eastern Europe and in the former Soviet Union after the fall of the Berlin Wall in 1989.

The clash between strong public demand for historical narratives painted in broad strokes, with identifiable heroes and villains, and the multiplicity of new perspectives germinating in academia, many of which challenged traditional depictions of the past, set the stage for heated debates, often characterized as episodes in "culture wars" about the interpretation of history. Although the historical cultural wars of the late 1980s and early 1990s in different countries focused on different issues, they shared certain common features. Throughout the Western world, a backlash against the cultural innovations of the 1960s had set in by the end of the 1970s, signaled by the election of the Conservative Margaret Thatcher as prime minister in Britain in 1979 and of the Republican Ronald Reagan as president of the United States in 1980. Both leaders had no patience for the new historiographical fashions they saw as having taken over the universities. "Though not an historian myself, I had a very clear—and I had naively imagined uncontroversial—idea of what history was," Thatcher wrote in her memoirs. "History is an account of what happened in the past," and history teaching, she insisted, was a matter of "memorizing what actually happened."[38] Reagan had less intellectual interest in what academic historians were doing, but he insistently painted a picture of the United States that emphasized only the most optimistic aspects of the past. In the post-Communist world, struggles over historical memory took the form of demands for the opening of archives and for an honest accounting of what had taken place during the decades of Soviet rule. Throughout the world, historians discovered that historiographical controversies, normally the exclusive concern of professionals, could, under certain circumstances, become major political issues.

One of the most explosive of the period's public historiographical controversies was ignited in 1986, when a conservative West German scholar, Ernst Nolte, set off what came to be called the *Historikerstreit*, "the battle of the historians," by challenging the notion that the extermination of the Jews carried out by the Nazis was a uniquely terrible crime that resulted from a special flaw rooted in German historical development. Nolte suggested that Hitler had merely followed a precedent set by the Communist regime in the Soviet Union. Opponents of Nolte, including the philosopher Jürgen Habermas and a number of prominent German historians, denounced his position, arguing that it amounted to a whitewash of the German past and an attempt to evade the country's collective responsibility for the events of the Holocaust. Positions similar to Nolte's were defended by several prominent historians, however, and they appeared to have the backing of the conservative West German government of the day, whose leader, Helmut Kohl, had triggered public controversy in 1985 when he had persuaded President Reagan to join him in honoring the graves of German soldiers, including members of the SS who had helped carry out killings during the war. The dramatic events following the fall of the Berlin Wall in 1989 and the subsequent unification of West and East Germany diverted public attention from the *Historikerstreit*, but debate about these issues flared up again in 1995, when the Hamburg Institute for Social Research opened a public exhibit devoted to "The Crimes of the *Wehrmacht* from 1941 to 1944," which documented the extent of the German army's involvement in the killing of Jews during the war and discredited the myth that the Holocaust had been the exclusive work of the committed Nazis in the SS.

The sudden and unexpected collapse of the Soviet system of satellite states in Eastern Europe in 1989, followed by the breakup of the

Soviet Union itself in 1991, appeared to vindicate Western political conservatives' insistence on the superiority of systems based on individual
freedom and capitalist economics. A prominent American political
commentator, Francis Fukuyama, boldly announced that this event
signaled "the end of history." To be sure, Fukuyama conceded, there
would still be changes in human affairs, but the conflicts about fundamental values that had generated the great historical dramas of the
past—clashes between civilizations, religious faiths, and rival political
ideologies—were over, since the whole planet now recognized that
there was no serious alternative to a broadly shared set of principles
rooted in the traditions of Western democracy. Implicit in Fukuyama's
thesis was the possibility that the discipline of history itself would
lose its interest, since it would amount to no more than a set of stories
about the bad old days in which human beings had not yet learned how
to get along with one another.

Fukuyama's prediction proved to be premature, but the events of
1989 did set off a widespread process of historical revision in societies
where Communist governments had rigidly controlled what could be
said about the past. Whatever aspect of the past they studied, historians who hoped to make successful careers in these societies had had to
adopt a Marxist perspective, taking class struggle as the fundamental
explanation for historical change, and, especially if they were dealing
with the recent past, they had to endorse the notion that integration
into the Soviet empire had been a beneficial event, supported by the
"masses" of the local population. After 1989, historians in these countries were suddenly able to write openly about crucial episodes of their
national pasts that had been blacked out under Communism, and outside scholars, who had operated under tight restrictions, were suddenly
given access to archives that had always been off limits to them. In the
former Soviet Union and the newly independent countries that broke
away from Russian dominance after 1989, there was unprecedented
discussion of controversial historical events. A Russian human rights
organization, "Memorial," founded in 1989, which set out to create
for the first time a comprehensive archive identifying the victims of
Stalin's regime, showed the impact that free historical inquiry could
have in a society that had long been deprived of it. One of the disquiet-
ing signs of the return to authoritarianism in Russia and other countries that were once part of the Soviet Union in recent years have been
government efforts to close down Memorial and similar organizations.

In many cases, archival documents that were opened to scholars after 1989 have now been locked away again.

In the former Soviet bloc countries of Eastern Europe, historians rehabilitated national pasts that had been condemned as obstacles to social progress during the Soviet period. The history wars in the former Communist countries were not always limited to the refutation of false claims made prior to 1989, however. In some countries, politicians, sometimes aided by nationalist historians, used "visions of past greatness" to rally particular ethnic groups against their neighbors.[39] In the former Yugoslavia, where the Communist regime had managed to hold several hostile groups together in a single state, the end of that government unleashed devastating conflicts. Slobodan Milosevic, the president of Serbia, Yugoslavia's largest component state, made especially virulent use of historical myths, blaming the neighboring Croats for collaborating with the Germans during World War II and unleashing a campaign of terror against Serbia's Muslim Albanian minority to avenge a defeat at the hands of Muslims in 1389.

The versions of the history wars that broke out in the United States in the first half of the 1990s were noisy but far less dangerous than the debates in the former Communist states. The history wars in the United States often saw academic historians defending a pluralistic approach to the past, inspired by the historiographical innovations that had begun with the new social history of the 1960s and continued with the linguistic and cultural turns of the 1970s and the development of movements such as feminist and non-Western history, against critics, often politically inspired, who insisted on what they called historical objectivity. This was particularly the case with the storm that enveloped a set of proposed "National History Standards," meant to guide curriculum development in American schools. The effort to develop guidelines dealing with American and world history was part of a larger movement for educational reform, spurred by a 1983 assessment of the country's schools entitled "A Nation at Risk" that had warned that the United States was falling behind other countries in a wide range of educational areas, including students' understanding of history. The movement to define goals for history classes initially brought together a broad coalition, including academic historians, schoolteachers, and politicians, including Lynne Cheney, who, in her capacity as director of the government's National Endowment for the Humanities under President Reagan, provided much of its funding.

Historians who had spent years drafting a proposal that sought to incorporate the new scholarship in the field while accommodating the concerns of dozens of different groups were outraged in 1994 when Cheney suddenly launched a media campaign against their work, claiming that it slighted the positive aspects of American history in the name of "political correctness." Journalists and conservative politicians quickly joined in, and before the controversy ended, the U.S. Senate had voted 99 to 1 for a resolution disavowing the proposed standards and demanding that any future history guidelines show "a decent respect for the contributions of Western civilization."[40] Although the timing of Cheney's denunciation, shortly before the congressional elections of 1994, suggested a political motivation, the debate about the proposed history standards and in particular the attempt to incorporate a more multicultural perspective into the curriculum had been under way for several years beforehand, and not all the critics of the new history were political conservatives. In 1992, the prominent political historian Arthur Schlesinger Jr., long associated with liberal political causes, had published *The Disuniting of America*, warning that emphasis on the oppression of minorities and women might undermine the common values on which the coherence of American society depended. The notion that "cultural literacy" required a shared base of factual knowledge, most of it related to Western civilization, was promoted in a best-selling book by that title written by E. D. Hirsch in 1987 and had a broad appeal.[41]

The controversy about the proposed national history standards coincided with an equally passionate and equally politicized controversy about a planned exhibition on the bombing of Hiroshima and Nagasaki at the National Air and Space Museum in Washington, D.C. The preceding years had already seen several other controversial exhibitions at museums that, like the Air and Space Museum, were part of the government-owned Smithsonian Institution, including a show devoted to the internment of Japanese Americans during World War II and another, "The West as America," that emphasized the violence and exploitation that had accompanied the country's expansion. The proposed Hiroshima exhibit, designed by the museum's professional staff, would have featured a display of the *Enola Gay*, the bomber that had dropped the first atomic bomb, but also artifacts dramatizing the devastation and human suffering caused by its use, and would have documented the debate at the highest levels of the U.S. government and military in

1945 about whether the new weapon should be deployed. Critics alleged that the exhibition amounted to an apology for the use of the atomic bomb and that it was disrespectful to American veterans. Like the historical standards, the *Enola Gay* exhibit became a political football. Faced with threats from congressmen to cut its funding, the Smithsonian abandoned the original plans for the exhibition and instead simply put a part of the famous plane's fuselage on display, with a minimum of commentary, and the museum's director resigned.

The controversy over the *Enola Gay* exhibition was clearly a defeat for those who thought the American public, or at least its political leaders, were ready to accept the new approaches to the past that had become generally accepted among academic scholars since the 1960s. The outcome of the "war" over the national history standards was less clear cut. In the long run, as the leaders of the history standards task force wrote in an account of the effort that they published under the militant title *History on Trial*, the political firestorm of 1994 did not prevent the gradual adoption of many of the changes in textbooks and curricula they had recommended. The solid factual evidence of the importance of minorities and women in the American past, the obvious changes in the world that required more attention to the histories of Asia, Africa, and Latin America, and the impact of a generation of new approaches to history in colleges and universities could not be ignored.

History wars in the 1990s did not always pit academic historians against politically motivated critics. Controversies about "Afrocentrism" saw mainline university scholars squaring off against opponents who were often also academics, but who claimed to speak for an oppressed subaltern group. "Afrocentric" scholars, often inspired by the work of the Senegalese author Cheikh Anta Diop (1923–1986), denounced what they saw as the historical profession's unjustified neglect of the contributions black Africans had made to world civilization. The publication of Martin Bernal's *Black Athena: The Afroasiatic Roots of Classical Civilization* in 1987 inspired furious controversy. Bernal—who, as it happened, was white—argued that the intellectual achievements of classical Greece were inspired, for the most part, by the earlier civilization of Egypt, and that ancient Egypt should be seen as an African culture. Although most academic scholars agreed that a reexamination of Africa's role in world history was long overdue, many of them accused Bernal of exaggerating and distorting the evidence to make his case. The title of classicist Mary Lefkowitz's polemical response,

Not Out of Africa: How Afrocentrism Became an Excuse to Teach Myth as History, exemplifies the tone of the debate. On the other side, self-identified spokesmen for Afrocentrism, such as Molefi Kete Asante, denounced "all European ideologies from dialectical materialism to postmodernism" as efforts to "protect the ruthless Eurocentric idea of white triumphalism and hegemony."[42] As the editors of a volume about the teaching of history in the United States have written "the passion of such debates suggests that the cultural meaning of knowledge, including knowledge about history, reaches deep into the social psychological life of American society."[43] The history wars of the last decades of the twentieth century often left scholars feeling beleaguered and misunderstood, but these conflicts did demonstrate how much the past still matters in our culture.

Notes

1. Jesse Lemisch, "Towards a Democratic History," (1967) and "The American Revolution Seen from the Bottom Up," in Barton J. Bernstein, ed., *Towards a New Past: Dissenting Essays in American History* (New York: Vintage, 1967), 29.
2. Eugene Genovese, *Roll, Jordan, Roll: The World the Slaves Made* (New York: Vintage, 1973), xvi.
3. Thomas L. Haskell, "The True and Tragical History of *Time on the Cross*," *New York Review of Books* 22 (Oct. 2, 1975), 38.
4. Clifford Geertz, "Thick Description: Toward an Interpretive Theory of Culture," in Geertz, *The Interpretation of Cultures* (New York: Basic Books, 1973), 5; Geertz, "Deep Play: Notes on the Balinese Cockfight," *Daedalus* vol. 134, no. 4 (Fall 2009), 86 (orig. 1972).
5. Hayden White, *Metahistory: The Historical Imagination in Nineteenth-Century Europe* (Baltimore: Johns Hopkins University Press, 1973), 2, 433.
6. Andrew Ezergailis, review of *Metahistory*, *Clio*, 5, no. 2 (1976), 240.
7. Paul Ricoeur, *Time and Narrative*, trans. Kathleen McLaughlin and David Pellauer, 3 vols. (Chicago: University of Chicago Press, 1984–1986).
8. Jean-François Lyotard, *The Post-Modern Condition: A Report on Knowledge*, trans. Beoff Bennington and Brian Massumi (Manchester, UK: Manchester University Press, 1985 (orig. 1979)), 37.

9. Reinhart Koselleck, *Futures Past: On the Semantics of Historical Time*, Keith Tribe, ed., (Cambridge, MA: MIT Press, 1985 (orig. 1979)), 29.

10. William Cronon, *Changes in the Land: Indians, Colonists, and the Ecology of New England* (New York: Hill and Wang, 1983), 170.

11. Robert Darnton, "Revolution sans Revolutionaries," *New York Review of Books*, Jan. 31, 1985, p. 23.

12. Gerda Lerner, "The Challenge of Women's History," (1977) in Gerda Lerner, *The Majority Finds Its Past: Placing Women in History*. Forward by Linda K. Kerber (Chapel Hill: University of North Carolina Press, 2005 (orig. 1979)), 142.

13. Joan Kelly-Gadol, "Did Women Have a Renaissance?" in Renate Bridenthal and Claudia Koonz, eds., *Becoming Visible: Women in European History* (Boston: Houghton Mifflin, 1977), 175–201.

14. Carroll Smith-Rosenberg, "The Female World of Love and Ritual: Relations between Women in Nineteenth-Century America," *Signs* 1 (1975), 1–29.

15. Natalie Zemon Davis, *A Life of Learning*, ACLS Occasional Paper no. 39 (New York: American Council of Learned Societies, 1997), 16.

16. Carolyn Bynum, "Interview," *The Historian* 59 (1996), 8.

17. Smith, *Gender of History*, 238.

18. Michelle Perrot, "L'air du temps," in Pierre Nora, ed., *Essais d'ego-histoire* (Paris: Gallimard, 1991), 292.

19. Edward Said, *Orientalism* (New York: Vintage Books, 1979 (orig. 1978), 3, 109.

20. Marshall Sahlins, *Islands of History* (Chicago: University of Chicago Press, 1985), 34.

21. R. A. Abou-El-Haj, "Historiography in West Asian and North African Studies since Said's *Orientalism*," in Arif Dirlik, Vinay Bahl, and Peter Gran, eds., *History after the Three Worlds: Post-Eurocentric Historiographies* (Lanham, MD: Rowman & Littlefield, 2000), 67.

22. Patrick Manning, *Navigating World History: Historians Create a Global Past* (New York: Palgrave Macmillan, 2003), 53.

23. Richard Price, *First-Time: The Historical Vision of an Afro-American People* (Baltimore: Johns Hopkins University Press, 1983); Richard Price, *Alabi's World* (Baltimore: Johns Hopkins University Press, 1990).

24. Gyan Prakash, "Subaltern Studies as Postcolonial Criticism," *American Historical Review* 89 (1994), 1480.
25. Dipesh Chakrabarty, *Provincializing Europe: Postcolonial Thought and Historical Difference* (Princeton, NJ: Princeton University Press, 2000), 7, 28, 43.
26. For a critical view of Chakrabarty, see Arif Dirlik, "Is There History after Eurocentrism? Globalism, Postcolonialism, and the Disavowal of History," in Dirlik, Bahl, and Gran, eds., *History after the Three Worlds*, 25–47.
27. Paul Fussell, *The Great War and Modern Memory* (New York: Oxford University Press, 1975), 35.
28. Pierre Nora, "General Introduction: Between Memory and History," in Pierre Nora, ed., *Realms of Memory: Rethinking the French Past*, trans. Arthur Goldhammer, 3 vols., 1:4.
29. Annette Wievorka, *L'Ère du témoin* (Paris: Plon, 1998), 150, 165.
30. Alessandro Portelli, *The Death of Luigi Trastulli and Other Stories: Form and Meaning in Oral History* (Albany: State University of New York Press, 1991).
31. Jay Winter, *Remembering War: The Great War Between Memory and History in the Twentieth Century* (New Haven, CT: Yale University Press, 2006), 6.
32. Tony Horwitz, *Confederates in the Attic: Dispatches from the Unfinished Civil War* (New York: Vintage Books 1998), 16.
33. Tony Horwitz, *Confederates in the Attic: Dispatches from the Unfinished Civil War* (New York: Vintage Books, 1998), 16.
34. Novick, *That Noble Dream*, 628.
35. François Dosse, *L'Histoire en miettes. Des "Annales" à la "nouvelle histoire"* (Paris: La Découverte, 1987), 256.
36. Georges Duby, *History Continues*, trans. Arthur Goldhammer (Chicago: University of Chicago Press, 1994), 90.
37. David Lowenthal, *The Past Is a Foreign Country* (Cambridge, UK: Cambridge University Press, 1985), 408.
38. Margaret Thatcher, *The Downing Street Years*, cited in Gary B. Nash, Charlotte Crabtree, and Ross E. Dunn, *History on Trial: Culture Wars and the Teaching of the Past* (New York: Knopf, 1977), 128.
39. Julie Mostov, "The Use and Abuse of History in Eastern Europe: A Challenge for the 1990s," *Constellations* 4 (1998), 376.

40. Gary B. Nash, Charlotte Crabtree, and Ross E. Dunn, *History on Trial: Culture Wars and the Teaching of the Past* (New York: Knopf, 1977), 4, 235.
41. E. D. Hirsch Jr., *Cultural Literacy: What Every American Needs to Know* (Boston: Houghton Mifflin, 1987).
42. Martin Bernal, *Black Athena: The Afroasiatic Roots of Classical Civilization*, 3 vols. (New Brunswick, NJ: Rutgers University Press, 1987; Mary Lefkowitz, *Not Out of Africa: How Afrocentrism Became an Excuse to Teach Myth as History* (New York: Basic Books, 1996); Molefi Kete Asante, *An Afrocentric Manifesto* (Malden, MA: Polity Books, 2007), 107. Two contrasting collections of essays on Bernal's work are Mary R. Lefkowitz and Guy MacLean Rogers, eds., *Black Athena Revisited* (Chapel Hill, NC: University of North Carolina Press, 1996), and Wim van Binsberger, ed., *Black Athena Comes of Age* (Berlin: LIT Verlag, 2011). See also Stephen Howe, *Afrocentrism: Mythical Pasts and Imagined Homes* (London: Verso, 1998).
43. Lloyd Kramer and Donald Reid, "Introduction: Historical Knowledge, Education, and Public Culture," in Lloyd Kramer, Donald Reid, and William L. Barney, eds., *Learning History in America: Schools, Cultures, and Politics* (Minneapolis: University of Minnesota Press, 1994), 5.

CHAPTER 7

History in a New Millennium

A s the year 2000 approached, historians joined journalists and others in pondering the significance of the end of a millennium and the imminent beginning of another. There was a flurry of conferences and publications about what the world had been like in the year 1000 and a good deal of discussion about why human beings attach so much meaning to the ends and beginnings of centuries, considering that the calendar is basically an arbitrary human device for marking the passage of time. The fact that this debate spanned the globe reflected one profound historical change that made the world of 2000 very different from that of the year 1000: as a result of the spread of European civilization, a calendar originally rooted in the beliefs of the Christian religion had become the common framework for the dating of events for almost all of humanity. In the year 1000, and for many centuries thereafter, this would not have been the case: at that time, the Mayans and Aztecs in Central America, the inhabitants of the Muslim world, and the populations of the Chinese Empire all counted the years according to entirely different systems. The kind of universal calendar posited by the philosopher Paul Ricoeur as one of the necessary conditions for the recognition of historical narratives as distinct from other kinds of stories did not yet exist.

A Historical Controversy to End the Millennium

From the point of view of historians in the Western world, the year 2000 was marked particularly by an unusual public courtroom case in which the issue of whether the methods of professional historical scholarship are in fact adequate to establish the truth about the past became a central issue. Judges are rarely called upon to decide controversies about historical claims, but this was an exception. The trial centered around the question of the historical evidence for the occurrence of the Holocaust. Even as documented evidence of the magnitude of the effort to exterminate the Jews of Europe has mounted over the decades, a determined band of neo-Nazi sympathizers has persistently tried to minimize or deny altogether the crimes committed by Hitler and his followers. To justify their efforts, Holocaust negationists have revived skeptical arguments about the unreliability of eyewitnesses that were used in the nineteenth century by the author of *Historic Doubts Relative to Napoleon Buonaparte*, and they have sometimes seized on the assertions about the impossibility of achieving absolute truth in history put forward by postmodernist historical theorists such as Hayden White. The coded language used by the Nazis themselves in documents concerning "the Final Solution" has served the negationists' purposes as well: few of these sources explicitly describe what happened at Auschwitz. In effect, one characteristic of genocidal episodes is that their perpetrators, if they are successful, are in a position to cover up or deny their actions, as the Turkish government has done for nearly a century with regard to the massacre of its Armenian population in 1915. As one scholar has pointed out, what is unusual about the Nazi Holocaust is not that some people try to deny that it happened, but that so many acknowledge that it did take place.[1]

Even before the David Irving trial in 2000, the debate about the status of historical knowledge launched by Hayden White in the early 1970s and the highly politicized "history wars" controversies of the earlier part of the 1990s had lost much of their energy. During the 1990s, a number of historians proposed middle positions between a sweeping postmodern rejection of the whole notion of historical truth and an indefensible positivist assumption that the facts about the past, if properly regarded, would speak for themselves. In a jointly written volume, *Telling the Truth about History* (1994), Joyce Appleby, Lynn Hunt, and Margaret Jacob outlined a position that they called "practical realism" and "qualified objectivity," meant to counter what they saw as the exaggerated skepticism about the possibility of achieving genuine knowledge of the past. Absolutely valid conclusions might be beyond the reach of the historian, they conceded, but this did not mean that any story about the past was as good as any other. Documents and other forms of evidence "constrain those who seek to find out what once took place," they insisted, as did the necessity for historians to follow rules of interpretation shared by their professional community. They did not deny that historians have to reconstruct the past through language, but they argued that language itself is a human invention generated by "contact with the world."[2]

In 1997, Richard J. Evans made a stronger defense of the notion that historical research can produce demonstrably true conclusions. "Objective history in the last analysis is history that is researched and written within the limits placed on the historical imagination by the facts of history and the sources which reveal them, and by the historian's desire to produce a true, fair, and adequate account of the subject under consideration," he wrote in the conclusion to his 1997 book, *In Defense of History*. Evans, writing before the Irving trial, at which he appeared as an expert witness for the defense, already cited the Holocaust as one issue on which historians could not afford to accept postmodernist positions about the impossibility of arriving at objective conclusions about the past. He undoubtedly spoke for most practicing academic historians when he wrote that "history is an empirical discipline, and it is concerned with the content of knowledge rather than its nature."[3] In 1998, perhaps sensing that the tide was turning against postmodernist positions, Keith Jenkins, one of Hayden White's leading disciples, responded by proposing to simply "wave goodbye to history." "There is no reason why . . . postmodernism need drag modernity's very particular and peculiar habits of historicizing time with it," he contended.[4]

The 2000 trial reaffirmed most historians' conviction that the search for historical truth was too important to be abandoned, as Jenkins proposed. The trial resulted from a lawsuit brought by a British author, David Irving, who had built up a certain reputation as a popular historian of the Hitler era, against an American university professor, Deborah Lipstadt. Irving claimed that Lipstadt had libeled him by labeling him a Holocaust denier in her 1993 book, *Denying the Holocaust: The Growing Assault on Truth and Memory*. In her book, Lipstadt had argued that postmodernists, by making it "difficult to talk about the objective truth of a text, legal concept, or even an event," were opening the way to distortions of the past.[5] Lipstadt had also specifically identified Irving as an author who pretended to be an objective scholar while in fact putting forward timeworn negationist arguments. In response to Irving's libel suit, Lipstadt and her publisher assembled a defense team that included many of the leading experts on the history of the Holocaust. On the witness stand and in the lengthy written documents they submitted, these historians showed exactly how scholars interpret historical evidence and demonstrated that it proved the truth of claims Irving had disputed. The trial, which brought out Irving's long-standing association with unsavory neo-Nazi groups, ended with a resounding judgment in favor of Lipstadt: the court came down firmly in support of the proposition that the procedures of historical scholarship could establish dependable knowledge about the past.[6] After decades of dispute among themselves and in various public forums, academic historians breathed a sigh of relief at knowing that they had successfully convinced a respected judge to rule that their professional methods could produce convincing accounts of past events.

Testimony at the Irving trial showed that Irving hardly deserved to be considered a historian. Several other widely publicized scandals in the early 2000s showed that even well-regarded members of the profession had violated its ethical rules. Among the cases that received such publicity in recent decades was that of Michael Bellesiles, accused of inaccurately describing or possibly inventing data to support his argument about the historical origins of the Second Amendment to the U.S. Constitution. Bellesiles's book was withdrawn by its publisher and he lost his academic position. Two prominent popular historians, Stephen Ambrose and Doris Kearns Goodwin, were blamed for plagiarism—copying passages from other historians' work without giving them proper credit. Another popular historian, Joseph Ellis, who also holds an academic position, ran into trouble for telling invented stories about his personal past to his students: he falsely claimed, for example, to have served in the U.S. military during the Vietnam War.[7] To outsiders, such outrage among historians about what may seem like minor sins— the presence or absence of quotation marks around a sentence, for instance—may seem excessive. To most professional historians, however, misrepresentation of sources and plagiarism are grave matters. Despite the peer review system, the edifice of scholarly research depends heavily on the integrity of its practitioners. If violators are not severely chastised, our discipline's claim to produce reliable knowledge about the past will be undermined, and all historians will be affected. The strong response among historians to these ethical lapses was an affirmation of their shared belief that members of the profession have an obligation to follow its guidelines.

The verdict in the Irving trial reassured historians that postmodern critiques had not in fact undermined their discipline's ability to establish certain truths about the past, and methodological disputes shifted to other areas. The idea that humankind might have reached "the end of history," as Francis Fukuyama had predicted after 1989, soon gave way to questions about how history should be written in the face of the new conflicts and crises that beset the world after the turn of the millennium. The spectacular terrorist attack on the World Trade Center and the Pentagon on September 11, 2001, the steady rise of China as an economic and military power, the world economic crisis of 2008, and the "Arab Spring" of 2011 and its violent aftermath all demonstrated that there was still no worldwide consensus on Western-style democracy and capitalism. The election of an African American president in the United States in 2008 and the rapidly developing movement for gay rights, on the other hand, showed that democracy itself was still capable of producing historical surprises. Increasing concern about the global effects of climate change led some historians, such as Dipesh Chakrabarty, to argue that, far from having reached a stable state, humanity had plunged the planet into an entirely new and dangerous "Anthropocene Epoch," in which human activity has come to be the dominant influence on the environment, and that historians needed to react by focusing on this problem, even if it means turning away from issues such as the legacy of colonialism. Chakrabarty has called for scholarship that would "put global histories of capital in conversation with the species history of humans."[8]

History in the Internet Era

The most significant historiographical developments in the years since 2000 have not been shifts in the balance between the various forms of history, but rather a new awareness of the importance of changes in the ways in which historical knowledge is communicated. No new methodological approach to historical research has as much impact on history in the past two decades as the development of the Internet. Many of the liveliest historiographical debates of recent years have had to do not with history as it is recorded in books and scholarly articles, but with the status of history on film, the representation of the past in museums, and the potentialities of other media, such as interactive video games, for changing the way we understand the past. Together, these developments are changing every aspect of history: methods of research, ways of teaching, and the connection between historical specialists and the general public.

The rapidity with which the availability of personal computers and the growth of the Internet have transformed historians' practices is undoubtedly difficult to appreciate for those who have grown up, like today's students, surrounded by digital devices. Scholars of my own generation, who began our careers taking notes on index cards, writing on typewriters, and communicating via letters, are more conscious of having lived through a continuous process of change, one that shows no sign of slowing down. The possibility of communication from one computer to another began to change historians' worlds toward the end of the 1980s, with the development of email. Suddenly, it was possible to exchange ideas with distant colleagues in "real time," instead of relying on the postal service. The possibility of sending the same message instantly to many people led to the creation of discussion lists for scholars with common interests. Today, H-Net, based at Michigan State University, maintains over a hundred such lists for historians in different fields, some of which have thousands of subscribers. On them, participants can share new ideas with colleagues, announce publications, organize conferences, and post questions in the hope that someone else on the list will know the answer. (www.h-net.org/) Many historians' lists post and archive book reviews; H-France, the list for French historians, goes further by organizing "forums" with multiple reviews of particularly important new publications, reviewing films of historical interest, and even posting podcasts of sessions at professional conferences (www.h-france.net/).[9]

Over the course of the 1990s, the Internet became steadily more versatile and more and more important in the lives of historians. In 1993, the World Wide Web, previously accessible only to a small number of scientists, was opened to the general public. Scholars soon realized that it was now possible to post source documents online, where they could be accessed by anyone else with a computer connection. By bringing together documents from different locations, websites can even create "archives" that do not exist outside of cyberspace. One example is the "Papers of the War Department" virtual archive: as its creators explain, the files of the U.S. War Department for its early years were destroyed in a fire in 1800. By bringing together 55,000 documents scattered in libraries and archives all over the country, this website strives to recreate an equivalent for this lost body of sources (http://wardepartmentpapers.org/). Early websites could only store text files, not images, and it took the development of web browsers to make it possible to find information easily. Other developments have followed in a steady cascade, so that today it is easily possible to access not only textual documents and images but also sound recordings and video clips, integrate them into a single presentation, and share the results with an audience all over the world. It is also now possible, thanks to the development of the "smartphone," to access information anywhere and at any time. Increased access to online information raises problems and also creates new possibilities. Plagiarism, for example, can now be accomplished by simply copying and pasting text found on line, although sophisticated search programs also make it easier for teachers to detect. Teachers giving examinations now have to ask themselves whether they can really be sure that students are not able to access information from outside.

Computers and the Internet have already changed every aspect of how historians do their work, and there is no doubt that even more changes lie ahead of us. Compiling a bibliography on a research topic used to mean hours of paging through printed subject indexes; now it means plugging a few keywords into a search engine. Many of the rare books that historians could only find in major research libraries can now be accessed online and read in the convenience of one's favorite armchair. Historians used to take notes on small index cards. Cards could be easily sorted by subject when one was ready to start writing, but they were hard to carry around and difficult to duplicate. Now, the smart historical researcher uses a note-taking program and stores the results in the "cloud," where they can be accessed on multiple devices. Research notes and drafts of writing can easily be shared with collaborators, making joint projects much more feasible than they used to be. Some older historians still find it easier to write first drafts by hand, but with the arrival of a new generation of students who did not learn cursive handwriting as children, almost all historical writing is now done directly on computers.

The scholarly journals in which academic historians publish their specialized research still exist, but many of the smaller ones have already stopped publishing on paper and appear only in online form. This has made the experience of reading articles different from what it used to be. Nowadays, most readers go directly to specific items that interest them; they no longer flip through a whole issue or volume of a journal, perhaps stopping to read something they hadn't originally been looking for. Computerized indexing makes it easier to find scattered articles on one's specific topic in many different journals, but when they are read piecemeal in this fashion, periodicals no longer function to create scholarly communities of readers with shared interests. Monographs, too, are increasingly available as "e-books" rather than in physical form. Although the Internet has the potential to make research more accessible, these changes raise serious questions about how the costly processes of peer review and editing can be financed if journals can no longer depend on income from subscriptions and publishers can no longer count on selling substantial numbers of their titles.

Computers and the Internet are transforming history teaching just as rapidly as they are changing research and publication. It is the rare history teacher who heads to class nowadays without a PowerPoint presentation; the old days of putting up a lecture outline on a chalkboard are gone, along with the chalk. With the development of online courses and "flipped" classrooms, even the notion of "heading to class" is being transformed. Students expect class information, assignments, and grades to be posted online, and when they are given research exercises, they automatically look for information on the Web rather than in the library. In classrooms equipped with screens, instructors can tap into a vast range of materials and integrate them directly into discussions. Like instructors in other disciplines, historians are experimenting with various kinds of online teaching methods. Lectures may be recorded as podcasts, so that students can listen to them at their own convenience, and in-person discussion classes may be augmented with or even replaced by online "chat" sessions. Faculty anxiously speculate about whether their courses will be replaced by MOOCs, "massive open online courses" transmitted over the Internet. Such courses might allow students from many campuses to learn about subjects not offered at their own schools, but they also raise the prospect of a world in which one star professor becomes the only authority on subjects such as the French Revolution or the Meiji Restoration, with students turning in essays to be graded by poorly paid adjuncts or even by computers. Like colleagues in other humanities fields, most historians continue to believe that there is something irreplaceable about the direct contact between teacher and students that occurs in the traditional classroom. In a world in which students can easily surf the Web during classes, however, instructors must find creative ways to keep them actively engaged.

Although history instructors do worry about losing students' attention in class, the teaching resources available on the Internet are too valuable to be ignored. The ubiquitous, "crowd-sourced" Wikipedia has largely replaced printed reference works; professors have come to rely on it as heavily as students, and comparisons with traditional encyclopedias show that it is generally at least as reliable, although its bias in favor of "the conventional and accepted wisdom on a topic" means that it often fails to reflect new research findings.[10] Students can be assigned to use the sources posted online on sites such as "Valley of the Shadow," a trove of information on the Civil War created by Edward Ayers and his collaborators that includes letters and diaries, newspaper articles, data from census and tax records, maps, and images, as well as a variety of tools for manipulating the data (www.valley.lib.virginia.edu). The Center for History and New Media at George Mason University in Virginia has been a pioneer in exploring the possibilities of Web-based teaching and research. Founded in 1994, its purpose is to use "digital media and computer technology to democratize history—to incorporate multiple voices, reach diverse audiences, and encourage popular participation in presenting and preserving the past." The Center, whose website receives 20 million visitors a year, has created online resources of its own and also gives users links to other sites and online resources (www.chnm.gmu.edu). Major research libraries and history museums have created their own online libraries and archives. Among those frequently used by students, teachers, and scholars are the Library of Congress's "American Memory" website, which offers direct access to such resources as the George Washington papers and "Voices from the Days of Slavery," audio interviews with former slaves conducted in the twentieth century (memory.loc.gov), and the site of the U.S. Holocaust Memorial Museum (www.ushmm.org).

In *Digital History: A Guide to Gathering, Preserving, and Presenting the Past on the Web* (2005), Daniel J. Cohen and Roy Rosenzweig, two of the creators of the Center for History and New Media, list the advantages of the Web as "accessibility, flexibility, diversity, manipulability, interactivity, and hypertextuality (or nonlinearity)." Capacity is the ability to store enormous amounts of data cheaply. By flexibility, the authors mean possibilities such as linking together various kinds of information about documents posted online. The Web has made it possible for many more people to contribute to historical discussions; as they note, "the number of authors of history web pages is likely greater than the number of authors of history books," and no special credentials are required to create a webpage. The Web facilitates new ways of using or manipulating historical data, such as word searches, and hypertextuality, the capability of "moving through narratives or data in undirected and multiple ways" and providing links that allow users to explore alternative possibilities, theoretically enabling historians to approach the past in entirely new ways.[11]

History has benefitted greatly from the new capabilities created by computers and the Internet. More people have more access to more historical information than ever before. Nevertheless, there are also some costs associated with the discipline's entry into this brave new world. At the same time as the Web facilitates the work of professional historians, it also has the potential to undermine the elaborate system of assessment and peer review on which academic historical scholarship has depended since the time of Ranke. Identifying herself as a "neo-Luddite," a critic of radical change, Gertrude Himmelfarb warned in 1996 that "the Internet does not distinguish between the true and the false, the important and the trivial, the enduring and the ephemeral . . . Every source appearing on the screen has the same weight and credibility as every other; no authority is 'privileged' over any other."[12] Another scholar who compared her own work with sources about her subject available on the Web noted that "professional historians . . . write history that contributes to a larger body of knowledge. Each article and monograph must clarify how it adds to the developing narrative patterns. By contrast, amateur historians write about isolated topics" and do not feel obliged to acknowledge other perspectives on their subject.[13] Sometimes, materials posted on the Web as historical are not only lacking in context but also completely false or misleading. Negationist groups that deny the reality of the Holocaust, for example, have created numerous webpages, and historians teaching the subject must warn students against making uncritical use of such materials, which may not be immediately recognizable as neo-Nazi propaganda.

Another concern about online historical materials is that of access. Electronic versions of scholarly journals and many invaluable data bases, such as the Readex "Early American Newspapers" collection, require expensive subscriptions. In practice, many of these materials are only available to users affiliated with major research universities, creating a two-class system in which some students and scholars have research opportunities from which others are shut out.

Whatever the pros and cons of the move to the Internet may be, however, there is no doubt that its existence has already changed historical practices in fundamental ways. Historians are notoriously bad at predicting the future, and it is difficult to guess which of the innovations of the past two decades will turn out to be the most significant. It is certain, however, that the historians of the future will research, communicate their findings, and teach in very different ways from their predecessors and that these changes in practices are bound to have an influence on the ways we understand the past.

History beyond the Printed Page

The development of the Internet has changed history in many ways. Nevertheless, the majority of the material about history available on the Web is still presented in the form of text, and it is by no means certain that Internet users looking for historical information have really abandoned the habit of reading in a linear fashion for the eager pursuit of hyperlinks. One of the major developments in history at the beginning of the twenty-first century, however, is the increasing prominence of nontextual representations of the past. Historical museums, historical films, graphic art, and even video games with historical settings are now being taken seriously as ways of communicating knowledge about the past and not merely as forms of amusement. As the historiographical debates that dominated discussions of written history from the 1970s to the 1990s have petered out, some of the energy that fueled them has migrated to thinking about nontextual forms of history.

Robert Rosenstone's exploration of the theoretical issues raised by the presentation of history through film are often relevant to these other media as well. What Rosenstone says about visual representations of history, in film and on television, namely that "to leave them out of the equation when we think of the meaning of the past is to condemn ourselves to ignore the way a huge segment of the population has come to understand the events and people that comprise history," certainly applies as well to museums and video games. So does his insistence that other media cannot be evaluated in the same way as traditional printed texts. History on film, he argues, must be judged on its own terms. "This visual form of historical thinking should not and cannot be judged by the criteria we apply to the history that is produced on the page."[14] Taking film versions of history seriously, Rosenstone recognizes, represents a major change in thinking for academic historians. He likes to quote a letter written in 1935 by a distinguished university professor of history to the president of the Metro–Goldwyn–Mayer film company, complaining about the historical inaccuracies in its productions and urging that "no picture of a historical nature ought to be offered to the public until a reputable historian has had a chance to criticize and revise it."[15]

In Rosenstone's view, this type of criticism, still common among scholars, is misguided, and literal accuracy cannot be the principal criterion for evaluating historical films. "The camera's need to fill out the specifics of a particular historical scene, or to create a coherent (and moving) visual sequence, will always ensure large doses of invention in the historical film," he writes. "All films will include fictional people or invented elements of character." Incidents also have to be invented, "to keep the story moving, to maintain intensity of feeling, to simplify complexity of events into plausible dramatic structure that will fit within filmic time constraints." Summing up his argument, he concludes that "on the screen, history must be fictional in order to be true!"[16] Nevertheless, he insists, not only can history be represented on film, but also film can communicate some aspects of the past in ways that prose cannot. "This new historical past on film is potentially much more complex than any written text, for on the screen, several things can occur simultaneously—image, sound, language, even text— elements that support and work against each other to render a realm of meaning as different from written history as written was from oral history," Rosenstone argues. History on film is "so different that it allows us to speculate that the visual media may represent a major shift in consciousness about how we think about the past."[17] Not surprisingly, Rosenstone identifies himself as a postmodernist historian, often citing the arguments of Hayden White. Indeed, in the context of discussions of film, White's emphasis on the underlying narrative structures in historical accounts has a plausibility that is not always so evident with respect to written texts.

Rosenstone's essays have done much to make historians take film seriously as a medium for the communication of knowledge about the past, but his eagerness to embrace even movies that flagrantly contradict established facts as "historical" bothers many scholars. Directors of recent blockbuster films such as Steven Spielberg's "Lincoln" (2012) and Ava Duvernay's "Selma" (2014), both of which won major awards, have defended their decisions to alter certain historical episodes to heighten their stories' intensity or to emphasize what they regard as the essence of the past. Natalie Davis, who served as historical advisor in the making of a highly regarded film about life in sixteenth-century France, "The Return of Martin Guerre," has argued that filmmakers should help viewers understand the difficulties of depicting the truth about the past, rather than simply creating narratives that seem to be beyond contestation. "Films can do much more to pose questions to their viewers about history-making and history-knowing" she writes. She suggests several ways in which filmmakers can let their audiences understand what sources they have drawn on, what liberties they may have taken with them, and what alternative ways of interpreting the stories they tell exist, without interrupting the flow of their story or putting a solemn "talking head" on screen to bestow an official seal of historical approval.[18]

Presentations of history on television share some characteristics with historical films, but there are significant differences between the two media as well. Documentary television miniseries, shown in episodes, can be much longer and comprehensive than films meant to be shown in theaters, and there are some techniques, such as the zeroing in on details of still photographs and the presentation of commentaries by scholars, that are frequent on television but rarely used in films. Film scholar Pierre Sorlin has written that the "fixedness" of photographs "and the time necessary to fully explore them are at odds with the permanent mobility characteristic of moving pictures."[19] Few professional historians have had anything positive to say about the ubiquitous History Channel, sometimes derided as the "Hitler Channel" because of its endless reruns of old documentaries on World War II. Nevertheless, its programs are undoubtedly one of the main ways in which general audiences and especially young Americans now encounter stories about the past.

Two dominant figures in the presentation of serious history on television in recent decades are the American documentary-maker Ken Burns and the transatlantic historian and media personality Simon Schama. Burns's ten-hour series on the Civil War, aired on public television in 1990, was an enormous success: the first two episodes alone attracted 23 million viewers. His subsequent projects, including "Baseball" and "Jazz," led one academic scholar to call Burns "the most famous historian in the country." Burns has enlisted professors to help in planning his projects and has featured them, along with prominent popular historians such as David McCullough and Shelby Foote, on the screen, but he is not intimidated by their authority. He told one interviewer that he was proud of his role in "breaking the stranglehold the academicians exercised over this discipline for the last hundred years." The impact of his projects has been amplified by the sale of books and DVDs of his productions, and his concern with reaching a broad audience has led him to speak in the language of commercial marketing. An academic who worked as an advisor on one of Burns's projects remembered being put off by "the presence of high-velocity words like *agony* and *horror* and *gargantuan* and *fantastic* and *colossal*" in the script, although he was impressed by the emotional force of the final result.[20]

Unlike Burns, Simon Schama is a professional scholar who has held positions at Harvard and Columbia University. From an early stage in his career, however, Schama has been interested in testing the limits of academic history and reaching out to broader audiences. Whereas other historians, in the wake of Hayden White's challenge, debated whether history shared the characteristics of fiction, in 1991 Schama produced a book, *Dead Certainties* (*Unwarranted Speculations*), in which he deliberately introduced made-up dialogue and incidents into his reconstruction of the past.[21] This particular venture was not well received by Schama's academic peers, but he has been more successful as the narrator of a number of television documentaries, including "A History of Britain" in 2000 and "The Story of the Jews," aired in 2014, while also authoring a number of successful books. Like Burns, Schama has been criticized for oversimplifying complex historical issues; like Burns also, he has unquestionably succeeded in bringing the past to life for audiences of a size that ordinary scholars can never hope to reach. Schama makes no secret of the fact that his programs convey a highly personal view of his subjects: unlike Burns, he appears on screen in his documentaries, and in the first episode of his series on Jewish history, he is shown presiding over his own Passover Seder. As one critic has written, although Schama has certainly demonstrated the potential of television for creating public interest in history, he and other program hosts have also made themselves into "culturally- and economically-constructed human commodities" who are "famous for their fame as much as for their profession."[22] Like David Hume in the 1700s, Schama's success has made him "opulent," but it also raises questions about when considerations of marketing can begin to overwhelm other issues in the presentation of the past.

The historical museum is another medium for the representation of the past that has increasingly become a focus of historiographical debates. If films give viewers the impression of watching past events unfold before their eyes, museums give them the opportunity to view objects that embody the past. In their most traditional form, historical museums may simply put these objects on display, with identifying labels, and leave it to visitors to decide for themselves what meaning they convey. For many years, for example, the Smithsonian Museum of American History in Washington, D.C., exhibited gowns owned by presidents' wives in its First Ladies exhibit, telling viewers only the year in which each dress had been made and who wore it. Increasingly, however, museum curators have seen it as their function to integrate their museum's treasures into meaningful historical narratives. In its current arrangement, the Smithsonian First Ladies exhibition informs visitors about the ways in which each of these women influenced public life during her husband's administration; it also comments on how changes in women's clothing have reflected changing styles of art and design.

Because they are usually public institutions, museums are often at the center of conflicts about how controversial aspects of the past should be represented, as the highly politicized dispute over the Air and Space Museum's Hiroshima exhibition in 1994 shows. Sometimes these are arguments between museum professionals who want to convey the findings of academic scholarship to the public and interest groups defending their particular vision of the past, but sometimes they are clashes between rival groups of experts. Museum curators, for example, are divided about whether historical museums should feature exhibits that try to reconstruct whole environments from the past, such as pioneer cabins, even if this means mixing authentic artifacts from the past with modern replicas, or whether they should display only historic objects, emphasizing that the incompleteness of the historical record is part of its "pastness" and challenging viewers to use their imaginations to fill in the missing context. Despite controversies such as that over the Hiroshima exhibit, museums in Western countries have become more willing to present visitors with alternative interpretations of the past; indeed, one criticism of the Smithsonian's Museum of American History is that it offers so many conflicting perspectives on the past that visitors have a hard time extracting any coherent message at all from the exhibits. Elsewhere, however, museum exhibits often insist on guiding viewers to conclusions that clearly serve political purposes, even if those purposes have changed over time. In China, where the main historical museums in the capital city of Beijing have been redesigned numerous times to coincide with shifting political winds since the death of Mao Zedong in 1976, the one constant, according to a Western scholar, has been the insistence that each version presents "the one and true account of China's modern past."[23]

A major milestone in the design of historical museums was the creation of the U.S. Holocaust Memorial Museum, also located in Washington, which opened to the public in 1993. Historians' understanding of the complexities involved in museum and exhibit design has been greatly advanced by Edward Linenthal's *Preserving Memory: The Struggle to Create America's Holocaust Museum* (2001), a detailed account of the many questions that had to be addressed in the institution's creation. As Linenthal shows, every decision, from the location of the museum just off the Washington Mall, the center of American historical memory, to the design of the building and the choice of which objects and photographs should be on display, had consequences for the way in which visitors experience the story of the Holocaust. As *Preserving Memory* demonstrates, the design of the museum involved many people other than professional historians. Architects, curators, and exhibition specialists, politicians and representatives of various interest groups, and above all, Holocaust survivors, represented by Elie Wiesel, among others, had their own points of view and concerns that had to be taken into account. The museum exhibit that viewers see is the result of long and involved debates that brought profound historiographical issues to the surface.

The Holocaust Museum has some unique features, but the issues raised in Linenthal's book are also pertinent to other historical museums, many of which have also been the subject of major controversies. Museums devoted to Native American history and culture have been major sites of contestation in recent decades. "Museums can be very painful sites for Native peoples, as they are intimately tied to the colonization process," one recent scholar has written.[24] Sometimes created more than a century ago by whites who wanted to preserve the memory of what they regarded as a "vanishing race," such museums now seek to play a positive role in communicating the fact that Native Americans are very much a part of present-day American life. Older exhibits that included human remains have disappeared, and Native American groups have been given a much greater role in drafting text for displays. At the same time, however, to attract visitors, these museums feel pressure to offer displays that may reflect older stereotypes about Indians, even if they try to educate viewers on their significance as seen by the people who created them.

Native Americans are certainly not the only group for whom historical museums have become an important way of preserving and communicating their own past, both as a way of defining a group identity and as a way of claiming a place in larger national historical narratives. Almost every American city has at least one "house museum," often located in the former home of a historically significant resident. The Rhode Island Historical Society's Museum of Work and Culture in Woonsocket, Rhode Island, stands out for its presentation of the experiences of the region's factory workers, most of them French-speaking immigrants from the Canadian province of Quebec, in the late nineteenth and early twentieth centuries. At a time when labor and social history has been somewhat in eclipse in academic scholarship, this museum, like the more ambitious People's History Museum in Manchester, England, has tried to counter this trend. Another example of a historical museum that serves as a show-window for a group whose experiences have received little scholarly attention is the U.S. Army Women's Museum in Fort Lee, Virginia, which combines a traditional museum function—the memorialization of military service to the country—with an innovative focus on gender as it traces the participation of women in the American military, from the cases of soldiers who concealed their sex to serve in the Revolutionary War and the Civil War through the history of the Army Women's Corps in the early twentieth century and the progressive integration of women into the army in more recent decades. Like many historical museums dedicated to rarely studied groups, the Army Women's Museum has become a depository for artifacts and documents, most of them donated by former women soldiers, and it encourages scholars to make use of its resources.

Visitors come to the U.S. Holocaust Memorial Museum expecting a serious educational experience, and specialized museums such as the Museum of Work and Culture and the Army Women's Museum make no secret of their pedagogical intentions. Historical theme parks that mix entertainment with information raise other questions, especially if they are run as money-making enterprises. In the United States, one of the most important of these theme parks is Colonial Williamsburg, which occupies an entire district of Williamsburg, Virginia, and is vital to the city's economy. Originally established in the 1930s by John D. Rockefeller Jr., a millionaire with a passion for historical preservation, Colonial Williamsburg at first openly celebrated the values of Virginia's eighteenth-century planter elite. Originally, the exhibits said nothing about the slaves who had made up half of the city's population in that era. In the Cold War years, its supporters saw Colonial Williamsburg as a way of teaching visitors patriotic values. In the 1970s, "slavery was discovered at Williamsburg," as one scholar has put it, and the presentation of the past offered to visitors was changed, but only up to a point: "Slave culture was one thing, slave revolts were another."[25] In more recent years, Colonial Williamsburg has tried to make its treatment of slavery more comprehensive, but these efforts have often encountered obstacles. A reenactment of a slave auction set off protests, and scenes in which actors playing slaves are mistreated sometimes provoke visitors to interfere. The museum has not always been able to find black actors willing to perform the roles of slaves. "You interview people, and they'll say: 'I just can't do it. I can't put on that costume,'" a museum official told a reporter in 2013.[26]

Whereas historical films and historical museums have been around for some time, video games with historical settings are a more recent development. As in the case of film, postmodernism has made it easier for some scholars to envisage this medium as a way of communicating certain truths about history. Just as Robert Rosenstone has argued that filmmakers necessarily have to take certain liberties with the past to produce representations that work as films, enthusiasts for historical games have emphasized that games do have to be fun to play if they are going to succeed and that the historical accuracy of their settings and narrative structure may take second place to engaging their users. The most important historical lesson that games can play, according to their advocates, is "the potential to understand history as a process." As one of their supporters puts it, "by constructing a virtual past and granting the player agency within it, video games have become the ideal medium for teaching the lesson of contingency."[27] Players of games such as "Civilization" are able to experiment with different decisions and see what the consequences of their actions are. Instead of being passive consumers of representations of the past, like book readers and film viewers, video-game players take an active role in constructing notions of the past.

Although most of the new ways of presenting history that have affected historiographical discussion in recent years have abandoned the printed page, comic art has shown that there are new possibilities even in the traditional format of the book. No work in this form has had more impact on history, as well as on several other fields, than Art Spiegelman's *Maus*, originally published in 1992. *Maus* uses comic-art techniques to tell the story of Spiegelman's father's ordeal during the Holocaust and simultaneously the story of how Spiegelman was affected by his father's narrative. It may seem odd to consider a book in which the Jewish victims of the Holocaust are depicted as cartoon mice and the Germans as cats as a serious effort at representing history. Spiegelman's intentions are serious, however, and he has used the comic medium as a way of conveying a historical story in ways that words alone cannot do, as he has explained in his own commentary on his work, *MetaMaus*. His approach "allowed me to approach otherwise unsayable things," he writes. "What makes *Maus* thorny is actually what allows it to be useful as a real 'teaching tool.' "[28] The special power of comic art is that its panels simultaneously communicate through words and pictures, and the interplay between the two is often more expressive than either one on its own. Although Spiegelman's use of cartoon-style animals takes his work out of the realm of realism, it has come to be recognized as a powerful evocation of the Holocaust and is frequently used as a reading in courses on the subject.

Larry Gonick is another comic artist who has employed that medium for historical purposes. His *Cartoon History of the Universe* and similar books about American and world history remind "serious" historians that humor can be an effective way of communicating historical ideas. Although his books are meant to be entertaining—"How come it's OK for a teacher to be funny, but it's not OK for a textbook to be funny?" he asks—they are also a serious project, which took him some thirty years to complete. His narrative begins with the creation of the universe, thus connecting natural and human history, and goes to the present. The historical volumes present a global history, deftly integrating Asia, Africa, and Latin America into the narrative. Gonick sees comic art as having some unique qualities that enable it to communicate aspects of history that conventional prose cannot. "Cartoons can put badly-needed life back into history," he told an interviewer. "There's no getting around it: historical figures are mostly dead. And traditional textbooks mostly leave them that way . . . Comics can restore our identification with past actors as living, feeling beings like ourselves." He has also argued that drawings can show "a wealth of historical graphic detail such as costumes, landscape, and architecture that isn't readily conveyed in text or even a normal illustrated book."[29] Academic historians can become irritated with the many minor errors of fact that litter Gonick's visual narrative, but he has something to teach us about getting readers interested in the drama of the past. Some academic historians are now starting to collaborate with professional graphic artists to exploit the medium's possibilities for engaging readers. In recent years, three scholars—Trevor Getz, Rafe Blaufarb, and Ronald Schechter—have worked with the artist Liz Clarke to produce "graphic histories" that combine historical narrative, illustrations, and selections from archival documents. Getz's *Abina and the Important Men* (2011), a microhistory based on the court case brought by an African woman seeking her freedom in 1876, has won widespread praise.

New Directions in Historical Scholarship

Even in a digital age in which history now comes to us in many other forms, it is still a dizzying experience to visit the book exhibit at a major historical convention, such as the annual meeting of the American Historical Association, and see the hundreds of new scholarly publications that have appeared in a single year. Just as there is much concern about the future of traditional employment in universities, there is much anxiety among historians about the future of the system of peer-reviewed scholarly publication on which academic history has come to depend, but for the moment, there is little indication that the rate at which new history books are appearing has diminished. Historians continue to practice all of the many varieties of scholarship we have discussed in earlier chapters, including political, economic, social, and cultural history. The bicentennial of the outbreak of World War I in

2014 has revived interest in diplomatic and military history, with a number of new monographs on the sequence of events that led to the start of hostilities and on the many ways in which the conflict affected the populations of the countries that were drawn into it.

The years since 2000 have not been marked by any transformations of history as profound or controversial as those that resulted from the linguistic and cultural turns of the 1970, the rise of feminism, and the challenge of postcolonialism, but the discipline continues to absorb new perspectives. One important tendency has certainly been an increased emphasis on history with a "world" or "global" perspective. Patrick Manning, one of the leading American proponents of this development, defines world history as "studies of the past working from the postulate of connection rather than the postulate of autonomy." What this means continues to be debated. Is a work of history "global" because it deals with phenomena that affect the entire planet, such as climate change, the spread of diseases, or trade networks? Does global history necessarily require the mastery of historical data from different countries or continents, or can it mean focusing on the history of one nation's relations with other parts of the world? Is the historical era we now live in unique because of the degree to which different parts of the world are now linked together, or does history suggest that such linkages were already important in previous epochs? This is a point Manning emphasizes when he says that the distinctive contribution historians can make to the understanding of globalization is to show that its present-day manifestations are "less . . . a radical disjuncture than . . . a set of recent nuances in a global pattern of fluctuations and gradual transformations."[30]

Global history remains a challenging field. Global historians often have difficulty fitting themselves into the paradigm of scholarly historical research, going back to Ranke's day, that dictates that the historian should work directly with archival sources. Few historians have the command of multiple languages or the time and energy that would be necessary to truly do such research in more than a few countries. Global history is thus more of a teaching field, especially at the undergraduate level, than a domain for original research, and many of the books published under this rubric are collections of articles by scholars working on different parts of the world. Nevertheless, some ambitious scholars have made efforts to treat significant aspects of the global past, although they necessarily must rely heavily on other historians' more specialized work. C. A. Bayly's *The Birth of the Modern World, 1780–1914*, published in 2004, has been one influential example. Bayly has explicitly challenged the postmodern aversion to grand narratives, arguing that they are necessary if a historian is to make sense of so much data and render it comprehensible to readers. Timothy Brook's *Vermeer's Hat* (2008), on the other hand, has demonstrated that the microhistorical approach can be adapted to global history. Tracing the origins of objects depicted in one of Dutch artist Jan Vermeer's detailed paintings from the seventeenth century, Brook shows that the world in that era was already tightly interconnected.[31] Even historiography has taken a global turn, with Daniel Woolf's *A Global History of History* (2011), which brings a global perspective to the subject, setting the Greek and Roman heritage that led eventually to modern Western history-writing in the context of other traditions of writing about the past.[32]

Global history is closely related to transnational history, another way of challenging the hegemony of national frameworks in studying the past. Transnational historical projects stress the interaction between events in two or more countries, but do not necessarily focus on issues that can be studied on a planetary scale. A transnational historical project may even treat events in the interior of a single nation if they have clear links to other societies. Thus Patricia Nelson Limerick, a leading exponent of the "new western history," which has overturned old assumptions about the history of the western United States, sees her work as adding a transnational dimension to regional history by emphasizing that the American West was not just the edge of white settlement spreading from the east, but "one of the great meeting zones of the planet," where whites, Hispanics, Native Americans, and African Americans came together to create a new society.[33] Her work exemplifies another American historian's call for "rethinking and deprovincializing the narrative of American history" to "integrate the stories of American history with other, larger stories from which, with a kind of continental self-sufficiency, the United States has isolated itself."[34] Perhaps the most successful example of transnational history in recent decades has been the field of Atlantic history, which one scholar has defined as the study of "the creation, destruction, and re-creation of communities as a result of the movement, across and around the Atlantic basin, of people, commodities, cultural practices, and values."[35] Bringing together the history of Europe, the Americas, and

Africa, giving a central position to the history of slavery, and crossing the borders between the different European empires, Atlantic history has also been highly interdisciplinary, attracting practitioners of every variety of scholarship, from economic history to cultural studies. Courses on Atlantic history have become standard at most American colleges and universities.

Although global history stresses interconnections between civilizations but usually accepts the notion that history begins only with the emergence of written records, Daniel Smail and his collaborators have challenged historians to think in terms of what he calls "deep history," which means extending our sense of the historical past to include much earlier periods of human existence that are normally labeled "prehistory." According to Smail, when scholars broke away from a chronology of the past based on the Bible and accepted the idea that the world and human beings had come into existence many thousands or millions of years ago, a development he calls the "time revolution" of the mid-nineteenth century, historians nevertheless continued to define their domain as covering only the six thousand or so years since the development of the first civilizations that used writing. He sees this tendency as a disguised survival of an essentially religious worldview, one that still wants to deny that "humans are part of nature, and that human systems are natural systems."[36] Aspects of the deep history approach can also be found in the movement for "big history," a label popularized by David Christian, author of *Maps of Time: An Introduction to Big History.* The proponents of "big history" want to present the human past as part of a larger "unifying narrative of life on earth," and even as part of the history of the cosmos. This idea has attracted the support of the billionaire Bill Gates, who is trying to persuade American schools to introduce the approach in their curricula.[37]

To practice deep history, Smail acknowledges, we will have to give up the insistence that historical narratives must be able to give the events they cover precise dates and that we must be able to identify specific individuals as historical actors in the past. "The study of deep history emphasizes trends and processes more than events and persons." Historians must also broaden their notion of what constitutes historical evidence and be willing to rely on archeological data and findings from some of the other natural sciences. "History can be written from every type of trace, from the memoir to the bone fragment and the blood type," he insists.[38] In addition to enriching our picture of the distant human past, the advocates of deep history contend that it gives us a broader perspective on the history of more recent periods. Two examples in the volume Smail co-edited with Andrew Shryock in 2011 are the sections on food, which uses biological and archeological evidence to point to the importance of meat protein in the human diet from the origin of our species to the present, and the chapter on human migration, which shows that a phenomenon often considered part of modern history can in fact be traced back thousands of years. Many of these findings reflect the use of DNA evidence, which has only become available in the past few decades. This is allowing scholars to give a much more detailed account of when and how the practice of agriculture spread from the ancient Middle East to the continent of Europe, for example, and has challenged the notion that this process involved the displacement of hunter-gatherers by settlers from outside, as opposed to the adoption of new methods by members of existing populations.

Evidence from DNA has had an impact on the understanding of more modern history as well; probably the most widely known example is the use of genetic testing to establish with near certainty that Thomas Jefferson had children with one of his slaves, Sally Hemings, a story that circulated during Jefferson's lifetime but that historians and biographers had long rejected. Annette Gordon-Reed's publications on this subject have led to a considerable change in how historians write about Jefferson's relations with blacks and slavery. Among other things, Gordon-Reed's work is an example of a third new historiographical development that has flourished since 2000: the "biographic turn" in historical studies. Biography and history have coexisted since the time of Plutarch, but academic historians have usually treated the chronicling of individual lives as a lesser form of scholarship, one that they were willing to leave to nonspecialists. Now, in the guise of the "new biography," historians have begun to use life stories to illuminate the connections between individual experience and broader historical themes. With the decline of historical grand narratives, Barbara Caine has written, "biography can be seen as the archetypal 'contingent narrative' and the one best able to show the great importance of particular locations and circumstances and the multiple layers of historical change and experience."[39]

The new biography offers the possibility of combining a traditional form of narrative with new theoretical insights. In her introduction to a volume entitled *The New Biography: Performing Femininity in Nineteenth-Century France* (2000), Jo Burr Margadant makes the notion of self-fashioning central to the new biographical approach and shows how it draws on ideas articulated by the literary scholar Stephen Greenblatt and the feminist theorist Judith Butler. The new biography posits "a method of analysis that recognizes the constructed nature of our conscious selves and views of others," she writes.[40] In his introduction to a forum devoted to "History and Biography," published in the *American Historical Review* in 2009, another scholar and biographer, David Nasaw, expanded on the potentialities of the genre. "It allows, even encourages, us to move beyond the strictures of identity politics without having to abandon its every-expanding and often useful categories," he wrote, adding that "it offers a way of transcending the theoretical divide between empiricist social history and linguistic-turn cultural history."[41]

Historiography itself has taken on a new tone in the years since 2000. Long concerned almost exclusively with the historical work of academic scholars, scholars of the subject now recognize, as written by the editors of the most comprehensive treatment of the subject published in recent years, the French two-volume collection *Historiographies: Concepts et Débats* ("Historiographies: Concepts and Debates"), that "professional historians have never had a monopoly on the writing of history" and insist on the necessity of taking into account the many ways in which history is transmitted to the public. The polemical tone of the historiographical debates in the second half of the twentieth century has faded; the editors of *Historiographies* emphasize instead history's "pluralism" of approaches.[42] The 126 articles in their collection no longer highlight only the contributions of French scholars, even those of the influential Annales school. Instead, they mention the work of historians from all over the world. The three-volume work of the American historian of historiography Donald R. Kelley, *Faces of History: Historical Inquiry from Herodotus to Herder* (1998), *Fortunes of History: Historical Inquiry from Herder to Huizinga* (2003), and *Frontiers of History: Historical Inquiry in the Twentieth Century* (2006), the most detailed account of historical writing in recent decades, confines itself to the tradition of history-writing in the Western world, but it, too, represents a broadening of perspectives. Rather than seeing the rise of Rankean "scientific" history in the nineteenth century as a sharp break with everything that came before, Kelley emphasizes continuity and urges a greater appreciation of the achievements of the historical writers of antiquity, the Middle Ages, and the Renaissance.

As the examples of global history, deep history, and the new biography demonstrate, historians continue to identify new approaches to their subject. Other new directions in historical research in recent years have included the history of the emotions and the history of material culture, the first taking research into the domain of psychology and the second involving historians with technology and the decorative arts. Major world events since the turn of the millennium have given historians opportunities to underline the continuing relevance of our discipline, as policy makers and journalists have turned to scholars to provide perspective on topics ranging from crises in the Middle East to the "Great Recession" of 2008. The historically-minded economist Thomas Piketty's *Capital in the Twenty-First Century,* for example, uses data spanning several centuries to argue that capitalist economies have an inherent tendency to increase social inequality. Critics immediately recognized that Piketty's presentation of history is highly relevant to current debates about public policy.[43]

The history of memory has turned out to have practical present-day significance as historians from countries with long histories of conflict have come together to try to agree on guidelines for school textbooks that will present clashing perspectives on the past in ways that can promote reconciliation. These initiatives, which have often been launched by high-school teachers rather than university scholars, have resulted in the publication of a jointly written book on French-German relations and in the publication of document readers for classes on Asian history taught in Korea, Japan, and China, where disputes about the Second World War remain burning issues.[44] Historians have taken advantage of the 150th anniversary of the American Civil War, from 2011 to 2015, and the 100th anniversary of World War I to share new perspectives with a broader public, stressing the role of blacks in the American conflict and the global dimensions of the "Great War." Intellectually speaking, there is no question that history remains a vital and creative discipline and that historiographic analysis continues to have a vital role to play. The future of history is not only a matter of intellectual activity, however; it also depends on there being professional employment opportunities for historians and on young people wanting to make careers in the history field. The next chapter looks at what is involved in becoming a professional historian, either as a university teacher or in some other career.

Notes

1. Cathérine Coquio, "À propos d'un nihilisme contemporain: négation, déni, témoignage," in Cathérine Coquio, ed., *L'Histoire trouée. Négation et témoignage* (Nantes: L'Atalante, 2003), 23–89.
2. Joyce Appleby, Lynn Hunt, and Margaret Jacob, *Telling the Truth about History* (New York: Norton, 1994), 247, 259, 255, 248. For dissents from their "pragmatic" position, see Perez Zagorin, "History, the Referent, and Narrative," *History and Theory* 38 (1999), 1–24, opposing any concession to the "linguistic turn," and F. R. Ankersmit, "In Praise of Objectivity," in David Carr et al., eds., *The Ethics of History* (complete reference), 1–22, defending a position close to that of Hayden White.
3. Richard J. Evans, *In Defense of History* (New York: Norton, 1997), 220, 217.
4. Keith Jenkins, "'After' History," in Alun Munslow, ed., *Authoring the Past: Writing and Rethinking History* (London: Routledge, 2013 (orig. 1998)), 28.
5. Deborah Lipstadt, *Denying the Holocaust: The Growing Assault on Truth and Memory* (New York: Plume, 1993), 18.
6. Lipstadt has recounted the trial from her point of view in *History on Trial: My Day in Court with a Holocaust Denier* (New York: Ecco, 2005). Another of the expert witnesses who testified on her behalf has also published a book on the trial: Richard J. Evans, *Lying about Hitler: History, the Holocaust, and the David Irving Trial* (New York: Basic Books, 2001). In *The Case for Auschwitz: Evidence from the Irving Trial*, a published version of the brief he submitted at the trial, architecture historian Robert Jan van Pelt has explained the documentary basis for our knowledge that gas chambers were used at Auschwitz, the central issue Irving had raised (Bloomington: Indiana University Press, 2002.)
7. The Bellesiles, Ambrose, Goodwin, and Ellis affairs are described at length in Peter Charles Hoffer, *Past Imperfect: Facts, Fictions, Frauds—American History from Bancroft and Parkman to*

Ambrose, Bellsiles, Ellis, and Goodwin (New York: Public Affairs, 2007), 141–229.

8. Dipesh Chakrabarty, "The Climate of History: Four Theses," *Critical Inquiry* 35 (2009), 208.

9. H-France is not affiliated with H-Net.

10. Roy Rosenzweig, *Clio Wired: The Future of the Past in the Digital Age* (New York: Columbia University Press, 2011), 55.

11. Daniel J. Cohen and Roy Rosenzweig, *Digital History: A Guide to Gathering, Preserving, and Presenting the Past on the Web* (Philadelphia: University of Pennsylvania Press, 2005), accessed online via the Center for History and New Media website.

12. Gertrude Himmelfarb, "A Neo-Luddite Reflects on the Internet," *Chronicle of Higher Education*, Nov. 1, 1996, cited in Cohen and Rosenzweig, *Digital History*.

13. Renée M. Sentilles, "Toiling in the Archives of Cyberspace," in Antoinette Burton, ed., *Archive Stories: Facts, Fictions, and the Writing of History* (Durham, NC: Duke University Press, 2005), 140.

14. Robert A. Rosenstone, *History on Film/Film on History* (Harlow: Pearson Education, 2006), 4, 37.

15. Louis Gottschalk to president of MGMY, cited in Rosenstone, *History on Film*, 20.

16. Robert A. Rosenstone, *Visions of the Past: The Challenge of Film to Our Idea of History* (Cambridge, MA: Harvard University Press, 1995), 68, 70.

17. Rosenstone, *Visions*, 15.

18. Natalie Zemon Davis, *Slaves on Screen: Film and Historical Vision* (Cambridge, MA: Harvard University Press, 2000), 131–36.

19. Pierre Sorlin, "Television and Our Understanding of History: A Distant Conversation," in Tony Barta, ed., *Screening the Past: Film and the Representation of History* (Westport, CT: Praeger, 1998), 213.

20. David Harlan, "Ken Burns and the Coming Crisis of Academic History," *Rethinking History* 7 (2003), 169; Gary R. Edgerton, *Ken Burns's America* (New York: Palgrave, 2001), 17; Samuel Hynes, "At War with Ken Burns," *Sewanee Review* 118 (Spring 2010), 261, 264.

21. Simon Schama, *Dead Certainties (Unwarranted Speculations)* (New York: Vintage Books, 1992 (orig. 1991)).

22. Jerome de Groot, *Consuming History: Historians and Heritage in Contemporary Popular Culture* (London: Routledge, 2009), 19–20.
23. Kirk A. Denton, *Historical Memory and the Politics of Museums in Postsocialist China* (Honolulu: University of Hawai'i Press, 2014), 74.
24. Amy Lonetree, *Decolonizing Museums: Representing Native America in National and Tribal Museums* (Chapel Hill: University of North Carolina Press, 2012), 1.
25. Mike Wallace, *Mickey Mouse History and Other Essays on American Memory* (Philadelphia: Temple University Press, 1996), 23.
26. J. Freedom du Lac, "Learning How to Portray a Slave at Colonial Williamsburg Is a Psychological Challenge," *Washington Post* "Style section," Mar. 9, 2013.
27. Harry Brown, cited in Andrew B. R. Elliott and Matthew Wilhelm Kapell, "Introduction: To Build a Past That Will 'Stand the Test of Time'—Discovering Historical Facts, Assembling Historical Narratives," in Andrew Wilhelm Kapell and Andrew B. R. Elliott, eds., *Playing with the Past: Digital Games and the Simulation of History* (New York: Bloomsburg, 2013), 11.
28. Art Spiegelman, *MetaMaus: A Look Inside a Modern Classic* (New York: Random House, 2011), 127.
29. Larry Gonick, interview with Matthew Johnson, "Media Smarts," Oct. 13, 2009.
30. Patrick Manning, *Navigating World History: Historians Create a Global Past* (New York: Palgrave, 2003), 116, 167.
31. C. A. Bayly, *The Birth of the Modern World, 1780–1914* (Oxford: Blackwell, 2004); Timothy Brook, *Vermeer's Hat: The Seventeenth Century and the Dawn of the Global World* (New York: Bloomsbury, 2008).
32. Daniel Woolf, *A Global History of History* (New York: Cambridge University Press, 2011).
33. Patricia Nelson Limerick, "The American West: From Exceptionalism to Internationalism," in Melvyn Stokes, ed., *The State of U.S. History* (New York: Berg, 2002), 289.
34. Thomas Bender, "Introduction," in Thomas Bender, ed., *Rethinking American History in a Global Age* (Berkeley: University of California Press, 2002), 5–6.
35. John Elliott, cited in Jack P. Greene and Philip D. Morgan, eds., *Atlantic History: A Critical Appraisal* (New York: Oxford University Press, 2009), 3.

36. Andrew Shryock and Daniel Lord Smail, eds., *Deep History: The Architecture of Past and Present* (Berkeley: University of California Press, 2011), xiii, 8.

37. David Christian, *Maps of Time: An Introduction to Big History* (Berkeley, CA: University of California Press, 2011); Andrew Ross Sorkin, "Everything Is Illuminated," *New York Times Magazine*, Sept. 7, 2014, p. 32.

38. Shryock and Smail, eds., *Deep History*, 14, 13.

39. Barbara Caine, *Biography and History* (New York: Palgrave Macmillan, 2010), 2.

40. Jo Burr Margadant, "Introduction," in Jo Burr Margadant, ed., *The New Biography: Performing Femininity in Nineteenth-Century France* (Berkeley: University of California Press, 2000), 8.

41. David Nasaw, "Historians and Biography: Introduction," *American Historical Review* 114 (June 2009), 576, 577.

42. Christian Delacroix, François Dosse, Patrick Garcia, and Nicolas Offenstadt, eds., *Historiographies. Concepts et Débats* (Paris: Gallimard, 2010), 1:13.

43. Thomas Piketty, *Capital in the Twenty-First Century* (Cambridge, MA: Harvard University Press, 2014).

44. On joint textbook projects, see Katerina V. Korostelina and Simone Lässig, History Education and Post-Conflict Reconciliation: Reconsidering Joint Textbook Projects (New York: Routledge, 2013).

CHAPTER 8

Historians at Work

One purpose of courses about historiography is to teach students "to think like a historian." The majority of college students who major in history, of course, do not intend to pursue history as a career, and professors know the realities of the job market too well to encourage all but the most dedicated and enthusiastic participants in their classes to make such a choice. To be able to think like a historian is an advantage in a wide variety of careers, however. It means having the skills to collect and evaluate different kinds of evidence, to organize and synthesize data, to draw conclusions and to communicate them effectively in speech and in writing, and to be able to analyze and explain complicated forms of human behavior. History graduates are well-trained and flexible generalists whose studies give them good preparation for many careers, including law, journalism, business, schoolteaching, public relations, work with nonprofit organizations, and government service. In 2014, voters in Nebraska sent Ben Sasse, a history Ph.D., to the U.S. Senate.

History teachers know from experience, however, that there will be a few stubborn students who enjoy the subject so much that they want to at least consider the possibility of becoming historians themselves. As we have seen in the previous chapter, being a historian today can mean many things, including working as a video-game developer or designing museum exhibits. Rapid changes in economy and society in the early twenty-first century are making it increasingly difficult to predict what careers in history will look like in coming years. Interest in the past remains strong, both in the United States and in other countries, and there will surely continue to be a demand for specialists trained to research and explain the past. Whether college and university teaching will continue to be the dominant career track for professional historians, as it has been for well over a hundred years, and what new opportunities for historians may develop as a result of new digital media and other innovations remain open questions. Just as enterprising historians in the past took advantage of the new possibilities created by the invention of the printing press and the spread of universities, tomorrow's professional historians will have to be ready to explore new ways of combining a fascination with the past with the challenge of making a living.

Even if many historians worry about its future, teaching at the college and university level remains the most common form of employment for historians, and students who imagine becoming historians are most likely to think of that possibility. A survey taken in 2013 showed that, among historians who earned their Ph.D.'s in the United States between 1998 and 2009, two-thirds held teaching positions at four-year colleges and universities, and another 5 percent had jobs teaching at community colleges.[1] The survey also showed that there are a wide variety of professional opportunities for historians that do not involve college teaching, including working in historical museums, employment in the historical offices of government agencies, and developing historical content for the media. Nevertheless, the number of such history jobs in each of these categories is still limited. Four percent of those surveyed were employed by federal, state, or local governments, 3 percent taught in elementary or secondary schools, 3 percent worked for nonprofit organizations and 3 percent for private businesses, 3 percent were "independent scholars," and 1.5 percent worked for libraries, archives, or museums.

As we have seen, being a historian has not always been so closely associated with teaching. Only in the nineteenth century did Leopold von Ranke establish the pattern according to which students who wanted to become historians would be specifically trained in research methods, with the expectation that they would eventually support themselves by becoming professors and that they would produce scholarship meant to be read primarily by other academics. For most of the nineteenth century, university historians were probably still outnumbered by nonacademic historians; until 1890, the president of Harvard at the time noted, most American colleges had "no teacher of history whatsoever."² The tremendous expansion of universities in the twentieth century, both in the United States and in most other developed countries, made professors the largest group among those who earn their living from history. Programs of graduate study in history, which are of course taught by academics, still serve mostly to prepare their graduates to become college and university professors. Under the impact of the current crisis in academic employment, faculty are working hard to come up with better ways to train students for other kinds of history careers, but how to do this effectively remains an unresolved question.

If university professors do encourage highly motivated students to consider careers in history, whether in academia or elsewhere, it is because we consider history important and we know that our work can be truly rewarding. At its best, a history career offers an opportunity for those who love the subject to make a living doing something that truly engages them. When their classes go well, professors have the satisfaction of seeing that they are changing the lives of intelligent young people by helping them to develop their abilities to think and communicate. "A teacher affects eternity; he can never tell where his influence stops," the nineteenth-century historian Henry Adams wrote.³ Those academic historians who have the opportunity to do research get to devote themselves to topics of their own choice, and, at least on some occasions, they enjoy the intoxicating experience of thinking that they have illuminated some aspect of the past better than anyone else before them. Professors love to grumble about the demands of their jobs, but they know that they have more flexibility in setting their schedules than most other people. It is hard to think of any other occupation whose practitioners get three-month vacations and, in many cases, periodical sabbatical semesters or years, time they can devote to their own interests. Up to now, college and university professors have also had a remarkable degree of job security, provided by the system of academic tenure. American university professors are not as well paid as many other professionals, but they usually earn enough to maintain a comfortable middle-class lifestyle. Jokes about "ivory tower academics" notwithstanding, university professors are generally respected in society.

For all its potential rewards, a career in history also has certain drawbacks. Becoming a professor or preparing for other careers in history requires a long period of apprenticeship, in the form of graduate study, and a long probationary period before one can hope to earn tenure and job security. Despite persistent efforts to shorten the time required to earn a Ph.D. degree, most history students take seven to nine years to complete their graduate studies. Graduate students are usually able to support themselves through fellowships and teaching assistantships, but the stipends they receive are fairly minimal, often driving students to postpone decisions about marriage and starting a family. Particularly since the economic crisis of 2008, the most desirable starting jobs for newly graduated Ph.D.'s—professorships on the "tenure track" at four-year colleges and universities—have become considerably more scarce, and there is much concern that educational institutions will increasingly rely on untenured teachers who will be offered lower salaries and much less job security than in the past. New Ph.D.'s entering the job market must be ready to move to distant parts of the country, or even the world, to pursue their careers: history is not an occupation where one can confidently hope to find employment in a specific region. This is a major concern for those who are not geographically mobile.

Those historians who do succeed in becoming tenured members of a college or university faculty may experience other frustrations inherent in the academic enterprise. Bringing history alive to students can be a creative challenge at the start of a career, but it can turn into drudgery, especially for teachers who have to repeat the same courses semester after semester. The outcome of history teaching is difficult to measure, even compared to many other academic disciplines. At the end of a semester, a language teacher can take satisfaction in hearing a student pronounce a sentence in a new language, and a mathematics instructor can measure whether a student can calculate the derivative of a function, but it is much harder to define what one has taught a student in a history course. Nor is everyone suited for the intense interactions with colleagues that make up the life of an academic department. In British novelist Kingsley Amis's classic satirical *Lucky Jim*, the hero suffers under the thumb of a pretentious department head who answers his phone with the words, "History speaking." The story ends with the young historian abandoning his teaching position for a more adventurous life. Every history department has its share of "burned-out" faculty who have lost all enthusiasm for their work but who cannot conceive of giving up the advantages of a tenured position to try some other career. To be sure, there is no occupation that guarantees lifelong stimulation and satisfaction, and surveys usually indicate that university professors, including historians, are among the most contented with their career choices. Nevertheless, students considering pursuing a career in history should have a realistic idea of what they are committing themselves to.

The Graduate School Experience

Setting out to become a professional historian is like embarking on a video-game quest. Overcoming the different challenges the future historian must face requires acquiring powers that may not be magical but are certainly difficult to obtain, making strategic alliances, and persevering in the face of sometimes daunting obstacles. The first stage of this quest is graduate school in history, the almost unavoidable starting point for anyone who wants to become a professional historian, either as a college professor or in public history. Graduate study in history is not simply a continuation of undergraduate work. Students' years of undergraduate study in American institutions are supposed to be a time for exploration and personal growth, and even courses intended exclusively for history majors are meant mainly to broaden their audience's intellectual horizons. In graduate-level classes, on the other hand, the majority of the students are planning to become professional historians, and historiography and research methodology are central emphases. Reading assignments in graduate courses are heavier than in those at the undergraduate level, and expectations for students' writing are more rigorous. On the other hand, graduate students are left largely on their own to complete their assignments, a situation that requires maturity and self-discipline.

Which students do decide to try to pursue professional careers in history? A sampling of historians' memoirs suggest that they are usually individuals who acquired an interest in stories about the past at an early age. Most remember being avid readers, attracted by dramatic tales about distant times and places. At first, fiction made a stronger impression on most of them than actual works of history, and the classic English novelist Charles Dickens has been a favorite for future historians from all over the world. His "unashamed rousing of feeling, his uproariously funny characters, his epic settings—cities of hunger and degradation, countries in revolution, the stakes being life and death not just for one family but for thousands," as the American historian Howard Zinn put it, taught many historians the power of dramatic narratives showing people confronted with vital choices. Childhood travel experiences, especially if they involved going to places that seemed to belong to an earlier era than the locations where future historians were growing up, stimulated many future historians' curiosity about the past. For many twentieth-century European historians, visiting the rural villages where their grandparents lived had this effect; for Americans, trips to Europe, with its ancient and medieval monuments, often helped generate "a feeling for the past, a sense of its continuous presence and endless fascination," as the historian of colonial America Henry May wrote.[4] Listening to older family members' stories about historical events they had experienced, such as reminiscences about immigration to the United States or service in one of the world wars, helped stimulate some future historians' vocations. Nowadays, as children grow up in different environments, the imaginations of future historians may be stimulated in new ways, perhaps by immersion in video simulation games such as *Oregon Trail* or *Assassins' Creed*.

Considering that many history majors in the United States intend to become social studies teachers, it is discouraging to see how few historian-memoirists remember their school classes as important in developing their interest in history. Leon Litwack, the son of Jewish immigrants and a future specialist in African American history, found high school history boring. The curriculum recounted "someone else's history, not my history, not the lives of my parents, friends, and neighbors," he recalled.[5] But most historians do have grateful memories of at least one inspiring college professor. The African American historian John Hope Franklin entered college in the early 1930s intending to major in English and go on to law school, but then he encountered such a teacher, Theodore S. Currier. "He was so animated that he was in constant motion before the class, pacing from one side of the room to the other . . . Embellished with anecdotes concerning real, live characters, ranging from kings and queens to prime ministers and presidents to industrial giants to common laborers, his lectures raised and answered questions of how and why events occurred," Franklin remembered years later.[6] Encounters with such teachers not only stimulate students' interest in the subject, but also, as the French historian Raoul Girardet wrote in his memoir, teach the lesson that "it could, after all, be a respectable thing for an adult to teach history and . . . . . . to consecrate his life to it."[7]

The first big challenge facing students who decide to apply to graduate school in history is preparing their application. Most graduate schools require students to take the Graduate Record Exam and submit a transcript showing their courses and grades, but a well-drafted application letter, a good writing sample, and strong letters of recommendation from undergraduate teachers are the most important parts of an application. Your application letter should explain why you want to study history. Applicants are not expected to know exactly what subfield they will go into, but mentioning a few professors in the department you are applying to whose work interests you shows that you have taken the time to familiarize yourself with the program you are applying to. Like your letter, the sample of written work you submit (if the application requests one) should be carefully proofread. It need not be too long—admissions committees often have to screen dozens of applications—but it should show your ability to integrate information from primary and secondary sources and to make a convincing argument. Letters of reference should come from instructors who know your work well. Applicants should talk personally to the teachers from whom they want to request letters and should make their requests well in advance of application deadlines.

As of 2014, there were nearly 120 universities in the United States offering Ph.D. degrees in history, as well as a number of institutions in Canada, and many more schools that offer an M.A. (master's) degree, so deciding where to apply can be difficult. The American Historical Association publishes a directory of history programs that lists universities with doctoral programs, their faculty, and the fields in which they offer graduate-level training. Graduate programs post extensive information online, including lists of their faculty and their fields of interest, details about the requirements for earning a degree, and instructions for submitting applications. Potential graduate applicants should not hesitate to contact the directors of graduate studies at departments they are interested in to ask whether they have the qualifications to be competitive for admission and financial aid; undergraduate advisors and faculty at the schools where students are receiving their B.A. degrees can also be helpful in answering these questions. History programs in the United States generally make genuine efforts to recruit a diversified student body. In 2010, 45 percent of recently graduated history Ph.D.'s were women, and 19 percent were members of racial and ethnic minorities (African Americans, Hispanics, Asian Americans, and Native Americans).[8]

Applicants must take many things into account in choosing a graduate school. The prestige of the graduate program where students earn their Ph.D. degree is important in determining their prospects on the job market, especially for those who hope some day to be hired at research universities. There is no universally accepted ranking of the quality of American graduate programs, but the majority of professors at research universities have Ph.D.'s from the fifteen or so programs that have dominated the discipline for many decades. This list includes many of the Ivy League campuses in the East—Harvard, Yale, Princeton, Columbia, Cornell, and the University of Pennsylvania—as well as long-established programs in the Midwest, notably the universities of Michigan, Wisconsin, and Chicago, along with leading schools in the South, such as Johns Hopkins in Baltimore, the University of North Carolina at Chapel Hill, and Duke University, and on the West Coast, where Stanford and the University of California campuses at Berkeley and UCLA stand out. Traditionally, students have been urged not to get their graduate degree at the same institution where they earned their B.A. Changing schools gives you a chance to learn from new professors and be exposed to a wider range of viewpoints. This is not an ironclad rule, however: the author of this book received both his B.A. and his Ph.D. degrees from the University of California, Berkeley.

The traditionally prestigious universities are not the only places where aspiring students can receive excellent training, and there are many reasons why applicants might consider other programs. A student may have special interests that will be best served by working with a particular professor who does not happen to be at one of the most high-profile universities, and there are fields, such as Latin American history, African history, and public history, in which the best departments are not necessarily those at the traditional big-name institutions. For personal or family reasons, some graduate students need to stay in a particular part of the country, which may limit their choices. A good fellowship offer from a less highly ranked program may make it a better choice than going to a high-prestige university without stable funding. Responsible graduate programs strongly discourage students from borrowing to finance their studies: the chances of finding a history job that will enable one to pay back loans are not good. Historically, earning a Ph.D. from a less-well-known university has not necessarily meant a poorer chance to finding a full-time history job after graduation, although it may affect the kinds of jobs for which such graduates are most competitive: they are more likely to be at teaching-oriented institutions or in nonuniversity venues. Undergraduates considering history study should not be scared off by the figures for tuition listed in the American Historical Association directory, since most programs offer financial support to applicants they admit, but it is important to know the odds on receiving an aid offer. Talking to students already enrolled in a program is a good way to learn important things about the atmosphere there that faculty and websites may not reveal: do faculty show a real interest in their students, and is there a congenial graduate-student community?

As students embark on the quest for a graduate degree in history, they must also think about what kind of degree they plan to earn: an M.A. (master's degree) or a Ph.D. The M.A., which usually takes two years to complete, can serve a variety of purposes. For some students, earning a master's degree is a way of testing whether they really want to commit themselves to the longer course of study required for the Ph.D. It is not unusual for students to earn an M.A. at one institution and then apply to continue for the Ph.D. elsewhere; among other things, this can be a way for students whose undergraduate records were less than stellar to show that they do have the abilities and the determination to succeed in graduate school. A master's degree in history may also be useful in combination with other professional training, such as a credential in secondary education, journalism, or international relations, and it qualifies graduates to teach in community colleges, as adjunct instructors in lower-division courses at four-year institutions, and in private high schools. (Teaching jobs in public schools usually require a teaching credential from an education school). Holders of an M.A. can apply for higher-level civil service jobs than those accessible with a B.A.

The Ph.D. degree is more prestigious than the M.A., but it is also a more specialized credential that takes longer to earn. Despite repeated efforts to speed things up, it takes most students seven to nine years after they graduate from college to complete a history Ph.D. Not all history Ph.D.'s will go on to become professors, and the skills demonstrated by completion of a Ph.D.—the ability to carry out a complicated research project that involves bringing together information from diverse sources, organizing data, and presenting it effectively in written form—can be valuable in other contexts. Nevertheless, anyone who knows from the start that college-level teaching is not their professional goal should think carefully about whether obtaining a doctoral degree is the best way of preparing for their intended career. Because the Ph.D. degree takes so much time and effort to complete, students are less likely to combine it with other credentials than in the case of the master's degree, although there are a few fields, such as legal history, where it may be necessary to earn another professional degree to be fully competitive.

Following in the tradition founded by Leopold von Ranke in the nineteenth century, most graduate courses are taught as seminars, with an emphasis on close analysis of assigned readings, although some graduate programs also use the tutorial method, in which students meet individually with professors to discuss their work. Ranke's seminars were largely devoted to learning to interpret primary source documents, but American graduate programs typically emphasize reading seminars, in which students systematically explore the most important secondary literature in their fields of study. The relationship of the professor to the course material is different in graduate courses compared to undergraduate classes. When teaching undergraduates, a professor may not have much firsthand knowledge on many of the topics covered: anyone giving a survey course on world history or United States history is bound to have to treat subjects that he or she really knows little about. In graduate courses, however, it is assumed that the instructor is truly an expert, personally familiar both with the primary sources in the field and with the secondary literature written by other scholars. Professors expect graduate students to take the subject matter in their courses as seriously as they themselves do and sometimes to embrace the professor's own approach to it. Joan Scott remembers one of her professors returning her paper, which contested his methodology, and "comment[ing] caustically that this was an example of how not to write history."[9] The resilience to survive such experiences is essential for survival in graduate school.

Students in graduate courses receive grades, as in undergraduate classes, but, in the quest for their degrees, they must also pass comprehensive qualifying examinations that are not directly linked to particular courses. Fields of graduate study may be defined in various ways: a student may do a field in the history of a particular country or civilization during a specified chronological period or a "thematic" field on a topic such as women's and gender history. Some graduate programs encourage students to do an examination field in a discipline outside of history. Traditionally, comprehensive examinations are "orals," in which a committee of professors with whom the student has worked pose questions that the candidate must answer verbally without consulting notes or other references. The purpose is to see whether examinees have grasped the major historiographical issues in the fields they have studied and whether they can "think on their feet." Qualifying exams may also involve a written component, in which students compose essays on topics set by their committee members. Whatever form qualifying examinations take, they inevitably provoke much anxiety; even students whose success was never in doubt usually remember their orals as the most stressful part of their graduate studies.

As graduate students have been preparing themselves taking courses and preparing for exams, they have usually been acquiring their first teaching experience. At most institutions, graduate students earn at least some of their financial support by working as teaching assistants. In that capacity, they typically lead discussion sections in large courses taught by regular faculty and grade written assignments. One goal of graduate programs is to give students some preparation for teaching, with training sessions on how to maintain classroom order, stimulate discussions, and provide constructive feedback on assignments. The first day in the classroom is, like the oral exam, an anxiety-provoking rite of passage. After many years in the role of learner, the budding historian suddenly must act as a teacher. Unconsciously learned lessons about how to run a class, absorbed from one's own teachers, are helpful, but it takes time for most graduate students to develop a classroom style that works for them. Advanced graduate students may get the chance to put together independent courses, in which they develop their own syllabus. This allows them to enter the job market with tangible evidence of their readiness to teach. Graduate students primarily interested in public history, as well as those who discover the hard way that they truly do not like teaching, should seek out internships at archives, museums, and other organizations to start to build up their credentials.

Like video-game players, Ph.D. students who successfully pass their qualifying exams then move on to face a new challenge: the writing of their doctoral dissertation. The dissertation is normally done under the supervision of one professor whose own expertise is relevant to the topic the student wants to pursue. The choice of a Ph.D. director is an important decision: as the German word "Doktorvater" ("doctoral father," or, nowadays, also "Doktormutter") suggests, the relationship between a student and his or her director has an emotional dimension as well as an intellectual one. The ideal Ph.D. director, like a good parent, knows how to give a student enough guidance and advice but not too much and recognizes that the goal of the relationship is to let the student develop the confidence to become an independent scholar. The doctoral director must be knowledgeable in the student's intended field of research to give the student good advice on designing and carrying out a dissertation project. In choosing a dissertation director, students must consider not only their personal compatibility with their mentor, but also the degree to which the director can be helpful in launching their careers. Recommendations from professors who are prominent in their fields will usually carry the most weight when students apply for fellowships and jobs. On the other hand, however, well-known professors are often the busiest members of a department's faculty and may not be willing to set aside the time dissertation students need.

Writing a Ph.D. dissertation involves developing an original research project significant enough to justify a study that may run from two hundred to five hundred double-spaced pages. Dissertation projects are expected to be based on primary source documents, although the nature of those documents will differ considerably depending on the nature of the project. To be accepted as a dissertation, a project must either deal with a subject that has not previously been studied or propose a new interpretation of sources and events. Often, the dissertation project will require the student to travel to distant archives and libraries in search of documents. Students are expected to be able to read their sources in the languages in which they were originally written, and even those working only with English-language materials usually must prove that they can read at least one foreign language.

For most historians, the Ph.D. dissertation is the moment when they first fully engage themselves in archival research, the closest thing the history discipline has to a unique defining characteristic. There are fields, such as ancient history, whose primary sources are not found in archives, but to be recognized as original research, the majority of scholarly research projects require scholars to use documents generated by actors in the past. No one has evoked the passion of archival research better than the French social historian Arlette Farge in her book *Le Goût de l'archive* (*"The Allure of the Archives"*). Reading documents, particularly manuscripts that were never intended for publication, "generates a sense of contact with reality that no printed text, no matter how obscure, can arouse," she writes. "Manuscript archives are living matter."[10] Handling actual pieces of paper covered with ink made centuries ago, the researcher has the heady feeling of bringing the dead back to life. As she reads her documents, however, the historian also recognizes that they do not tell their own story. Archival research is a dialogue between the scholar and the documents, which must be "delicately questioned in order to reveal their meaning." The apprenticeship in archival research that graduate students receive in the course of doing their dissertations is the time when they develop the skills of finding and interpreting such traces of the past. Working through a mass of archival documents looking for those that reveal something significant can be tedious—"one cannot say often enough how slowly archival work goes," Farge writes—but out of it comes a level of understanding that cannot be generated in any other way.[11]

Archives come in many forms. Government documents, the basis for the majority of historical research projects, may be housed in massive building complexes, like the U.S. National Archives, whose main site, in College Park, Maryland, holds billions of items generated by federal agencies. Hundreds of employees work to preserve and organize these documents and to make them accessible to researchers. To accommodate researchers, the National Archives has a large reading room, an on-site cafeteria, and other facilities. Like all major public archives, the National Archives catalogs its holdings in series, usually based on their source, the branch of government that generated them. Series are in turn usually broken down into cartons, large boxes holding a certain number of files or dossiers. If researchers are lucky, an archivist will have prepared an inventory of the documents in each series, giving a brief indication of the nature of the contents of each carton and thus sparing the historian from having to undertake the proverbial search for a needle in a haystack. At the other extreme from well-organized public archives are the innumerable collections of documents belonging to private individuals, business corporations, and other institutions, which may be nothing more than cardboard boxes stuffed with unorganized pieces of paper whose importance and fragility may not be recognized by their owners.

Writing in 1989, Arlette Farge was already conscious that technology was changing the nature of archival research. She lamented the fact that scholars were increasingly being forced to rely on microfilmed versions of documents rather than being allowed to handle the originals.

In the years since, changes have become even more dramatic. Instead of submitting to the slow process of leafing through the contents of an archival carton, researchers can now often be seen frantically photographing documents with their cell phones to be able to read them later on their computer screens. On my own most recent archival research trip, I even saw colleagues taking digital photographs of microfilmed documents, producing images at two removes from the original. A growing number of documents, such as those concerning the Spanish colonial empire, can now be consulted online, making an actual trip to the archive unnecessary. Digital transcription tools that automatically convert hard-to-read handwriting, such as that found in medieval manuscripts, into modern print hold out the prospect that students will not have to acquire the specialized skills that have been needed up to now simply to make out the words in such documents. Online archives hold out important new possibilities for research—they can alert scholars, for example, to the existence of related archival documents from other locations—but they are also rapidly changing the relationship between historians and their sources.

In addition to showing that its author has learned to deal with original sources, the Ph.D. dissertation is supposed to demonstrate a student's abilities to define a meaningful historical question, to find as many relevant sources as possible, to situate his or her own work in relationship to the existing historiography in the field, and to communicate findings effectively in written form. To keep their projects manageable, students are usually encouraged to make them fairly limited. Having to devote several years of work to a narrowly defined project can become discouraging, and it is unfortunately not unusual for well-qualified students to get stalled at this stage of their work or even to abandon graduate school altogether. University professors continue to agree, on the whole, that this difficult apprenticeship is necessary for future historians to learn how knowledge of the past is generated. Whether the traditional Ph.D. dissertation is the best preparation for students who may be headed for other kinds of history careers is an open question.

Continuing a tradition that goes back to the universities of medieval Europe, most graduate programs require Ph.D. students to "defend" their completed dissertation in an oral examination conducted by a committee of faculty. Ph.D. students are challenged to explain why they have chosen to research their particular subject and how they have carried out their work and to justify the conclusions they have reached. Historiographical issues are often at the heart of Ph.D. defenses, as students argue for the methodological approach they have adopted. The dissertation defense is also an opportunity for the student's mentors to offer advice on how the student's work might be used as the basis for future scholarly publications. Assuming all goes well, the candidate emerges from the defense with the title of "doctor of philosophy," ready to take on the responsibilities of teaching history at the university level or working in some field of public history.

Searching for a Job in History

As graduate students are completing their dissertations, they must also embark on a new quest: the search for a job. The vast majority of full-time college teaching jobs are now advertised online, especially on the website of H-Net (www.h-net.org), which applicants looking for employment learn to follow religiously. These positions will attract applicants from all over the country and even abroad; it is not necessarily an advantage to have lived or studied close to the job's location, although this may be helpful in finding part-time teaching. Many public history openings are also advertised online. Some openings appear on H-Net, but applicants must also consult the website of the National Council on Public History (www.ncph.org). Job openings with federal agencies can be found by searching civil service listings at www.usajobs.gov, entering the keyword "history." Depending on their nature, such positions may or may not attract a national pool of applicants; building up personal contacts with local public history institutions is an essential part of a job-search strategy in this field.

When applicants see a job listing that appears to fit them, they submit an application, which normally includes a cover letter explaining their qualifications, a *curriculum vitae* giving details of their education and accomplishments, such as graduate fellowships, talks at professional meetings, scholarly publications, and teaching experience, and letters of recommendation from professors with whom they have worked. Applicants for teaching positions are often also asked to submit a writing sample as evidence of their research abilities and course syllabi and classroom evaluations to demonstrate their teaching skills. Nowadays, these materials are usually submitted online.

In the case of teaching positions, a hiring committee made up of faculty goes through the applications it receives and selects a "short list" of candidates it considers most promising. In most cases, these candidates will be invited to participate in screening interviews, either in person at a professional meeting such as the annual conference of the American Historical Association or, increasingly, online. These interviews are an opportunity for hiring committees to get a sense of candidates' personalities and their ability to communicate their enthusiasm for their subject effectively. They can also give candidates a chance to learn something about the department they might be joining: they can ask questions about the hiring institution and observe whether the committee members appear to get along well together or whether there are visible tensions among them. Even under the best of circumstances, however, these interviews are stressful for candidates, who know they have only thirty to forty-five minutes to make their best impression. The online job wikis where candidates post news and rumors about ongoing searches that spring up every time a history teaching job is advertised reflect the anxieties that beset applicants as they wait for news of their prospects.

Once the hiring committee has digested the results of its screening interviews, it will usually invite between two and four candidates for on-campus job interviews. These campus visits, which are paid for by the hiring institution, normally last for a day or a day and a half, during which the candidate gives a public talk about his or her work and often also teaches a sample class. The job talk usually requires the candidate to make an effective case, not only for the originality of his or her research, but also for the value of its methodological approach: this is one situation in which the ability to articulate historiographical concerns can be essential. On-campus job interviews also include meetings with the chair of the hiring department and with higher-level college or university administrators involved in the hiring process. Candidates often have a chance to talk informally with a group of undergraduate history majors and, if the hiring department has graduate students, with some of them as well. If the candidate is lucky, there will be time set aside for a brief tour of the campus and of the city in which it is located. Almost always, there will be a dinner at a local restaurant with members of the faculty, which functions as a test of the candidate's social skills and a reminder that being hired as a professor means joining a campus community as well as filling a job slot.

Candidates usually know little about the heated debates that often take place in the hiring department once all the finalists have had their interviews. Colleagues may disagree about the strength of the candidates' qualifications, but these debates also often reflect deeply held convictions about what constitutes the proper approach to history; in other words, such debates are one of the occasions when historiographical issues have a direct effect on historians' careers. Eventually, in most cases, the job is offered to one of the candidates. Budding historians with the most impressive credentials—an exciting dissertation project, enthusiastic letters of recommendation from prominent scholars, and imaginative ideas about teaching—may be in the fortunate position of having several job offers to choose from and being able to bargain with potential employers. In the present climate of scarce opportunities, however, most historians looking for their first job feel fortunate if they receive one offer of a tenure-track position.

Most new Ph.D.'s are resigned to the fact that their first job is likely to be a temporary or part-time one. A few will be offered prestigious postdoctoral appointments at leading universities, such as Harvard and Stanford. These positions are highly sought after, although they last only for a few years, because they offer their holders excellent opportunities to continue and expand their research while teaching a small number of classes and because being selected for them sends a signal about the candidate's potential. Other new Ph.D.'s may be hired for temporary positions called lectureships or instructorships, which usually do not offer the possibility of eventual tenure and often involve large teaching loads and minimal support for research. Unfortunately, many graduates find themselves forced to scramble for part-time or adjunct positions, teaching one or two courses for a small amount of money and few or no fringe benefits. Job seekers who end up with these less desirable positions hope that the professional experience they acquire will put them in a better position to obtain a full-time position. Some do succeed, but others find themselves permanently relegated to a floating pool of underemployed part-time academic labor, unable to compete with new Ph.D. recipients with more promising research records. If they do not find a full-time teaching job after several years of searching, many of these would-be professors have to make the difficult decision to pursue other careers.

Although the majority of new Ph.D.'s do look for teaching jobs, an increasing number also consider positions in public history. The term "public history" covers a wide field. The comprehensive survey of the topic edited by Barbara J. Howe and Emory L. Kemp includes chapters on career opportunities in archives and libraries, the editing and publishing of historical documents, the fields of historic preservation and industrial archeology, museums, historical societies, the organization of public programs such as heritage festivals, federal and state government history offices, the National Park Service, and private businesses, as well as the possibility of supporting oneself as an independent scholar.[12]

Candidates interested in pursuing careers in public history must be enterprising in seeking out openings by contacting institutions such as state historical societies and museums on their own; internships are often an essential steppingstone to future employment. Faculty in academic institutions rarely have much familiarity with public history, unless they are specialists in the field, and it is hard for them to be as helpful to students as they can be in finding academic jobs. Opportunities for what one might call freelance historical work may only be advertised by word of mouth. A graduate classmate of mine saw an opportunity, for example, when he learned that a local synagogue wanted someone to write a history of its congregation. He never completed his Ph.D., but this first project launched him on a successful career both as the author of books on Jewish history and as a Jewish community educator. Today's generation of Ph.D.'s includes others with a similar entrepreneurial spirit, who are on the lookout for possibilities such as providing historical content to websites. Other Ph.D.'s conclude that they will do better to use the skills they have developed in graduate school in jobs that have no direct connection to history. As one history Ph.D. who has made a career as a business consultant has written, "the dissertation is an entrepreneurial venture," requiring advanced organizational skills that can be applied in other situations.[13]

The Quest for Tenure

Even those aspiring historians who complete graduate school and find a full-time job often know little about the new challenges they will then face. Those in college-level teaching positions will find themselves in a fairly structured environment, where the main question is whether they will receive the guarantee of permanent employment, known as tenure. Public history situations are much more varied: civil service positions with the federal government offer security and benefits equivalent to those enjoyed by tenured faculty, but other public history jobs may be defined as temporary in the first place, and career paths are usually less clearly laid out. For those who go into academia, tenure is a highly coveted prize: having it means that a professor cannot be dismissed from his or her job except for egregious misconduct or failure to perform his or her duties. In a world where fewer and fewer jobs in any profession offer such security, tenure is one of the great attractions of academic life.

The vast majority of American institutions of higher education adhere to standards for the definition of tenure and the procedures for granting it worked out by the American Association of University Professors and the Association of American Colleges in 1940. Tenure is not merely a special privilege for professors: as the 1940 statement says, it is meant to serve society by safeguarding "the free search for truth and its free exposition." Tenure is meant to guarantee that instructors cannot be punished for the content of their research or their teaching. Tenure is also meant, as the 1940 statement indicates, to provide "a sufficient degree of economic security to make the profession attractive to men and women of ability."[14] From the point of view of the colleges and universities that grant it, tenure gives their faculty a major stake in the success of their institution. It encourages professors to identify with their institutions and to be willing to put in extra time and energy to help their students succeed and to keep their departments and schools functioning well.

The tenure system has been a major feature of academic life for many decades, but whether it will continue in its present form in future decades is increasingly uncertain. Tenure is certainly open to abuses: faculty who have it are under little pressure to perform, either in the classroom or as scholars. From the institutional point of view, the tenure system limits colleges' flexibility in responding to new patterns of student demand and changes in financial conditions. The tenure system in public schools is under increasing attack, with critics blaming it for students' poor performance, and these challenges have had an effect on attitudes toward tenure at the college and university level. In a survey in 2013, more than half of the provosts of American colleges and universities agreed with that the statement that "future generations of faculty in this country should not expect tenure to be a factor in their employment at higher education institutions."[15] Tenure for university professors in Great Britain was abolished in 1988; faculty who did not have tenure at the time or who have changed jobs now work on renewable contracts of variable length and are required to demonstrate their productivity as scholars and teachers to keep their positions. The abolition of tenure has not meant the end of college teaching in Britain, and young people have continued to enter the profession, but it has certainly raised the stress level among academics.

In the less centralized American academic system, tenure cannot be abolished by government fiat, as it was in Britain. Most American professors continue to defend tenure as a justified form of compensation for the long years of insecurity spent in graduate school and in the early part of their teaching careers and for the relatively low salaries that faculty earn compared to many other professions. The tenure guidelines require colleges and universities to evaluate full-time faculty for tenure by the end of their sixth year of employment; professors cannot be kept waiting indefinitely to learn whether they will receive it. (Some institutions now allow faculty to postpone coming up for tenure if they take parental leave after the birth of a child or for certain other reasons.) From the time they are hired, new professors nervously watch their "tenure clock," trying to make sure that they will meet the standards for performance set by their institutions by the time they are considered for this reward.

Professors' Work

To gain the coveted prize of tenure, newly hired professors must show that they are capable teachers and productive researchers. Although most history graduate students get some teaching experience before they finish their Ph.D.'s, few are really prepared for the experience of full-time teaching. On paper, the teaching workload of a college history professor looks easily manageable: at American research universities, most professors are expected to teach two three-hour classes per semester, and even at teaching-oriented institutions, assignments rarely exceed four courses per semester. The idea that professors only spend six to twelve hours a week on their teaching is misleading, however. Many hours of preparation are needed for every hour actually spent in the classroom. Long before the semester begins, a professor must choose books and materials for each class. By the beginning of the semester, the professor must draw up a syllabus for each course, figuring out the sequence of topics to be covered, the reading related to each topic, and the schedule of exams and other assignments. Even if they have taught a course many times, few professors can enter a classroom ready to lecture or begin a discussion without having recently reviewed their material. Usually, instructors also want to prepare audiovisual materials to put on the screen and sometimes also handouts for students to discuss. As the semester moves along, professors must make up tests and other assignments for their students and then grade the results. Professors are also expected to hold regular office hours to talk to students in their classes. Most of these encounters are congenial, but some can be confrontational, when students are upset about their grades. A single case of student plagiarism can consume many hours of a professor's time if the offender chooses to contest the accusation. The end of each semester sets off a rush to get final papers and exams graded and to calculate students' overall results and report them to the campus registrar.

A new professor's first year of full-time teaching is an exhausting struggle to stay one step ahead of the students. Over the years, teaching becomes less time-consuming: repeating an established course is easier than teaching it for the first time. With experience, professors develop a teaching style that works for them. Those with a bit of the ham in their personality are often particularly successful as lecturers, drawing their students into their subjects with dramatic classroom performances. Others learn that they are more comfortable leading discussions with smaller groups of students. Certain professors have more of the patience and understanding needed to guide students doing individual research projects, whether at the undergraduate or the graduate level, than others. Nowadays, faculty are also expected to be able to teach courses using the Internet in various ways: lectures may be delivered as video podcasts, for example, and online "chats" with students may replace classroom discussions. Evaluating teaching performance fairly is difficult and causes much anxiety for faculty being considered for tenure. Most institutions rely heavily on student course evaluation forms, although these may reflect how generously the professor grades as much as they do the quality of the teaching. Older faculty members may observe untenured professors' classes, and promotion committees may also look at course syllabi and assignments to get an idea of how their colleagues handle their classroom duties.

Meanwhile, newly hired professors are also trying to move forward with their research, which means learning to navigate the arcane world of scholarly conferences and "peer-reviewed publication." As the constantly repeated mantra "publish or perish" reminds new faculty members, few institutions will grant tenure without at least some record of publication. At research universities, this aspect of professors' work usually weighs more heavily than teaching in the decision about tenure, and even at schools where faculty are judged primarily on their success in the classroom, at least some evidence of activity in research is usually required. For most historians, demonstrating productivity means publicizing the results of one's research, in the form of talks to scholarly audiences and the publication of books and articles. These activities are essential to establish one's reputation beyond the campus where one teaches. They demonstrate that the newly minted professor is a member not only of a campus community, but also of the professional community of the discipline.

Most beginning scholars start the process of publicizing their work by giving papers at professional conferences, sometimes even before they have completed their Ph.D.'s. These gatherings are an essential part of scholarly life. Some conferences, such as the annual meeting of the American Historical Association, attract historians from every corner of the discipline and serve as venues for other purposes, such as hiring interviews, in addition to the discussion of scholarship; the American Historical Association often attracts as many as five thousand participants. More specialized meetings, such as those of the Byzantine Studies Association or the Society for the History of American Foreign Relations, may have one hundred to five hundred attendees. They are opportunities for faculty to meet other researchers in their field, to find out about the latest work in that area, and to make personal contacts with those who share their interests. Most departments encourage faculty to attend at least one conference per year and often make travel funds available for this purpose. Public historians participate in history conferences in their fields and organize their own professional meetings.

Scholars who want to present some of their work at a conference watch for the "call for papers" announcing the dates of an upcoming meeting, which is normally circulated well in advance. Conference organizers encourage would-be participants to organize panels of papers on related themes, although they will often also consider individual paper proposals. Panels at history conferences are highly ritualized performances. A typical panel features three presenters, who give twenty-minute talks about some aspect of their research, a commentator, who reads the papers in advance and critiques them, and a panel chair, who introduces the others. If the chair has kept the speakers to their allotted time limits—always a difficult challenge—there will be some time left over for questions from the audience. When the panel ends, the participants and the audience dash out, some to attend other conference sessions, others to socialize with friends whom they otherwise rarely see during the course of the academic year. Giving one's first few conference papers is, like many other things that new historians do, a nerve-wracking experience: although the audience may be small, on the order of fifteen or twenty, speakers are conscious that many of those listening to them are true experts on their subject.

Successful conference talks help establish a new scholar's reputation, but, for professors, scholarly publication is even more important. At the beginning of their careers, most historians try to make sure that at least part of the content of their dissertation gets into print. Since a historian's Ph.D. dissertation is normally equal in length to a good-sized book, it might seem that meeting this challenge should not be difficult, and indeed in other countries, dissertations are frequently published with little or no revision, sometimes at the expense of the author. This serves to make the author's research findings available to other scholars, which is, after all, the supposed purpose of research. In the United States, however, it is generally assumed that a Ph.D. dissertation is not yet fully ready to be shared with the world. A typical dissertation often begins, for example, with an extensive discussion of the historiography on the topic to underline what is new about the author's research. Ph.D. students are also usually eager to show how much research they did, which means that their dissertations can become excessively detailed. In the course of completing their dissertations, many students come to realize that they must do additional research to convert their project from a narrow study of one aspect of a topic into a more coherent account of the subject. Having already spent a number of years contending with their subjects, new Ph.D.'s thus realize that they will need to devote even more time to it before they have produced a publishable manuscript.

It is not enough for beginning professors to convert their dissertation into a book manuscript or to turn parts of it into shorter articles: these publications must also appear in appropriate places. Most universities and colleges push faculty, especially those who do not yet have tenure, to get their work published in recognized peer-reviewed venues. The system of "peer review" is an essential part of the definition of professional academic research, as it has developed in history and other disciplines since the time of Leopold von Ranke. Peer-reviewed scholarship has been carefully scrutinized by other academic experts in the scholar's field before being published, and scholar-authors must respond to the criticisms and suggestions that these usually anonymous reviewers have made, often modifying their work considerably. The peer-review system distinguishes scholarly history from work written for a general audience: publishers of books on popular history are more concerned with whether a work is written in a lively style than whether it uses all available sources and engages with the existing historiography on the subject.

Most peer-reviewed works of history are published either by university presses or by independent publishers who aim at a scholarly audience. Peer-reviewed scholarly journals are often sponsored by professional scholarly organizations, such as the American Historical Association, which puts out the *American Historical Review*, and the Organization of American Historians, which publishes the *Journal of American History*. Whereas commercial publishers often balk at issuing books with footnotes, arguing that they scare off ordinary readers, presses publishing peer-reviewed historical scholarship insist that authors indicate their sources: the presence of footnotes or endnotes and of a full bibliography is one of the main signs that a book is intended to be a piece of professional scholarship. Footnotes are also an almost universal feature of articles published in scholarly journals. Most major historical journals are still published in paper form, but almost all of them are now also available online. Even when a scholarly journal appears only in digital form, however, it still needs to follow the time-honored processes of peer review in selecting its content if it wants to be taken seriously within the profession.

Is There Life after Tenure?

Finally, the fateful year for the tenure review arrives. The anxious candidate helps her department chair or the chair of her department's promotion committee to assemble all the materials required for the process: a minutely detailed *curriculum vitae* listing every tangible bit of evidence of her scholarly productivity, her teaching, and her other contributions to the department and the campus. At research-oriented institutions, this dossier is then sent to a certain number of specialists in the candidate's field who teach at other colleges and universities, who are asked to read the materials and offer a considered judgment on whether the candidate deserves to receive tenure, which is normally also accompanied by promotion to the rank of associate professor. The "outside letters" written by these reviewers, who are presumed to be better versed in the candidate's field than colleagues in her own department and who are also supposed to be less liable to be biased for personal reasons, are a crucial part of the promotion dossier. At places where the candidate's teaching is the main consideration, the outside letters may be written by professors from other departments on the same campus.

Once the outside letters have arrived, the candidate's tenured colleagues will read them, along with the other contents of the dossier, and express their own opinions. Like hiring decisions, decisions about granting tenure can cause bitter divisions within a department. The fact that participants are deciding on the fate of a person they have come to know personally makes these decisions highly emotional. Once the department has made its recommendation, the promotion dossier goes to the administrators of the institution. Normally, the dean of the unit in which the history department is housed is the most important figure in the promotion decision, but other officials— provosts and presidents, as well as various advisory committees—may also have to give approval. The majority of candidates who reach the point of being considered for tenure at American institutions do in fact get it, but no applicant ever feels completely reassured until the final written confirmation arrives. Failure to get tenure is not necessarily the end of a scholar's career; some prominent members of the profession have rebounded from such a setback and gone on to good careers at other institutions. Being turned down for tenure is certainly an unpleasant experience, however, and it does often lead faculty to decide to pursue careers outside academia. Unsuccessful tenure applicants usually have some possibility to appeal a negative decision; if they have reason to suspect that they were discriminated against on the grounds of race, ethnicity, or gender, they may even file suit against their institution. Academic institutions try to avoid finding themselves involved in such cases, which sometimes become public issues on campus; this is one reason why procedures for considering tenure cases are so elaborate and bureaucratic.

The biggest surprise for professors who have been approved for tenure is that receiving this coveted status does not necessarily mean that they will teach and research happily ever after. Some surveys have shown that faculty satisfaction with their careers often goes down once tenure is achieved. A newly tenured history professor has usually spent the previous fifteen years of his or her life working toward clearly defined goals: to pass qualifying exams, complete a dissertation, find a job, and earn promotion. For much of that time, he or she has usually worked on a single research project, first as a dissertation and then as a book manuscript whose publication has probably coincided with the promotion application. When the long-awaited notification finally arrives, its recipient suddenly realizes that he or she has no obvious new goal to strive for. For a surprising number of professors, in history as well as in other academic disciplines, obtaining tenure sets off a crisis of motivation. "An associate professor starts to think: why I am I doing what I'm doing?" one veteran academic has said.[16] For many, this is in the end a process of personal growth that ends with engagement in new projects, either in their disciplinary field or in academic administration, but for some, it can become a permanent condition, often aggravated as they see more goal-oriented colleagues moving ahead in their careers.

The most ambitious and successful historians become professional stars, able to move to more prestigious and better-paid positions than their original jobs. The majority rise through the ranks at the campus where they received tenure, achieving promotion to the rank of full professor and gradually growing into the role of senior members of their campus's faculty. Compared to most Americans, college and university professors generally have adequate retirement plans—one of the compensations for their relatively modest salaries—and many look forward to having time to spend with family, to travel, and to pursue personal interests once they are no longer teaching full time. One of the advantages of being a historian is that one can remain active as a scholar even in retirement. Some historians have undertaken and completed major new research projects in their seventies and eighties. A surprising number have written autobiographies and memoirs, histories of their personal lives, in which they reflect on how their careers have been affected by the public events of the times in which they have lived.

History Careers Beyond Academia

Whereas there is a recognizable pattern to the lives of historians who make careers as college and university teachers, it is harder to generalize about the experiences of historians who pursue their interest in the past in other ways. Many nonacademic historians work in the area of public history. As the home page of the National Council on Public History puts it, "public historians come in all shapes and sizes. They call themselves historical consultants, museum professionals, government historians, archivists, oral historians, cultural resource managers, curators, film and media producers, historical interpreters, historic preservationists, policy advisors, local historians, and community activists, among many other job descriptions."[17] Whatever they do, public historians need a good background in the discipline of history. In contrast to academic historians, they are less likely to do much regular teaching and they may not do original research, but, depending on their position, they may need to acquire other skills. Museum professionals need to know about the preservation, restoration, and display of historical relics; archivists need to learn how to classify documents. Graduate programs in public history, offered at a number of universities, have students take some of the same courses required for future professors, along with specialized courses designed for their needs.

A common element of many public history jobs is the ability to communicate historical information to the general public or to collaborators from other professions who may have little background in the subject. Guides welcoming visitors to historical sites must be able to capture and hold the attention of audiences of all ages and be prepared to answer questions that are far less predictable than those asked by students. Historians working for large government agencies or for private businesses must be able to convince their employers of the value of the work they do and of the desirability of promoting historical work that meets professional standards, rather than just trying to put the best possible light on its sponsors. Oral historians may need to persuade subjects to share their stories; they also must learn to pose questions that may be uncomfortable for their subjects without losing their trust.

A second characteristic of many public history positions is that they involve more interdisciplinary and collaborative work than most university professorships. Academic historians are used to operating on their own in the classroom and in their research; public historians often work as part of a team, often in cooperation with colleagues who have no specific historical training. Creating an exhibit for a historical museum, for example, requires the contributions not only of historically trained curators, who can ensure that the information being communicated is accurate, but also of conservators who care for the objects being exhibited, of designers who can lay out a visually effective display, and of educators who can create materials to help visitors understand what they are seeing. The historical offices of the different branches of the U.S. military work together to compile official histories of the country's armed conflicts, such as the ongoing series on the Vietnam War, which already runs to more than a dozen volumes. Some bear the names of individual authors, but each volume fits into the overall plan for the massive project, an enterprise that no individual scholar could possibly complete.

Most public historians are relatively anonymous, although there are exceptions, such as Donald Ritchie, the longtime official historian of the U.S. Senate, who is regularly quoted in the media whenever questions about the traditions of that institution come up and who is recognized throughout the profession for his contribution to the techniques of oral history.[18] Even if they do not often get to put their names on their work, public historians make vital contributions to the understanding of the past and the vitality of the history discipline. Visits to historic sites inspire young people with the desire to learn more about the subject and keep adults interested in it long after they have completed their education. Museum exhibitions focus public attention on important issues and often introduce general audiences to the new perspectives generated by academic scholars; sometimes they also help send scholarship in new directions. Reports by preservationists help protect historic buildings and artifacts from needless destruction, and archivists ensure that future scholars will have the data they need. Historians working for the various levels of government help create institutional memory and provide input on policy decisions. The current crisis in academic history in the United States is having the effect of drawing attention to the opportunities in public history. Important as these opportunities are, however, they do not guarantee jobs for all the history students who might want to work in the field. Government public history offices have suffered from funding cutbacks in recent years, and students considering public history should be aware that the vast majority of opportunities in the field are in U.S. history.

The handful of popular authors who have written successful books about the past for general audiences are among the most visible but also the least typical of those who make a living from history. College professors often envy such authors for their ability to reach a broad audience, for the royalties they earn from their bestsellers, and sometimes for the public influence they are able to exercise. When Barack Obama convened annual "historians' dinners" at the White House, at least half the participants were nonacademic presidential historians, including the best-selling biographers Robert Caro and Doris Kearns Goodwin. Some popular historians have graduate-level training in history, but the biographies of many of them reveal that they were from the start more interested in writing than in the mechanics of historical research. As David McCullough, probably the most widely read historian in America today, told an interviewer, "I never had any intention of writing except in the narrative form"; he claims that "he never took an American history course after high school." McCullough majored in English in college and got his first job working for *Sports Illustrated*. He was well over forty when his first book, *The Johnstown Flood*, was published in 1968. His first books were well received, but they did not guarantee him a stable income. Like most self-supporting writers, he had to depend on advances from his publishers, and when the writing of one project took him longer than he expected, he and his family "were holding our breath, wondering how to pay the bills."[19]

When their books are reviewed in the journals of professional historians, books by popular historians are regularly criticized for putting too much emphasis on the actions of individuals rather than on the importance of impersonal sources, for relying on a narrow range of documents, and for ignoring the work of other scholars. The review of McCullough's Pulitzer Prize–winning biography of president Harry Truman in the *American Historical Review* said that the author wrote "as a storyteller, not as an analyst" and insisted that "the master biographer must also come to terms with all pertinent information, even if it is deemed dull." Reviews of the same books in newspapers and magazines, usually written by other professional authors rather than by university professors, and those posted by readers on websites such as Goodreads, evaluate the same books in terms of their readability and appeal to nonspecialists and tend to be more favorable. Comments on the popular book-review website Goodreads about McCullough's Truman biography often come from readers who make it clear that "I'm no historian." Ordinary readers praised the book for providing "a narrative that flows like the story from a novel" and expressed amazement that the author could motivate them to get through a book of almost a thousand pages.[20]

Academic critics often complain that popular historians focus exclusively on wars, catastrophes, and the lives of familiar figures such as American presidents. This is not entirely true: Jared Diamond, for example, has enjoyed great success with his books on environmental history, such as *Guns, Germs, and Steel* (1997), and the journalist Gail Collins scored a hit with her narrative of the feminist movement, *When Everything Changed: The Amazing Journey of American Women from 1960 to the Present* (2009). A few university professors, such as Emmanuel Le Roy Ladurie, Simon Schama, and Niall Ferguson, have shown that one can be both a successful popular author and a recognized scholar. They have adopted the popular historians' pattern of taking on widely varied subjects; many of their readers may not even realize that they also hold academic positions. Other scholar-authors have written bestsellers that feature the footnotes and scholarly apparatus of a standard monograph but that provide a readable synthesis of scholarship on a subject of interest to general readers. Often, these are books about wars, such as James McPherson's *Battle Cry of Freedom* (1988), an overview of the Civil War that was equally successful with academic readers and the general public, and, more recently, Christopher Clark's highly acclaimed *The Sleepwalkers: How Europe Went to War in 1914* (2012).

Popular historians and their best-selling books perform an essential function for the discipline of history: they keep it from turning into an arcane body of knowledge accessible only to initiates, as some other scholarly disciplines have become. There is, however, no simple formula for becoming a best-selling historical author. Superior writing ability is certainly an advantage; so is the willingness to make firm assertions about one's subject, rather than engaging in the judicious weighing of multiple possibilities that is prized in academic scholarship. Those who decide to strive for a career as a freelance historian must recognize that the odds of rapid success are slim; for every history book that makes it to the bestseller list, there are many more that are sell poorly and are quickly forgotten. Popular writers usually work with professional literary agents, who help them identify topics likely to interest general readers and figure out effective ways of telling their stories. Most commercial publishers are reluctant even to consider a manuscript sent in by an author who is not represented by an agent; they count on agents to identify authors and projects that have some real promise and to weed out those that have little potential.

Not all of those who are vitally engaged in studying and preserving the past do so as part of a professional career. History is also kept alive by numerous men and women who engage themselves with it because of their passion for the subject, without expecting to be paid for their efforts. Local history societies and museums are usually heavily dependent on volunteers, and every group and community is likely to have its amateur historian-archivist, an individual who actively seeks out documents and artifacts that testify to its past. Some historians who have chosen other careers still find the time to embark on scholarly projects that result in publications. The French "Sunday historian" Philippe Ariès, mentioned in a previous chapter, became a major influence in the development of cultural history and the history of everyday life despite having to do his research and writing in the time left over from his regular job in the French civil service. The vast majority of undergraduate history majors will not become professional historians, but for those who have the desire, there are many ways to remain engaged with the subject.

In the end, like all men and women, historians, whatever the pattern of their careers, must resign ourselves to "becoming history." If we have been lucky, those of us who have had professional careers in the field will be able to say that we had the good fortune to spend our working lives doing things that truly engaged us and not just earning a living. As members of a professional community, historians are able to share our passion for learning about the past and feel that we are contributing to an enterprise of enduring value, one that will continue to exist even when its individual practitioners have passed on. One would like to think that our familiarity with the long chain of generations that have lived before us, whose stories have been the material for our research, our teaching, and our writing, will help us accept this universal fate.

Notes

1. Survey results in *Perspectives in History* (the newsletter of the American Historical Association), December 2013. Of the 66 percent of Ph.D.'s teaching in four-year colleges and universities, 51 percent were in tenure-track positions and 15 percent in non-tenure-track positions.

---

2. Cited in Nash et al., *History on Trial*, 34.
3. Henry Adams, *The Education of Henry Adams* (Boston: Houghton Mifflin, 1971 (orig. 1918)), 300.
4. Howard Zinn, *You Can't Be Neutral on a Moving Train* (Boston: Beacon, 1994), 169; Henry May, *Coming to Terms: A Study in Memory and History* (Berkeley: University of California Press, 1987), 57.
5. Leon F. Litwack, "The Making of a Historian," in *Historians and Race*, eds. Paul A Cimbala and Robert F. Himmelberg (Bloomington: Indiana University Press, 1996), 18.
6. John Hope Franklin, *Mirror to America: The Autobiography of John Hope Franklin* (New York: Farrar, Straus and Giroux, 2005), 44–45.
7. Raoul Girardet, "L'Ombre de la guerre," in *Essais d'ego-histoire*, ed. Pierre Nora (Paris: Gallimard, 1987), 148.
8. Robert B. Townsend, "Who Are the New History PhDs?" *Perspectives on History*, March 2012.
9. Joan Scott, "Finding Critical History," in James M. Banner Jr. and John R. Gillis, eds., *Becoming Historians* (Chicago: University of Chicago Press, 2009), 32.
10. Arlette Farge, *Le Goût de l'Archive* (Paris: Seuil, 1989), 12, 23. Farge's book has been translated into English as *The Allure of the Archives* (New Haven, CT: Yale University Press, 2013).
11. Farge, *Goût*, 22, 71.
12. Barbara J. Howe and Emory L. Kemp, *Public History: An Introduction* (Malabar, FL: Krieger, 1986).
13. Joshua Wolff, "A New Course: Converting a Passion for History into a Private Sector Career," *Perspectives in History*, Jan. 2014.
14. "1940 Statement of Principles on Academic Freedom and Tenure," http://www.aaup.org, under "Reports and Publications."
15. Scott Jaschik, "Skepticism about Tenure, MOOCS and the Presidency: A Survey of Provosts," *Inside Higher Education*, Jan. 23, 2013.
16. Robert A. Rhoads, quoted in Robin Wilson, "Why Are Associate Professors So Unhappy?" *Chronicle of Higher Education*, June 3, 2012.
17. National Council on Public History, "What Is Public History?" http://www.ncph.org/cms/what-is-public-history/, accessed July 7, 2014.

18. Donald A. Ritchie, "Historians in the Federal Government," in Richard S. Kirkendall, ed., *The Writing and Teaching of American History* (New York: Oxford University Press, 2011), 306–16; Donald A. Ritchie, "The Oral History/Public History Connection," in Howe and Kemp, eds., *Public History*, 57–69.

19. *New York Times*, Aug. 12, 1992; David McCullough, "The Art of Biography No. 2," interview with Elizabeth Gaffney and Benjamin Ryder Howe, *Paris Review*, no. 152 (1999).

20. Donald R. McCoy, review of McCullough, *Truman*, *American Historical Review* 98 (June 1993), 974; readers' comments on Goodreads, accessed July 17, 2014.

CHAPTER 9

Conclusion

As we have seen in the preceding chapters, the discipline of history has had a long and complicated history. From the origins of written history in ancient Greece and China to the vociferous "history wars" at the end of the twentieth century, scholars and others have continued to argue about the proper way to represent the past. At the beginning of a new millennium, historians are no closer to consensus on the major issues with which historiography deals. Diversity is undoubtedly the major characteristic of the field of history today: diversity in subject matter, diversity in methodological approaches, and an unprecedented diversity in the media through which history is communicated. After a century during which it was often assumed that being a historian meant being a college teacher, we are also now increasingly conscious of the many different professions historians can embrace. Depending on one's perspective, the present day is either an exciting time to be a historian, with so many different possibilities to pursue in trying to reconstruct the truth about the past, or a frustrating moment, in which the sense of the historical enterprise has become increasingly difficult to define.

For many historians, anxiety about the future of the discipline is bound up with concern about the job prospects of those who seek careers as college professors. This concern, which is certainly not limited to the United States, is a real one, especially for students considering graduate study in the field, but it should not lead us to despair about the future of the subject of history. There are also promising signs for the future of history, such as the growing public interest in history museums, a worldwide phenomenon, and the continuing success of popular literature about the past. A discipline that has adapted to so many different situations over the centuries and that addresses so many deep human questions is not likely to disappear, even if the institutional arrangements that have supported it change.

And what of historiography itself? Like history as a whole, historiography is very much an ongoing enterprise. Once we recognize that reconstructing the past can never be restricted simply to the collection of facts, we are inevitably drawn into thinking about the processes by which historical data are assembled, interpreted, and presented—in other words, we cannot avoid historiographical questions. The study of historiography also teaches us that the discipline of history has its own history: studying the past has meant different things in different eras and different places. If the basic lesson of all history is that human actions take place in a particular temporal context, that lesson applies as much to the study and interpretation of the past as to every other aspect of human activity. Rather than limiting the value of history, this insight should help us appreciate it even more. It tells us that every search for the truth about the past, no matter how limited or obscure, is an action taken in the present, with consequences for our own lives.

To say that historians will never reach complete consensus about the past does not mean that they can say anything they want about it. The increasingly elaborate procedures that scholarly historians from Lorenzo Valla through Leopold von Ranke to the present have developed for interpreting evidence give us better tools for studying the past than our predecessors had. If we cannot always be completely sure about what happened in the past, we can at least use these tools, as one of my own teachers used to say, to disprove many erroneous assertions and narrow the range of issues we need to argue about. After decades of debate, for instance, about whether the German army massacred large numbers of civilians in Belgium and northern France at the beginning of World War I, the carefully documented work of two British historians, John Horne and Alan Kramer, has drawn on evidence from all sides in the conflict and established beyond reasonable doubt that such massacres did occur and that they were not, as even some scholars had long claimed, a response to a popular uprising by the local population.[1] The special status of academic history—historical research conducted in accordance with these procedures—is that it invites other historians to validate its conclusions and gives them the wherewithal to do so. By explaining their methodological approaches and providing references to their sources, scholars allow their peers to look over their shoulders and see whether they are doing their work properly and making justifiable arguments.

The fact that we can exclude certain assertions about the past as inaccurate does not mean, however, that sufficiently dedicated study of the sources will enable us to settle all historiographical arguments. In the case I have just mentioned, Horne and Kramer have documented a series of events and demonstrated that the popular uprising described by many Germans at the time was, so to speak, a "nonevent" that did not take place. They have also tried to explain the reasons for these massacres and for the German claims about civilian resistance. Their explanations are certainly plausible, but they depend on assumptions about human psychology that are not subject to confirmation or refutation in the way that their findings about the numbers of killings that took place on particular dates and in particular places are. Historiographical debate about the motivations for the atrocities that occurred in 1914 will continue, even if historians now accept Horne and Kramer's account of what actually happened.

The reason why historiographical debates are not subject to clearcut resolution is that they are ultimately debates about fundamental issues of values and meaning. Historians will see the past differently depending on the understanding of human nature that they have developed out of their personal experiences as well as their studies. One historian may be convinced that human behavior is most strongly influenced by calculations of material interest; another may see religious beliefs or cultural conditioning as more powerful. For one historian, the value in history may consist in the most detailed possible reconstitution of the facts; another may put more emphasis on conveying an intuitive sense of the meaning of past events. Careful observation of scholarly protocols may enable historians with different values to reach agreement on some historical questions, and indeed judicious historians are usually willing to admit that there is no single, simple answer to any significant question about the past and to incorporate more than one perspective in their presentations. To expect all historians to agree on a common set of answers about historical issues, however, is no more reasonable than to expect them to agree on the ultimate meaning of life.

Two things have united historians over the millennia, however. One is the shared conviction that the human past is meaningful and interesting. Whether they have seen the purpose of historical reconstruction as maintaining the memory of great deeds, providing lessons for the present, or broadening understanding of human nature, historians from Herodotus to the present have been deeply absorbed in the effort to find out about the past and transmit their discoveries. The other common passion historians have shared is a dedication to the truth about the past. Historians' definitions of historical truth have differed widely, as have their judgments about how close scholarship can come to it, but those who have abandoned all faith in its possibility have usually found themselves essentially excluded from the community of historians and ignored by a public that wants historical knowledge. Even visitors to historical theme parks want to believe that what they are being shown has some basis in historical fact, and, as one historian has argued, entertainment corporations such as Disney have made some real efforts to satisfy them.[2]

Truth is an important human value. We depend on it in our everyday lives: if we do not know the true amount of money in our bank accounts, serious consequences may ensue. We are even more concerned about it in our human relationships: when someone tells us, "I love you," we only regard their statement as meaningful if we judge it to be true. The fundamental reason for studying historiography, then, is that it teaches us about the ways in which we can seek truth about the past. To be sure, we learn that historical truth is not easy to obtain and, indeed, that we may never be able to achieve it completely. We may even conclude that the best we can do is to guard ourselves against believing falsehoods about the past. Nevertheless, by learning the lessons of historiography, we make ourselves part of a tradition of truth-seekers, committed to carrying on the effort to come as close to the elusive essence of the past as the powers of the human mind allow.

Notes

1. John Horne and Alan Kramer, *German Atrocities, 1914: A History of Denial* (New Haven, CT: Yale University Press, 2001).
2. Mike Wallace, "Mickey Mouse History: Portraying the Past at Disney World," in Mike Wallace, *Mickey Mouse History and Other Essays on American Memory* (Philadelphia: Temple University Press, 1996), 133–57.

SUGGESTIONS FOR FURTHER READING

The literature on historiography is vast and extremely varied. Many of the works that have influenced historians are discussed in the text; listing them here would be redundant. The titles listed here are just a small selection of the many stimulating works that can help students get a fuller picture of the subject. This bibliography is limited to works in English; it therefore omits many important publications in other languages.

Reference Works and Journals

Reference works containing short articles on historiographical subjects include Michael Bentley, *Companion to Historiography* (1997), and, for a postmodernist perspective, Alun Munslow, *The Routledge Companion to Historical Studies* (2000). For those who read French, the two volumes of C. Delacroix, F. Dosse, P. Garcia, and N. Offenstadt, eds., *Historiographies: Concepts et Débats* (2010), will be useful. Scholarly journals devoted to historiography and published primarily in English include *History and Theory, Rethinking History,* and *Storia della Storiografia.*

Introductions to History and Historical Methods

Among the most useful of the many books in this category intended primarily for undergraduate historiography students are John Tosh, *The Pursuit of History* (5th ed., 2010), Ludmilla Jordanova, *History in Practice* (2nd ed., 2006), Mark T. Gilderhus, *History and Historians:*

A Historiographical Introduction (7th ed., 2010), and Mark Donnelly and Claire Norton, *Doing History* (2011). Two collaborative books with contributions from a number of authors are Peter Lambert and Phillipp Schofield, eds., *Making History: An Introduction to the History and Practices of a Discipline* (2004), and Stefan Berger, Heiko Feldner, and Kevin Passmore, *Writing History: Theory and Practice* (2003). Four older works that are still worth reading are Marc Bloch, *The Historian's Craft* (1953), the reflections of one of the founders of the Annales school; R. G. Collingwood, *The Idea of History* (1946), from a philosophically "idealist" perspective, E. H. Carr, *What Is History?* (1961), a plea for historical relativism, and G. R. Elton, *The Practice of History* (1967), a response to Carr. More essayistic works include John Lewis Gaddis, *The Landscape of History: How Historians Map the Past* (2002), and H. Stuart Hughes, *History as Art and as Science* (1964).

Primary Sources

Useful collections of excerpted passages from leading historians are Peter Gay and Gerald J. Cavanaugh, eds., *Historians at Work*, 4 vols. (1972–1975), Donald R. Kelley, ed., *Versions of History from Antiquity to the Enlightenment* (1991), and Fritz Stern, *The Varieties of History, from Voltaire to the Present* (1956). Thomas R. Martin, *Herodotus and Sima Qian: The First Great Historians of Greece and China* (2010), provides excerpts from the founders of historical writing in Greece and China.

General Overviews of the History of History-Writing

Ernst Breisach, *Historiography: Ancient, Medieval, and Modern* (1983), is a standard overview. Donald R. Kelley's three volumes, *Faces of History: Historical Inquiry from Herodotus to Herder* (1998), *Fortunes of History: Historical Inquiry from Herder to Huizinga* (2003), and *Frontiers of History: Historical Inquiry in the Twentieth Century* (2006), are more challenging and often give interesting alternative perspectives on major authors. John Burrow, *A History of Histories: Epics, Chronicles, Romances and Inquiries from Herodotus and Thucydides to the Twentieth Century* (2008), is a lively survey of major historical works. Mary Spongberg, *Writing Women's History since the Renaissance* (2002), is a useful introduction to the tradition of women's historical writing. Daniel Woolf, *A Global History of History* (2011), treats European historiographical traditions alongside those of other civilizations.

Works Covering Limited Periods and Specific Historiographical Movements

Arnoldo Momigliano, *The Classical Foundations of Modern Historiography* (1990), reinvigorated the study of the ancient historians. Walter Goffart, *The Narrators of Barbarian History* (1988), provides a dense commentary on major early medieval historians; Joseph Dahmus, *Seven Medieval Historians* (1982), includes some later medieval authors, both Christian and Muslim. Donald R. Kelley, *Foundations of Modern Historical Scholarship: Language, Law, and History in the French Renaissance* (1970), revived interest in the historical traditions of the Renaissance. Jorge Cañizares-Esguerra, *How to Write the History of the New World: Historiographies, Epistemologies, and Identities in the Eighteenth-Century Atlantic World* (2001), argues for the importance of Latin American traditions in shaping modern history. Peter Hanns Reill, *The German Enlightenment and the Rise of Historicism* (1975), challenges the notion that historicism was a nineteenth-century invention. Georg Iggers, *The German Conception of History: The National Tradition of Historical Thought from Herder to the Present* (1968), has long been the standard study of the nineteenth-century German historical school; for a new approach to the subject, see Frederick Beiser, *The German Historicist Tradition* (2011). The older work of G. P. Gooch, *History and Historians in the Nineteenth Century* (1913), is still useful for its treatment of nineteenth-century history-writing outside of Germany. Theodore H. Von Laue, *Leopold Ranke: The Formative Years* (1950), is a biography of the German tradition's leading figure.

The French Annales school has inspired several major studies, including Peter Burke, *The French Historical Revolution: The Annales School, 1929–1989* (1990), and François Dosse, *New History in France: The Triumph of the Annales* (1994), as well as Carole Fink, *Marc Bloch: A Life in History* (1989). Burke has also edited *New Perspectives on Historical Writing* (2001). Peter Novick, *That Noble Dream: The "Objectivity Question" and the American Historical Profession* (1988), is a magisterial survey of professional historical scholarship in the United States. Jacques Revel and Lynn Hunt, eds., *Histories: French Constructions of the Past* (1995), offers an overview of the work of influential French historians since 1945. For a pioneering survey of the evolution of historical scholarship since the 1960s, see Geoff Eley, *A Crooked Line: From Cultural History to the History of Society* (2005).

Thematic Studies

Linguistic and Cultural Turns: Hayden White, *Metahistory* (1973), has been at the center of historiographical debates since its publication. Keith Jenkins, *Rethinking History* (1991), and Frank Ankersmit, *Meaning, Truth, and Reference in Historical Representation* (2012), are statements by two of White's main followers. Lynn Hunt, ed., *The New Cultural History* (1989), was crucial in defining the "new cultural history"; another volume she edited, *Beyond the Cultural Turn* (1999), reevaluated the movement ten years later.

Women's and Gender History: Bonnie G. Smith, *The Gender of History: Men, Women, and Historical Practice* (1998), offers a feminist critique of the profession. Gerda Lerner, *The Majority Finds Its Past: Placing Women in History* (2005), collects groundbreaking essays by one of the pioneers of women's history. Pamela S. Nadell and Kate Haulman, eds., *Making Women's Histories: Beyond National Perspectives* (2012), includes articles on women's history in different countries.

Postcolonialism and Global History: Dipesh Chakrabarty, *Provincializing Europe: Postcolonial Thought and Historical Difference* (2000), is a fundamental contribution to the debate about postcolonialism in history-writing. Arif Dirlik, Vinay Bahl, and Peter Gran, eds., *History after the Three Worlds: Post-Eurocentric Historiographies* (2000), offers a contrasting perspective on many issues raised by Chakrabarty. Michel-Rolph Trouillot, *Silencing the Past: Power and the Production of History* (1995), is a powerful statement against the neglect and misinterpretation of non-Western history. Patrick Manning, *Navigating World History: Historians Create a Global Past* (2003), is an overview of issues in global history by one of its leading practitioners. Jo Guldi and David Armitage, *The History Manifesto* (2014) is a polemical plea for historians to tackle broader topics and to make their work more relevant to debates about public policy.

History in the United States: Ian Tyrrell, *Historians in Public: The Practice of American History, 1890–1970* (2005), and Robert B. Townsend, *History's Babel: Scholarship, Professionalization, and the Historical Enterprise in the United States, 1880–1940* (2014), cover the rise of professional history in the United States, and August Meier and Elliott Rudwick, *Black History and the Historical Profession* (1986), tells the story of African American historians. Richard S. Kirkendall, *The Organization of American Historians and the Writing and Teaching of American History* (2011), gives an overview of the history and activities of one of America's major organizations of professional historians. Thomas Bender, ed., *Rethinking American History in a Global Age* (2002), offers an international perspective on American history and historiography. Barbara J. Howe and Emory L. Kemp, *Public History: An Introduction* (1986), although somewhat dated, provides a useful survey of the varieties of public history in the United States.

"**History Wars**": The public controversies of the 1980s and 1990s have generated a large literature. Some major contributions are Gary B. Nash, Charlotte Crabtree, and Ross E. Dunn, *History on Trial: Culture Wars and the Teaching of the Past* (1997); Edward T. Linenthal and Tom Engelhardt, eds., *History Wars* (1996); Stuart Macintyre and Anna Clark, *The History Wars* (2004) (about Australia); Rudolf Augstein, ed., *Forever in the Shadow of Hitler? Original Documents of the Historikerstreit* (1993); and Charles Maier, *The Unmasterable Past: History, Holocaust and German National Identity* (1988). Wim van Binsbergen, ed., *Black Athena Comes of Age* (2011) and Mary R. Lefkowitz and Guy MacLean Rogers, *Black Athena Revisited* (1996) give contrasting views of the controversy over a major "Afrocentric" publication of the period. Katerina V. Korostelina and Simone Lässig, eds., *History Education and Post-Conflict Reconciliation: Reconsidering Joint Textbook Projects* (2013) discusses successful and unsuccessful efforts to promote transnational history textbooks.

History and the New Media

A broad survey of history outside the academy, drawing primarily on British examples, is Jerome de Groot, *Consuming History: Historians and Heritage in Contemporary Popular Culture* (2009). On history and the Internet, Daniel I. Cohen and Roy Rosenzweig, *Digital History: A Guide to Gathering, Preserving, and Presenting the Past on the Web* (2005), is indispensable. Robert Rosenstone lays out his argument for taking film seriously as a form of history in *History on Film/Film on History* (2006); see also Marnie Hughes-Warrington, *History Goes to the Movies: Studying History on Film* (2007), and Natalie Zemon Davis, *Slaves on Screen: Film and Historical Vision* (2000). Among the literature on historical museums, particularly interesting works are Mike Wallace, *Mickey*

Mouse History and Other Essays on American Memory (1996), Edward Linenthal, *Preserving Memory: The Struggle to Create America's Holocaust Museum* (2001), Daniel J. Walkowitz and Barbara Weinstein, eds., *Contested Histories in Public Space* (2009), Amy Lonetree, *Decolonizing Museums: Representing Native America in National and Tribal Museums* (2012), and Kirk A. Denton, *Historical Memory and the Politics of Museums in Postsocialist China* (2014). Andrew Wilhelm Kapell and Andrew B. R. Elliott, eds., *Playing with the Past: Digital Games and the Simulation of History* (2013), explores the emerging field of video-game history.

Historical Writing: Peter Gay, *Style in History* (1974), is a classic essay on the meaning of style in historical writing. Anthony Grafton, *The Footnote: A Curious History* (1997), illuminates the origins and function of one of history writing's distinctive characteristics. David Carr, Thomas R. Flynn, and Rudolf Makkreel, eds., *The Ethics of History* (2004), considers the ethical dimension of history-writing. Antoinette Burton, ed., *Archive Stories* (2005), offers perspectives on the relationship between archives and historical writing.

Historians' Careers: Edward Gibbon's *Memoirs*, originally published in 1796, is a classic autobiography that still speaks to history scholars. Theodore Hamerow, *Reflections on History and Historians* (1987), although somewhat dated, still offers some thought-provoking comments on the life of the academic historian in America. Thomas Bender et al., *The Education of Historians for the Twenty-First Century* (2004), is a report commissioned by the American Historical Association. James M. Banner Jr., *Being a Historian: An Introduction to the Professional World of History* (2012), is an impassioned plea for historians to recognize the possibilities of careers outside of academia. Jeremy D. Popkin, *History, Historians and Autobiography* (2005), discusses historians who have written about their own lives and includes a bibliography listing some three hundred accounts by professional history scholars. Recent years have seen the publication of a number of volumes of shorter autobiographical essays by historians. These include James M. Banner Jr. and John R. Gillis, eds., *Becoming Historians* (2009); Paul A. Cimbala and Robert F. Himmelberg, eds., *Historians and Race: Autobiography and the Writing of History* (1996); Eileen Boris and Nupur Chaudhuri, eds., *Voices of Women Historians: The Personal, the Political, the Professional* (1999); and Laura Lee Downs and Stephane Gerson, eds., *Why France? American Historians Reflect on an Enduring Fascination* (2007).

INDEX

France, historical writing in, 51, 83–4, 103, 141, 149–50
See also Annales school of historiography; French Revolution
Franckesche Stiftung, 55
See also museums, historical
Frank, André Gunder, 141
Franklin, John Hope, 115–6, 201
French Revolution, 70–1, 83, 141–2
French Rural History (by Marc Bloch), 23, 112
Freud, Sigmund, 106
Friedan, Betty, 142
See also feminism
Froissart, Jean, 45, 47
Frontiers of History (by Donald R. Kelley), 191
Frye, Norbert, 136
Fukuyama, Francis, 158, 170
Fukuzawa Yukichi, 86
Furet, François, 141
Fussell, Paul, 149
See also memory, history of

Gaguin, Robert, 51
Galileo, 58
Gandhi, Mohandas, 120
Garcilaso de la Vega, El Inca, 52
Gaulle, Charles de, 113
Gay, Peter, 114
Geertz, Clifford, 135, 142
See also anthropology, impact on history; cultural history
gender history
See Foucault, Michel; Scott, Joan W.
Gender of History, The (by Bonnie Smith), 144–5
General History of Africa, 121
Genovese, Eugene, 131
See also African-American history
Geoffroy of Monmouth, 43
German History in the Nineteenth Century (by Heinrich Treitschke), 82
See also nationalism
Germany, historical writing in, 73, 82–3, 100–3, 113, 157
See also Historikerstreit; Ranke, Leopold von
Getz, Trevor, 185
G.I. Bill, 114
Gibbon, Edward, 8, 63–4, 77
See also Decline and Fall of the Roman Empire; Memoirs
Ginzburg, Carlo, 140
See also microhistory

Girardet, Raoul, 201
global history, 22, 186–8
Global History of History, A (by Daniel Woolf), 187
Gobineau, Arthur de, 87
See also race theories
Goffart, Walter, 39
Golden Legend, The (by Jacobus de Voragine) 44
Gonick, Larry, 184–5
See also graphic art, history and
Gooch, G. P., 79
Good War, The (by Studs Terkel), 152
See also oral history
Goodreads web site, 224
Goodwin, Doris Kearns, 169, 224
Gordon-Reed, Annette, 189
Göttingen, university of, 62
Goût de l'archive, L' (by Arlette Farge), 207
Graduate Record Exam, 201
graduate school, 200–10
application procedures for, 201–2
doctoral degree (Ph.D.), 204–7, 209–10, 218
examinations in, 205–7, 209–10
master's degree, 204
programs, 202–3
teaching in, 206–7
Graetz, Heinrich, 83
See also Jews
Grafton, Anthony, 47, 77, 80
"grand narratives," critique of, 137
graphic art, history and, 176, 184–5
See also Gonick, Larry; Spiegelman, Art
Great Depression, 110, 115
Great Divergence, The (by Kenneth Pomeranz), 22
Greek historians, 31, 33, 34, 36
See also Herodotus; Thucydides
Green, Gerald, 154
Greenblatt, Stephen, 190
Gregory of Tours, 39–40
Griffiths, D. W., 105
Guicciardini, Francesco, 13, 19, 44, 50
Guizot, François, 81, 83
Gulag Archipelago, The (by Alexander Solzhenitsyn), 141
Guns, Germs, and Steel (by Jared Diamond), 225
Guns of August, The (by Barbara Tuchman), 116
Gutenberg, Johannes, 53
Gutmann, Herbert, 132